Arbitration
in
Practice

Arnold M. Zack, editor

ILR Press
New York State School of
Industrial and Labor Relations
Cornell University

Cover design by Kathleen Dalton

Library of Congress number: 83-22667
International Standard Book Numbers: cloth 0-87546-103-4,
paperback 0-87546-104-2

Library of Congress Cataloging in Publication Data

Main entry under title:

Arbitration in practice.

   Bibliography: p.
   Includes index.
   1. Arbitration, Industrial—United States.
2. Arbitrators, Industrial—United States—Handbooks,
manuals, etc.   I. Zack, Arnold.
KF3424.A75 1983   344.73'0189143   83-22667
ISBN 0-87546-103-4   347.304189143
ISBN 0-87546-104-2 (pbk.)

Copies may be ordered from
ILR Press
New York State School of Industrial and Labor Relations
Cornell University
Ithaca, New York 14853

Printed in the United States of America
5   4   3   2

Contents

Preface

ARBITRATION of labor-management disputes has come to be accepted as an essential element of national labor policy and as a viable, voluntary procedure for conflict resolution. Arbitration has thrived in the private sector for nearly fifty years. It has expanded into the public sector and is now being adapted to resolve disputes in fields other than labor-management.

This volume has been compiled in response to the needs of both new and experienced arbitrators. Despite the expanding use of arbitration, there is a tendency for those who use the system to turn to the more experienced "old timers" as their arbitrators. Many of the new arbitrators entering the profession have little insight into the standards that have guided the profession over the years.

Arbitration, unlike law, medicine and other professional callings, has had no requirement of continuing education. The result is a dearth of written material for training new arbitrators, upgrading the skills of practicing arbitrators, or showing the parties how arbitrators think. Experienced arbitrators may reflect on how their individual cases fit into the larger patterns of conflict resolution. Unfortunately, too few take the time, or are willing to make the time, to share these thoughts with others. Some have written papers or volumes on labor relations subjects, often intended for a broader audience than those who actually participate in arbitrations. Few arbitrators have had any opportunity to write informally for other arbitrators or for practitioners on the substantive or procedural issues one confronts in daily practice.

Although this book has value as a training tool for new arbitrators, it has a larger purpose. Experienced arbitrators, practitioners, and students in arbitration courses will profit from the insights and philosophy offered by these practitioners. The diversity of approaches presented here underscores the strength of this private judicial procedure, the survival of which is testimony to the voluntary support it has achieved and maintained within the labor relations community.

The chapters here present informed, yet informal insights from a number of experienced arbitrators into their methods of dealing with various arbitration problems. They were adapted from speeches made during a training program for new arbitrators conducted at the University of Michigan Law School in 1975 by the Institute of Continuing Legal Education, under the auspices of General Electric Company and the Internation Union of Electrical Workers, and with cooperation from the American Arbitration Association and the Federal Mediation and Conciliation Service. At the suggestion of Ted St. Antoine, then dean of the law school, I edited the transcript, presented the edited versions of their presentations to the speakers for revision, and put together this collection. In the case of Richard Mittenthal, who used a speech presented previously to the National Academy of Arbitrators in 1960, it was decided to reproduce the more comprehensive original paper. We thank the Bureau of National Affairs for permission to publish that paper.

The authors sought to retain the informality of their oral presentations in recognition that they deal with subjective attitudes toward various elements of the arbitration process. This volume is not intended as an academic or legalistic survey of arbitration. It seeks to present a relaxed view of the substantive and procedural problems considered by arbitrators to be important issues and an explanation of how they deal with those issues.

A number of the authors discuss the role of arbitration in our society; others focus on problems arising during the conduct of the arbitration hearing. Contributors of the latter portion of the book examine substantive issues considered by arbitrators on the merits or specific aspects of the decision-making process.

I gained a good deal of insight from the preparation of this volume, and for this I am indebted to my colleagues who have contributed their work and especially to Ted St. Antoine for stimulating this project. I also want to thank these friends in a more personal way: for still being around, for still being active, and for still being devoted enough to their profession to labor with me on the revision of these chapters.

A Word to the Arbitrator in Training

Rolf Valtin

IN CHOOSING to become arbitrators, you presumably have been motivated by a mixture of considerations. You have thought about the privilege of doing responsible work, about the lofty role of judge and peacemaker, about the prospect of becoming a self-employed person and the commonly recognized advantages that go with it, and about the fact that success in the profession yields a comfortable standard of living. I had thought about all of these things. They are thoroughly legitimate motivating factors. But no one should expect to have a job that brings only good things. In this sense, the job of an arbitrator is the same as all other jobs. It has its drawbacks. I want to mention three of them because I was less than aware of them when I strove to become an arbitrator.

One is loneliness. Unless you have a practice that includes a lot of mediation or a lot of work on tripartite boards (meaning a lot of discussion in arriving at the disposition of cases), you have to be prepared to spend most of your working life quite by yourself. I do not mean only the traveling and the hotel life but the working life in the office. No one will come to you to discuss a problem and thus to jar you into action. No one will ask you to attend meetings. Sometimes days go by without so much as a telephone call. It can be awfully quiet and lonesome. Indeed, it *has* to be quiet and lonesome for the arbitrator to be productive. For there is no way to be productive without being in the process of either reading or writing. Pencil sharpening and unnecessary phone calls bring temporarily welcome diversions. But they do not spell progress on undone cases. There is an endless need to go into action by means of one's own will power, to pull yet another case record from the files and start the study process.

A second inherent difficulty in the job is the need for stamina in the face of unpopularity and pressure. It is not easy to do one's level best only to be blasted for it. This does not happen all the time or even most of the time. But when it does happen, it can be very rugged. It can be in the form of cutting insults or, worse still, a bitter comment by a genuinely disappointed party. The answer frequently given is that an arbitrator must be thick-skinned. The difficulty is that there often is no great difference between being thick-skinned and being insensitive—and I do think that sensitivity is an important part of being a good arbitrator.

The third drawback is the huge discrepancy between the lofty position of arbitrator and the daily tasks of the job. There is no escaping the close reading and analysis of the record, which is sometimes very long, sometimes quite complex, and sometimes plain dreary. And once that is done, there is no escaping the need for careful and clear writing. Good writing— good organization, clarity, and precision of expression—is a requisite condition of good arbitration. Good writing is also synonymous with hard work.

The Ideal Arbitrator

Let us examine the question of the ideal arbitrator.

First, there is no such thing as *the* ideal arbitrator. Ours is not a system of one set of national parties setting the terms of employment and the tone of industrial relations for all of industry and all of organized labor. Ours is a system that permits, indeed, emphasizes, freedom by any particular set of parties to respond to its particular needs. Uniformity is the antithesis of our free collective bargaining system. Thus, no one person can be equally effective, let alone ideal, for all parties making use of arbitration. And thus also, we have had arbitrators who had highly different characteristics, whose styles are marked by contrast rather than likeness, and yet who have each been viewed as a giant in the field.

Consider the contrast between my mentors. I did my graduate work under George Taylor—who as much as anyone deserves the title of founder of our unique system of arbitration as the terminal point of the grievance procedure. Then, after two or three years in beginning industrial relations jobs and four years as a federal mediator, I became an apprentice under Ralph Seward, an overloaded steel umpire. Taylor cherished informality; sought behind-the-scenes conferences; believed that working things out through compromise was the better way in almost every circumstance; and wanted, as often as not, to teach parties how to make their bargaining process work. His role was particularly suitable in the early days of collective bargaining. Seward cares no less for fairness and justice. But he is incapable of sweeping to end results. The language of the agreement and its logical implications are his first concern. This is not to say that he is a mere semanticist. He himself has described arbitration as involving the mediation "between the Agreement and the problem, between language and life, between rules and special needs" (Seward, 1964). But freewheeling is foreign to him. He works in seclusion, and he cannot bring himself to make a broad pronouncement except as he can make it stand up under the language of the agreement.

Another contrast among arbitrators is worth mentioning. There are arbitrators who care deeply about due process, and there are other arbitrators who care quite as deeply about expedition and economy for the parties. Highly respected practitioners are found in each camp. I am not prepared to say that the one camp is right and the other is wrong. I *am* prepared to say that the two goals—due process and hearing seven or eight cases in a day and disposing of each case in a paragraph or two—cannot be met simultaneously.

These contrasts illustrate why the adoption of a new Code of Professional Responsibility (see Appendix) was an undertaking of enormous difficulty. It is not that we had a contest between the good guys and the bad guys or between the forward-looking and the conservatives or between those who are commercially motivated and those motivated by public service. The difficulty lay in the fact that American labor arbitrators are anything but a monolithic group.

The second general comment I want to make is that the same individual might operate very differently depending on which set of parties he or she might be working with. It has happened to me. As the umpire under the GM-UAW agreement, I soon learned that suggestions for settlement, except in very rare and clearly appropriate circumstances, were taboo. Further, I came to conclude that the parties' attitude toward mediation by the arbitrator was well-founded and wise. Their needs and purposes were such that they correctly insisted on the judicial role of their umpire. At the same time, I was serving as the permanent arbitrator for a small steel company and the steelworkers union in the Philadelphia area. Years ago, for a variety of good reasons, the mediatory approach was useful and suitable to these parties. To this day, they welcome it, and so I pursue it with great enthusiasm.

I do not feel sheepish about playing both roles, and should you someday find yourself adopting very different approaches according to whom you are working with, you should not denounce yourself as a chameleon. Rather, I think, it is to be regarded as the constructive accommodation to the varying needs of different sets of parties.

Elements of Good Arbitration

Having made these general observations about the arbitrator's job, I want to point out the elements that are common to good arbitration.

Courage is an overused word, but I think it has to be listed. Your judgment is what the parties have hired, and you must be prepared to declare yourself. Splitting for the sake of retention of acceptability is awful. Moreover, it is not likely to achieve the desired result. Most parties are smart enough to see through it. The great fortune of our work is that morality and practicality fall together. Straight shooting and intellectual honesty are virtues and are respected by the parties. Keeping a scorebook on wins and losses and making arbitration a popularity contest are the surest ways to go down the drain.

Promptness in hearing and deciding cases is very important to the parties. We must all strive to achieve it. But for me, the need for promptness poses a never-ending dilemma: doing quality work is equally important. One cannot be a speed demon while also pursuing standards of excellence. Time consumption, sometimes inordinate time consumption, is the price of quality. This is a problem you will have to confront and work out as you become a busy arbitrator. If you find that you are not someone who can "knock them out," you will have to learn to say no to assignment offers—or else, you will mar your life with the awful pressures that go with falling badly behind.

Balanced conduct at the hearing is a vital feature. You must be in control, and you must be prepared to make procedural rulings, preferably with explanations. But this is not the equivalent of being overbearing, nor is it the equivalent of brusquely barging in whenever you feel like it.

On the question of the passive versus the active arbitrator, my vote is in favor of the latter. I understand the argument that an arbitrator ought to be content with what the parties place before him or her and on that basis to decide the case. But I don't accept the argument. I don't think that an arbitrator has an obligation to be a sphinxlike creature. He or she should ask for clarification when things are left unclear, and, though generally not until the parties have finished their presentation, he or she should be free to ask searching questions going to implications and contractual principles. The test, before the arbitrator leaves the hearing, should be whether he or she has been given enough information to intelligently decide the case.

At the hearing, try not to get overinvolved in the minutiae of the case. Try to think of the case as a whole and of what is centrally presented. When you do that, pertinent questions will be framing themselves in your mind.

There is, last, the matter of opinion writing. No one should expect to come up with a quality document without hard work, and next to the soundness of the holding itself, good opinion writing is the most important element both in the furtherance of your career and in what the parties must have to maintain confidence in the process of arbitration. The losing party may not become convinced that it should have lost, but it can live with the result—and if given a sound and understandable rationale for the result, its representative can live with his or her constituents.

Fundamentally, the opinion requires treatment of the losing party's contentions. But sometimes there are so many contentions and subcontentions that a judgment has to be made as to what to treat and what to ignore. This can be difficult and hazardous. But it needs to be done if overly long and wandering opinions, and therefore unpersuasive opinions, are to be avoided. The trick is to determine what the losing party is really saying, contrasted to all that it has literally said.

A statement of the facts should never be left out. It need not be a long dissertation of what the parties are factually contending and why you side with one side or the other on the facts.

But there must be an express finding of the facts. That much is necessary for the parties to understand what is being decided. That much, together with well-reasoned and well-stated support for the holding, will in the long run serve the parties' best interests, not only in terms of the acceptability of the arbitration process but also in terms of keeping the losing party from running to the courts to get the award set aside. Hard work on the opinion is worth it.

The Arbitration Process

1

Arbitration and the Law

Theodore J. St. Antoine

LABOR ARBITRATION, the voluntary resolution of disputes between union and employers by mutually acceptable third parties, is a unique contribution of the American system of industrial jurisprudence. But it is relatively young. Indeed, through the 1930s only about 10 percent of all collective bargaining agreements in the United States provided for arbitration. The mass production industries have been the principal locus for the development of this central facet of industrial jurisprudence. World War II gave arbitration its biggest boost. The National War Labor Board had the responsibilty for setting the terms of contracts when the parties themselves could not negotiate them, and the board often inserted arbitration clauses into those contracts when the parties failed to settle on their own. By the mid-1940s the rate of use for arbitration had risen to 30 to 40 percent. Arbitration has continued to grow. The most recent surveys show that about 95 percent of major collective bargaining agreements now have provisions for final and binding arbitration as the last step in the grievance procedure.

From Interest Arbitration to Grievance Arbitration

This is quite different from other countries. In the United Kingdom, for instance, the parties have diametrically opposed views about what issues are appropriate to present to an outsider to arbitrate. While only 2 or 3 percent of all collective bargaining agreements in the United States have provision for new contract or *interest* arbitration, that is virtually the only kind of arbitration that exists in the United Kingdom. Until very recently, British emphasis was on new contract arbitration and not on grievance *rights* arbitration under an existing contract. In the United States, employers and unions have traditionally accepted, almost as an article of faith, the notion that voluntary collective bargaining is the only proper way to arrive at the terms of a new contract. But, once there is an agreement, the outside third parties, the arbitrators, can be brought in to interpret its provisions. They may not change or add to the contract, of course. The British believe that each shop is unique and the problems that arise are so particular that outsiders could not possibly understand the nuances of employer-employee relations. Yet, the broader wage and benefit policies and conditions of employment can appropriately be dealt with by outsiders because these are matters of nationwide economic principle and need not be tailored to fit the needs of a particular shop or plant. Thus, the British and Americans have directly opposing philosophies concerning interest and grievance arbitration. In a number of states in this country, however, there seems to be a growing recognition that when public employees, such as police and fire fighters, are denied the right to strike, it makes sense to have compulsory arbitration of new contract terms at the request of one of the parties if their negotiations fail.

Different approaches have been tried in the various states. Michigan started with a statute that simply provided that each party would make a presentation and the arbitrator would determine whatever terms he or she felt were appropriate. Now there is an increasing trend toward last-best-offer arbitration. Each party presents its last best offer to the arbitrator who then must choose one or the other. The theory is that, because of the fear that if either side is too unreasonable the arbitrator will choose the other offer, this will draw the parties as close together as possible and also encourage voluntary settlement. In some states there must be a choice between one complete package and the other, while other states provide the option of choosing between the parties' different positions on each issue.

Some legislation provides for last-best-offer consideration of economic matters but leaves the arbitrator more flexibility on noneconomic issues (of course, there is always the possibility of a dispute over whether a particular issue is economic or noneconomic).

In addition to this somewhat limited use of interest arbitration, many states authorize *factfinding* for certain public employees, such as school teachers, where there is less concern about danger to public health and safety in the case of a strike than there would be regarding police or fire fighters. Factfinding is very similar to arbitration in format, the difference being that the factfinding report is not final and binding. It is a set of recommendations.

All of us who handle interest arbitration and factfinding do so with a certain amount of trepidation. In the arbitration of a grievance, the collective bargaining agreement establishes the standard of decision. But in interest arbitration or factfinding, the arbitrator is let loose on a broad sea with no fixed compass but with the mandate to produce a contract for the parties from scratch. Actually, the lack of guidelines may be more apparent than real. The contracts negotiated for comparable groups of employees in comparable communities are handy and helpful references.

There is a widespread belief that interest arbitration may have an enervating effect on the parties' negotiations. There is a tendency to rely less on negotiations and to go directly to arbitration, at least on some issues, to "save something for the arbitrator." Although this is unfortunate, it may be the best alternative in cases where the right to strike is denied. Otherwise, public employee unions are left with little effective means of applying any leverage to effect a settlement. Furthermore, recent studies indicate that arbitration has had less adverse effect on voluntary dealings between the parties than was originally feared. One must concede, however, that any form of compulsory arbitration will probably have some tendency to dilute the collective bargaining process.

There was initially some concern that outsiders coming in to arbitrate interest disputes—such as academics who had never had to meet a payroll—would write unrealistic contracts. That does not seem to have occurred. I think that most arbitrators, in either grievance or interest arbitration, are likely to be conservative in the sense that they are not trying to blaze new paths but rather to make their own decision a genuine substitute for that of the parties. They seek to come as close as possible to the settlement the parties would have concluded had they been able to reach an accord. To assist in attaining that goal, statutes typically set forth a number of factors to be taken into consideration by the arbitrator in making the decision. They include such criteria as cost of living, ability to pay, the employment market, and comparability to similar communities.

Changing Judicial Attitudes

The common law did not favor arbitration. As far as the judges were concerned, arbitrators were upstarts from outside the judicial system who were trying to usurp the courts' business. In many common law decisions, the courts simply said they would not enforce an executory agreement to arbitrate. So unless an award had already been issued, there would be no enforcement of an agreement to arbitrate. That was pretty much the doctrine in England and the United States for a long time. Eventually, many states in this country passed statutes that made executory agreements to arbitrate legally enforceable. Even the common law became sufficiently modified so that agreements to arbitrate were sustained insofar as they covered the arbitration of disputes about the meaning of existing contract terms. At that point, apparently, no one had thought much about new contract arbitration. The notion of parties actually agreeing to arbitrate the substantive terms of a labor contract in case they could not voluntarily negotiate one was probably not viewed as a practical option. The assumption seems to have been that the courts would not hold such agreements legally enforceable. Decisions on this point are still divided.

There has been little government emphasis on interest arbitration over the years. The Railway Labor Act (RLA), which provides for both new contract and grievance arbitration, declares that if the parties cannot agree on a new contract, or cannot settle during a rather extended procedure, the National Mediation Board will try to nudge them into arbitration. It has no power, however, to force the parties to arbitrate unless they both agree. Congress on occasion has had to step in and push the parties into "mediation to a finality," which, no matter what you term it, smells suspiciously like compulsory arbitration. Under the RLA there is also an established statutory procedure for grievance arbitration, administered by the National Railroad Adjustment Board. The statute permits either party to invoke procedures before the board, and then arbitration becomes compulsory in the sense that if either party wants it, the other party is obliged to participate. For the most part, the arbitration panels are composed of union and employer representatives, with some limited participation by outside neutrals.

The Civil Service Reform Act of 1978 governs the labor relations of the federal government's own employees. If negotiations break down and mediation proves unsuccessful, either party may request intervention by the Federal Service Impasses Panel. The parties may agree on binding interest arbitration if the panel approves. Otherwise, the panel recommends or establishes appropriate procedures, which may include advisory or binding factfinding. The Postal Reorganization Act, covering postal workers, is more rigid in prescribing binding arbitration if an impasse in negotiations remains unresolved. The Civil Service Reform Act also requires that a grievance procedure capped by binding arbitration be included in all collective bargaining agreements.

The Taft-Hartley Act covers nearly all of American industry outside of the railroads and airlines and certain exempted employees, such as agricultural workers, domestic servants, and the public employees provided for by federal and state law.

The 1947 congress that enacted the Taft-Hartley Act was extremely concerned about the great wave of strikes that swept the country at the end of World War II, especially because many of these strikes occurred in the face of collective bargaining agreements and no-strike clauses, which should have prevented them as a matter of law. It was difficult, however, under state statutes to get jurisdiction over a union because of the problems of securing service of process on unincorporated associations. As a result, in 1947, the first Republican congress since the New Deal, concerned with redressing a perceived imbalance in the union-management power relationship, decided to enact a statute that would provide for jurisdiction in the federal district courts for the enforcement of collective bargaining agreements in the event of alleged breaches. The result was section 301 of the Taft-Hartley Act. It refers to "contracts between an employer and a labor organization," going beyond collective bargaining agreements and making any type of contract between union and employer arguably enforceable under section 301. Although agreements between unions and employers had been enforceable under state substantive law as contracts between private parties, that had not been the case under federal law, which technically has no such component as common law (the only federal law is the Constitution and the statutes enacted under it). After some debate over whether it was constitutional for the federal courts to decide these matters, it was resolved that section 301 constituted an authorization to the federal district courts to put together a substantive body of federal law for the interpretation and enforcement of contracts between unions and employers. Now, the Supreme Court of the United States, rather than the individual judiciaries of the states, would have the final say on the law governing collective bargaining agreements.

In the Supreme Court's decision in *Lincoln Mills*, 353 U.S. 448(1957), Justice Douglas stated that this new federal "common law" of labor contracts could be based upon state law, federal statutes, and the national labor policy. All would be absorbed into the developing body of federal law of labor contracts. Probably the greatest milestone in this effort of the federal government to ensure the enforceability of collective bargaining agreements came with the Supreme Court's decisions in the Steelworkers Trilogy in 1960.

The Steelworkers Trilogy lays down guidelines on the arbitrability of contract issues and the review and enforcement of arbitration awards. Justice Douglas was almost embarrassingly effusive in lauding labor arbitrators for their transcendental powers of insight into the rules and customs of the shop. The first and most important principle or arbitral law is that in a suit to enforce an agreement to arbitrate, a court is to resolve all doubts in favor of arbitration. An issue in dispute is to be held subject to arbitration if it is covered by the language of the arbitration clause, in the absence of the clearest and most unequivocal kind of exclusion. The fact that the claim is frivolous in the eyes of the court and the union should plainly lose the grievance on the merits is not a basis for rejecting the demand for arbitration. Even though the court knows that any sane arbitrator will throw out the grievance, it must still rule that the matter is arbitrable.

Employers were taken aback, even enraged, by this broad approach to arbitration. The Section of Labor Relations Law of the American Bar Association castigated the Steelworkers Trilogy and suggested that it could cause the downfall of the whole arbitration system in the United States. It was predicted that once they realized that such a broad interpretation could be applied to them, employers would not sign agreements to arbitrate. Some employers sought to establish extensive and precisely drawn exclusionary provisions in their contracts. But the Steelworkers Trilogy has not done the damage to labor relations that many feared. Part of this is due to self-policing by the parties. They have exercised common sense, and, since arbitration is time-consuming and expensive, unions wash out many more claims than they take to arbitration. Furthermore, even the arbitration of frivolous claims may have some thera- peutic value. Sometimes the scheduling of a case for arbitra- tion pressures the parties into detailed preparation and leads to the discovery that it is a case that should be settled. Some- times this revelation comes too late—at the arbitration hearing when one of the union or company witnesses discloses previ- ously unknown information. But this too may help the parties let off steam and thus serve a worthwhile function. Even if the parties know all the facts of the case before the hearing, they may be so wrapped up in their theories of the case that they do not realize that these will make no sense to an outsider. Presenting a case to a third, impartial party is quite different from presenting the same case across the table to the opposi- tion. To prevail in dealing with a person to whom you must appear reasonable, your position must have rational merit, and outlandish rhetoric will sound very hollow even to your own ears.

The issue of *substantive* arbitrability (whether the claim is covered by the contract's arbitration clause) is a matter for the courts to decide, not the arbitrator, and that should help to reassure those who believe the Steelworkers Trilogy leaned too far toward arbitration. The issue is to be resolved in favor of arbitration unless the exclusion is clear. Some contracts have a provision that assigns the question of arbitrability to the arbitrator. But otherwise, that issue is ultimately for the courts. According to a survey by Russ Smith and Dallas Jones, even if a court has ordered arbitration, many arbitrators are prepared to say that there is no contract provision under which they can grant relief, and thus they rule out arbitration under a somewhat stiffer standard than the courts would apply.

Even though an arbitrator to whom a case is referred by the court as being substantively arbitrable might find that the case is not substantively arbitrable, this decision will be based upon interpretation of the contract rather than upon an interpretation of the law. One question is arbitrability under the law as the courts interpret it; the other is a question of arbitrability under the contract as the arbitrator interprets it. Smith and Jones concluded that when arbitrators initially consider the question of arbitrability they will be tougher than the courts would be permitted to be under the Steelworkers Trilogy.

Questions of *procedural* arbitrability go to the issue of whether or not the moving party has fulfilled the necessary prerequisites to arbitration, such as timely submission of the grievance, and appeal from one step to another. In the absence of any express provision to the contrary on the part of the parties, procedural arbitrability is for the arbitrator to determine, not the courts. The courts deal with substantive arbitrability; the arbitrator deals with procedural arbitrability.

Coverage of the Arbitration Clause

Arbitration clauses differ from contract to contract, but there are two or three common arbitration arrangements. One is the so-called standard arbitration clause, under which the union or the employee or—sometimes—the employer will be entitled to take any grievance, any dispute concerning the interpretation or application of the terms and conditions of the contract, through the grievance procedure. If the issue cannot be resolved at one of those steps, the union, the grievant, or in some cases the employer, may submit the unresolved grievance to final and binding arbitration by some tribunal. Notice that this confines arbitration to the interpretation and application of contract terms.

More rarely, there is an open-ended arbitration or grievance arrangement whereby any dispute between the employer and the union may be taken up, at least through the grievance procedure. It is extremely rare for this kind of case to go to final and binding arbitration. That is in essence new contract arbitration, since it is not based on the terms of an existing contract.

Finally, a very common arrangement is an arbitration clause that, like the standard provision, covers any dispute over the interpretation or application of any term of the contract but adds a series of either generalized or specific exclusions from arbitration coverage. A quite detailed set of exclusions, for example, is found in the contracts in the electrical manufacturing industry.

Enforcement of Awards

Warrior and Gulf, 363 U.S. 574(1960), and *American Manufacturing*, 363 U.S. 564(1960), the first two cases of the Steelworkers Trilogy, dealt with the rules of arbitrability and the enforcement of the agreement to arbitrate. The third case of the trilogy, *Enterprise Wheel*, 363 U.S. 593(1960), dealt with the enforcement of the award once rendered. What standards should be applied by a court in reviewing and enforcing an arbitrator's award? It is quite clear that the reviewing court is not to pass on the merits de novo; it is not to second-guess the arbitrator on the merits. As the Supreme Court declared in *Enterprise Wheel*, the court is to enforce an award, whether or not it agrees with the award, as long as it was within the arbitrator's jurisdiction and it is not inherently deficient as being irrational or subject to some form of fraud, corruption, or similar defect.

There is one subtle question that has been troublesome over the past few years and remains a subject of controversy. In *Enterprise Wheel*, the Supreme Court emphasized that the arbitrator interprets the contract; that is his or her function. The award must "draw its essence" from the collective agreement. The arbitrator is not to base decisions on the provisions of "enacted legislation." That is what the Court says. Just what does it mean? Should the Court's statement be taken at face value?

Obvious conflicts can arise, such as a discrepancy between a straight reading of the contract's seniority provision and what may be an appropriate interpretation in light of Title VII of the Civil Rights Act of 1964. An administrative regulation on safety and health, veterans' preference statutes, and the union security provisions of the National Labor Relations Act (NLRA) are just a few of the many different areas in which there may be a conflict between what appears to be a mandate of the contract and what appears to be a mandate of the statute.

What should the arbitrator do? One view is that the arbitrator interprets the contract and lets the parties and the courts worry about the statutes. If the arbitration award is issued in accordance with the contract and is in violation of the statute, that is a matter for the courts to review. The arbitrator has fulfilled his commission from the parties. Another view is that it is wasteful and improper to have arbitrators issue awards that are supposed to be final and binding but are not in accord with the law. This view encourages the arbitrator to take applicable statutes into account in making a decision.

Probably the majority position among arbitrators, and certainly my own, is that if conflict between law and contract is unavoidable, the arbitrator should go by the contract. The parties have asked the arbitrator to "read" the contract for them, and that is all the arbitrator is empowered to do. But a lot of this controversy is a tempest in a teapot. In many cases the contract is ambiguous, and that gives the arbitrator a good deal of flexibility. You do not have to say that there is an irreconcilable conflict between the contract and the statute. You can simply interpret the contract so that it agrees with the statute. The contract was presumably intended to be interpreted in light of the existing law.

Arbitration and the NLRB

The relationship between arbitration and the National Labor Relations Board (NLRB) has been a puzzling problem for the NLRB and, more recently, for the courts. The NLRA forbids discrimination against employees because of union activity.

Many contracts also contain a provision that forbids employer discrimination against employees because of union activity or on the basis of race, sex, religion, and so forth. In addition, of course, Title VII of the Civil Rights Act contains a similar prohibition. So in effect, there are parallel streams—contract and statute—both of which provide rights to employees with accompanying remedies.

In my view, contracts are meant to be enforced by the arbitrators initially, and, ultimately and more technically, by the courts acting on arbitrators' interpretations. A statute is meant to be enforced by whatever tribunal the statute prescribes (the NLRB in the case of a National Labor Relations Act violation, and the EEOC and the courts in the case of a violation of the Civil Rights Act). The NLRB was informed by the Supreme Court in *C & C Plywood*, 385 U.S. 421 (1967), that it was entitled to handle a refusal to bargain charge in a case that arguably involved a matter of contract interpretation and enforcement. In that case, the employer had unilaterally granted pay increases to a whole group of employees. The contract gave the employer the right to grant individual merit increases, but that did not in terms include the right to grant group increases. Nonetheless, the employer maintained that if it could grant increases to individuals, then it could add them up and do the same thing for a group. Thus, it should not be considered a unilateral change of working conditions in violation of Section 8 (a) (5) of the National Labor Relations Act. The Board and the Supreme Court disagreed. Although there was no arbitration clause in the C & C Plywood agreement, lower courts have since held that even with an arbitration clause, there may be cases where the NLRB can take jurisdiction and deal with a matter that is also subject to the contract's grievance and arbitration procedure. Courts have thus apparently held that there can be concurrent jurisdiction by arbitrators and labor agencies over the same subject matter.

When should there be deferral by one tribunal to the other, or the "honoring" of the award of one by the other? To what extent should the different tribunals be totally independent? Once there has been a fair hearing in one forum, it can be argued, the other forum should accept the results. It seems to me, however, that different rights are involved: contract rights under the contract, and statutory rights under the statute. There is no inherent inconsistency in letting both the contract rights and the statutory rights be enforced. Yet we should still try to avoid excessive duplication of procedure, and we do not want cumulative remedies for the same situation. We simply want to make the employee whole for any injury that has been done. Suppose the arbitrator has already rendered an award. Under the *Spielberg* doctrine, 112 N.L.R.B. 1080 (1955), the NLRB will usually defer to that award if certain conditions are fulfilled. In the case of an employee fired for what he says is union activity, the arbitrator hears the case and decides there was no discrimination. The Board will ordinarily honor that award, assuming that there was a full and fair hearing, the statutory issue was presented to and decided by the arbitrator, all the parties agreed to be bound, and the result does not conflict with national labor policy. I would prefer to have the Board say that this is not a matter of honoring the award as a whole; it is a matter of accepting the factual determinations made by the arbitrator, which are also necessary to the Board's own determination. The Board cannot delegate its power to apply the NLRA, but it can avoid excessive litigation by accepting the factual findings as long as it is satisfied that the arbitration proceedings have been fair. But the Board does not describe the decision that way; it talks in terms of honoring the award.

In the case of *Alexander* v. *Gardner-Denver,* 415 U.S. 36 (1974), which involved the arbitration of an employee's racial discrimination claim, the Supreme Court emphasized that the arbitrator's award had no binding effect in a subsequent EEOC or court action under Title VII. Not even the *Spielberg* standards were applicable. The employee was not bound by the adverse arbitral award under the contract because he had a separate and independent statutory right. Title VII rights may be considered peculiarly personal—they belong to the individual—as well as exceptionally sensitive, in contrast to NLRA rights, which are more organizational and institutional. In *Gardner-Denver,* however, the courts were told that they could give such weight as seemed appropriate to the results of any arbitration proceeding. In what has become a famous footnote in the opinion, footnote 21, the Supreme Court went on to say that if the arbitral decision gave "full consideration" to the employee's Title VII rights, the award could be accorded "great weight." The Court explicitly noted that this might depend not only on the observance of all procedural safeguards, but also on the "special competence" of the particular arbitrator. Otherwise, the Court carefully sidestepped the question of what standards were to be applied in weighing the arbitration record.

Subsequent to the *Spielberg* case, the Board turned to other cases where there were claims of a violation of section 8 (a) (3) (discrimination because of union activity) or section 8 (a) (5) (refusal to bargain, specifically, a unilateral change in working conditions) but where there had not been any appeal to the parties' grievance and arbitration system. In the *Collyer* case, 192 N.L.R.B. 837 (1971), the Board dealt with an alleged unilateral change in working conditions that was arguably permissible under the contract. In a hotly controverted decision, the Board laid down the rule that if the matter in dispute was subject to the contract grievance machinery and the unfair labor practice issue might well be disposed of in the arbitrator's decision, then the Board would defer to the arbitrator and not handle the charge itself. The NLRB could reassert jurisdiction to examine the award for fairness in light of the *Spielberg* doctrine after it was issued.

After vacillating on the issue, a closely divided Board now holds that it will not defer to arbitration in cases involving alleged discrimination against individual employees. If *Gardner-Denver* and *Collyer* are distinguishable in part on the ground that the former is more concerned with personal statutory rights and the latter with group contractual rights, charges of section 8 (a) (3) violations may appropriately be classified as more in the nature of personal claims and thus properly not subject to the deferral doctrine.

Initially, the Board also extended the *Spielberg* doctrine to issues that could have been raised at the arbitration proceeding but were not. An example would be an employee who was fired for alleged drunkenness and the discharge was arbitrated on that issue. Thereafter, the employee raises with the NLRB for the first time the claim that he or she was terminated because of union activity, which would be a violation of section 8 (a) (3). In *Electronic Reproduction Service Corporation*, 213 N.L.R.B. 758 (1974), the Board held that it would honor the arbitration award with regard to every matter that the parties could have brought to the arbitrator even though, in fact, certain matters were not presented. In *Suburban Motor Freight*, 247 N.L.R.B. No. 2, 103 L.R.R.M. 1113 (1980), however, the Board changed this decision. It will no longer honor the result of an arbitration under *Spielberg* unless the unfair labor practice issue was both presented to and considered by the arbitrator. This increases the temptation for parties to hold back claims and thus proliferate litigation, but it also reduces the likelihood that legitimate claims will be lost by default.

2

New Contract Arbitration in the Public Sector: The Michigan Example

Robert G. Howlett

WHILE COLLECTIVE bargaining has existed in the public sector for many decades, the modern world of collective bargaining for public employees commenced with the first Wisconsin statute in 1959, followed by Executive Order 10988 in 1962. In 1965 Connecticut, Delaware, Massachusetts, and Michigan adopted public employment relations acts. At present, there are thirty-nine states, the District of Columbia, Puerto Rico, the Virgin Islands, and numerous cities that have some type of legislation authorizing or requiring collective bargaining for some or all of their government employees.[1] In some states the authorization for collective bargaining was initiated by court decision or attorney general opinions.

The Michigan Employment Relations Commission (MERC) evolved from the Labor Mediation Board created in 1939,

---

1. In one state, collective bargaining exists by executive order, and in Michigan, because of an unusual constitutional provision, state employees have collective bargaining rights by virtue of a Michigan Civil Service Commission rule.

when the Michigan legislature enacted a private sector statute that recognized the right of private employees not covered by the NLRA to engage in collective bargaining. In 1947 the legislature enacted a public sector statute concerned primarily with mediation. The Michigan statute, like most other public sector collective bargaining laws, authorizes collective bargaining in the public sector while adhering to the common law rule that strikes by public employees are illegal.

Most of the early statutes provided for factfinding as the terminal step for public sector impasses. In some states the factfinding has been viewed as adversarial; in others, it has been treated as investigatory. The factfinder hears evidence, writes a report, and makes recommendations to the parties that in his or her opinion will resolve the impasse. If the procedure is recognized as investigatory, the factfinder may go outside the record for information for the report and recommendations. Occasionally factfinders in Michigan have done so.

Anyone familiar with the public sector recognizes that the strike looks over the shoulder of the bargainers, even though in most states it is illegal by statute, court decision, or attorney general opinion. Public employees do engage in strikes. Strikes have been more prevalent in Michigan than in other states, perhaps because we rely more on collective bargaining than any other state in the union.

To the surprise of many of us who have been involved in public sector labor relations and lobbied for such legislation, the school teachers have been the most militant public employees. There have been more strikes by elementary and secondary school teachers than any other group of public employees. If anyone had told me in 1965 that this would be the case, I would have thought him or her a fit subject for a mental institution. In 1966 the school marms and their male counterparts "hit the bricks," and they have been doing it ever since—not only in Michigan, but elsewhere. The employees in the uniformed forces—police, fire fighters, and prison guards—have been generally less prone to engage in job actions, although strikes and blue flu do occur from time to time.

The prohibition of the strike is based on several concepts, including the theory that government services are essential to public safety and health. There is some basis for this theory, and while reliance on it is exaggerated, there is little dispute with respect to police and fire fighters. They are responsible for essential services, which if not performed endanger the public safety. In recent years it has been proposed that if police and fire fighters cannot strike, it is reasonable and perhaps obligatory to provide them a substitute method for resolving contract disputes, namely interest arbitration.

Grievance arbitration has worked in the private sector as an effective substitute for strikes—and for litigation. Why not adopt the example of some industries in the private sector, i.e., the printing and transit industries (Young 1966, Kuhn 1952, Barnum 1971, Platt et al. 1973), to resolve disputes over new contract terms for public sector employees?

The idea has already borne fruit. Wyoming, Pennsylvania, and Rhode Island were the first states to try it; others have followed. The Wyoming statute applies to fire fighters; the Rhode Island statute to police and fire fighters; and the Pennsylvania statute to police, fire fighters, prison guards, mental hospital employees, and court employees.

In 1967 a study committee, appointed by Michigan governor George Romney, recommended that Michigan experiment with interest arbitration for police and fire fighters. The members of the committee were a prestigious group: Russell A. Smith as chairman, Gabriel N. Alexander, Edward L. Cushman, Ronald W. Haughton, and Charles C. Killingsworth. The report and recommendations were issued February 15, 1967; in 1969 our law was enacted.

Later state statutes have expanded legislated arbitration from uniformed forces to employees who perform services deemed by the legislature, or decreed by a state agency or court, to be essential. Typically in these states, employees not subject to the arbitration process are authorized, with limitations, to use the strike as a means of persuading public employers to agree with their proposals. If they are prohibited from striking, there is arbitration of unresolved issues. Currently, twenty-six states provide for some form of permissive or mandatory legislated arbitration. In addition, the city of New York and a number of smaller cities provide for arbitration as an impasse-resolving procedure in collective bargaining.

Interest arbitration has become recognized as an intelli-

gent, civilized means of resolving impasses where service interruption causes serious damage to the public. I believe, as one of
a small minority, that all impasses in collective bargaining in
both the private and public sectors should be resolved by some
judicial or quasi-judicial process. In this complex world where
people are starving and do not have adequate housing, not to
mention a life of dignity, any work stoppage that reduces the
flow of goods and services so greatly needed borders on the
immoral. But I suspect I will be dead many years before the
world catches up with my intelligent approach to problem solv-
ing in collective bargaining.

There has been objection to legislated arbitration on the
grounds that it damages collective bargaining, that it is unconstitutional, and that it will not prevent strikes.

The charge that arbitration seriously damages collective
bargaining has not been validated, although there are situations where public employers or public sector unions, or both,
prefer the decision of an arbitrator to serious collective bargaining. In Michigan we have found that interest arbitration
has not seriously damaged collective bargaining. Most issues
are resolved in negotiations and mediation, and only the most
difficult remaining issues are submitted to arbitration—the few
horror stories notwithstanding. In a few cases, the prospect of
having to go to arbitration has had an adverse impact on serious negotiation and effective mediation. Usually this is rem-
edied by forceful mediators who push the parties toward settlement. The evidence shows that interest arbitration has been
working well in other states.

The constitutionality of legislated arbitration is no longer a
significant issue. It has been sustained by most of the appellate
courts that have been confronted with the issue. When our
statute was first upheld by the Michigan Supreme Court in a
two-to-two decision, a dissent by Justice Levin found the law
unconstitutional as an unlawful delegation of legislative power,
Dearborn Fire Fighters v. *City of Dearborn*, 394 Mich. 229, 231
N.W.2d 226 (1975).[2] This is the attack made on statutes by

---

2. Three justices did not participate. Subsequently, the statute's constitutionality was upheld by a four-to-three vote in *City of Detroit* v. *Detroit Police
Officers Ass'n*, 408 Mich. 410, 294 N.W. 2d 68 (1980).

municipal officials throughout the country. They point out that the neutral arbitrator does not have to face the voters and is thus insulated from political accountability. The other dissenter in the Michigan case held that the constitutional objection could be resolved by an amendment to the statute providing for continuing politically responsible arbitrators, presumably something like a labor court, or a panel of arbitrators appointed by the governor, or perhaps the panel chairperson drawn from our commission.

The statute was amended to provide for the appointment of a panel of arbitrators by MERC. The panel chairmen are selected from the group, and they take the public official's constitutional oath of office.

Standards in Interest Arbitration

In some states, constitutionality has been attacked on the ground that the statute does not have standards to guide the neutrals. A number of statutes, including the Michigan statute, have standards; others are silent on standards.

The standards imposed by the statutes vary. The Michigan and Rhode Island statutes, in which the standards are almost identical, provide that the panel must consider (1) the lawful authority of the employer, (2) stipulations of the parties, (3) the interest and welfare of the public, and (4) the ability of the unit of government to meet the costs of the award (cities, counties, and school districts usually argue that they cannot afford anything beyond their first on-the-table offer).

Other standards listed are (1) comparison of the wages, hours, and conditions of employment of the employees involved in the arbitration proceeding with the wages, hours, and conditions of employment of other employees performing similar services and with other employees in public employment in comparable communities, or in private employment in comparable communities; (2) the average consumer prices for goods and services, commonly known as the cost-of-living; (3) the overall compensation presently received by the employees, including fringe benefits; (4) changes in any of the foregoing circumstances during the pendency of the arbitration proceedings; and (5) such other factors as are normally or traditionally taken into consideration in the determination of wages, hours, and conditions of employment through collective bargaining, mediation, factfinding, arbitration, or otherwise between the parties in the public sector or in private employment. The long list of standards affords the panel a wide choice of criteria on which to rely. The Michigan Supreme Court has emphasized that the panel must consider the applicable (not necessarily all) standards, and the opinion must disclose the standards used in reaching decision, and its reasons for it, *City of Detroit* v. *Detroit Police Officers Ass'n.*

State statutes also vary as to whether the arbitration decision is subject to appeal. In Michigan the statute provides for an appeal and reversal for the traditional grievance arbitration reasons. It also provides that the award must be "supported by competent, material, and substantial evidence on the whole record." Given the importance of interest arbitration in government, there should be an appeal procedure. This is consistent with Anglo-American jurisprudence: one appeal is a matter of right.

Michigan Law

Under the Michigan statute, thirty days of mediation is a condition precedent to arbitration. One of the issues that has been debated is what mediation entails. The arguments run from one extreme—all that needs to be done is to have a mediator *appointed* thirty days before the request for arbitration, even though the mediator never meets with the parties—to the other—thirty days of mediation means that there must be meetings between the mediator and parties for thirty days, without which there is no entitlement to arbitration. This issue has caused MERC some trouble. Certainly the legislature intended that there be a serious effort by the parties to work with a mediator to try to resolve their impasse. That is what we try to get them to do. Sometimes when I was MERC chairman, I withheld appointment of an arbitration panel chairman until the parties met with a mediator and made a serious effort to settle. I used the withholding as an extralegal lever to force effective mediation.

After the thirty days of mediation, either the public employer or the public sector union may institute an arbitration by serving a written notice on the other party, with a copy to the commission. The filing of the notice starts a schedule under which each of the parties is to appoint a delegate to the tripartite panel. Formerly, the two delegates then attempted to select a panel chairman. If they were unsuccessful, the chairman was appointed by the MERC chairman within seven days. In about one-third of the cases, the parties notified me that they had agreed on the chairman. Since the amendment of the statute, MERC sends three names to the panel with the request that they indicate their order of preference. Appointment is made by MERC.

The statute requires that the panel chairman is to schedule the hearing within fifteen days, although experience discloses that usually both parties want more time to prepare. The panel holds the hearing and then issues a decision. The panel chairman prepares an opinion, which must be signed by at least one other member of the panel. Before the statute was amended to provide for last offer on economic issues, we had a substantial number of cases in which there were unanimous decisions. This suggests that there was mediation and compromise among the three members of the panel.

When the law first went into effect there was a campaign against the proceedings by the public employers on the ground that it did not prevent strikes, that it damaged collective bargaining, and that the economic awards were inordinately high. Since the early months, there has been little trouble with the acceptance of the awards, although a few have been appealed.

There is merit in both interest arbitration and in interest factfinding by a tripartite panel. If the neutral can persuade the two "side judges" in a tripartite panel to level with him, he can often formulate a recommendation in factfinding or an arbitration award that is satisfactory, or at least reasonably acceptable, to both parties.

The reaction of employer groups in Michigan to this legislation has been interesting. Before the law went into effect, the Michigan Municipal League opposed the legislation on the ground that collective bargaining had no place in the public sector. After the law went into effect, the league took the interesting position that legislated arbitration was unacceptable because it damaged collective bargaining.

In the first year or two under the law, the awards were high for police and fire fighters because they had previously exercised restraint in collective bargaining and had not used the strike or threat of a strike. This resulted in their falling behind in wages compared to the more aggressive teachers. Some catching up was appropriate in those early years.

When the law first came up for renewal, it was renewed for three years by the almost unanimous vote in both houses of the legislature, and when it came up the next time, the termination date was removed. If legislators reflect their constituents' desires, it is reasonable to conclude that the public is generally satisfied with the law in Michigan.

The opposition of the city officials seems to have been muted, although the Michigan Municipal League has adopted a resolution favoring strikes in the public sector as preferable to interest arbitration. This is a complete reversal from the position taken by the league a few years earlier.

When the law was before the legislature for renewal in 1972, the political situation was such that a provision for some kind of last offer arbitration was necessary in order to ensure enactment by the Senate. This may have been caused by the proposal of President Nixon that final offer arbitration was appropriate for the transportation industry.

The amended and renewed legislation limited the last offer provision to economic issues. The panel had the right to determine whether or not an issue was an economic issue (this can be a really sticky problem in some gray areas). Each economic issue is submitted separately to the panel, which selects either the public employer's last offer or the public sector union's last offer. It cannot split the baby down the middle. The act does not specify when the offers are to be made, but the practice is to have them submitted at the end of the evidence.

The theory of last offer arbitration is that it will cause each of the parties to be more realistic in its bargaining and to approach the middle ground, thus resulting in more settlements. Final offer selection was first tried on a package-by-package basis in Indianapolis and Eugene, Oregon. It was criticized by the arbitrators in both cases, because there were both good and bad proposals in each of the packages.

Some jurisdictions have adopted the package-by-package choice; others have empowered the arbitrator or panel to choose either the employer's last offer or the union's last offer on each issue; one state has added the factfinder's recommendation as a third alternative (Rehmus 1975, Benjamin 1978, Bowers 1973, Long and Feuille 1974, Whitney 1973, Loewenberg 1975).

Our experience in Michigan discloses that the last offer arrangement has worked. Before the introduction of final offer (October 1969 through December 1972), most cases were settled by collective bargaining or through mediation. But of those that did not settle and were submitted to arbitration, there were 105 awards and 71 settlements during the arbitration process. In a comparable period after final offer was introduced, we had 51 awards and 121 settlements, better than a two-to-one ratio. This suggests that the law is doing what the legislators intended, pushing the parties closer together. When they see they are close enough, they settle. This has not occurred solely by the parties' efforts. In some cases panel chairmen have engaged in mediation, a significant factor in the resolution in some of the cases.

The Role of the Arbitrator

This phenomenon raises a philosophical question: should the chairman of a tripartite panel in either factfinding or interest arbitration—or even a single factfinder or interest arbitrator—try to mediate? One view is that the proceeding is judicial, and therefore there should be no mediation. The other view is that settlement is the name of the game, hence it is proper for the factfinder or arbitrator to assist the parties in reaching an agreement if they indicate that a mediated settlement is possible.

When the teachers first went on strike in Michigan, there were so many cases to be mediated that MERC's mediation staff could not handle them all. To meet the need we designated factfinders (we called the process instant factfinding) and told them to mediate. It appeared to be a mistake for three reasons: (1) We found that many arbitrators had not had experience in collective bargaining and, because mediation is very different from arbitration, were not comfortable or effective as mediators. (2) We were fearful—too much so as it turned out—that we would damage the confidentiality of the mediation process, which works, in part, because the parties have confidence in the mediator and afford him information that they know he or she will not tell the other party until the right time. If you put a factfinder in that position, the parties may not level with him because of concern that information offered in confidence may influence him or her in the later role as factfinder. (3) We found that our mediators' noses were out of joint because they felt that telling a factfinder to mediate was suggesting that the mediators had not done their jobs effectively. So then we told our factfinders not to mediate but to confine themselves to factfinding. Some of them did not comply with our orders—fortunately—and secured settlements.

Later, the problem disappeared. The mediators were no longer concerned. We found that there was no damage to the confidentiality of the mediation process, and that some of our arbitrators are competent mediators. So when there is a particularly tough factfinding case, we select a factfinder who has experience in collective bargaining. Such an individual knows what goes on at the bargaining table and is able to get the parties together even though, on occasion, he or she may have to be a little rough about it. Arbitrators who have not had bargaining experience, by and large, are not as good at mediation.

Some mediators and lawyers have proposed that the last offer be submitted at the end of the mediation process rather than after the parties have submitted their evidence to arbitration. That has been rejected on the theory that the parties are not ready to admit their truly final offer until they have heard the evidence before the panel and have learned the weak and strong sides of both parties' cases. To submit the final positions at the end of the evidence is akin to the system of private sector deadlines and strikes. In private sector collective bargaining there is a "final" offer as a package. Then comes the decision whether to strike. Sometimes there is another "final" offer on each side, and maybe more, until there is a settlement—or a strike, or occasionally a lockout.

Examination of the cases decided by the arbitration panels

in the several states that use final offer arbitration discloses that the comparability factor is the most significant in the decision-making process. The panels look to comparable units of government and possibly to some private enterprises for both economic and noneconomic issues.

There is a theory that an arbitrator should, based on the evidence, do what is right, fair, and equitable. The other theory is that the award should seek to direct the solution the parties would have reached had they proceeded in collective bargaining and had they the right to strike or lock out. Although there is some overlap of these roles in individual cases, I favor the former approach.

Generally, arbitrators have not been innovative in awarding new collective bargaining provisions. This is as it should be. New procedures should be adopted by agreement of the parties; they should not be imposed. The arbitrator may suggest that the issue be taken up in direct negotiations for the next contract. This, in a sense, is an element of the comparability standard. The arbitrator looks at the area, cities and counties of the same size, and uses comparability as the prime guide. When dealing with comparability, each side picks the statistics it believes are best for its case. The panel must weigh the two submissions.

There are issues of a philosophic nature that should not be decided by an interest arbitrator. Most arbitrators have firmly held personal views on such issues as binding grievance arbitration and union security. Either you believe in binding grievance arbitration or you do not. Either you believe in union security or you do not. It is difficult to secure hard evidence on that type of issue. On union security, either you believe that everyone who receives a service should pay for it—that there should be no free riders—or you believe that no person should be required to pay tribute to hold a job. Arbitrators may decide such issues on the basis of personal conviction, or they may conclude that the prevailing practice in comparable communities forces them to one conclusion or the other without regard to their personal convictions.

The Conduct of the Hearing

3

Running the Hearing

Ronald W. Haughton

THE MOST important thing for you as an arbitrator to remember is that the parties own the hearing. They agreed to your selection; they hired you; they wrote the contract. You should not treat the process as yours; you should not be arrogant; you should not act like a judge; and you should not talk too much. Let the parties do the talking, work out the problems. You will be surprised how many knotty issues will be resolved during the hearing if you just ask the other side to respond, and then ask the original side to add something, and so on. By the time they have killed off each other's contrariness, the problem has disappeared.

Do not try to take their procedure away from them. Give it back whenever they try to abdicate or place the burden of procedure on you. For example, it is an old ploy for one party or the other to say, "Mr. or Ms. Arbitrator, do you want us to put in some evidence on this subject?" This can put you into a trap. If your answer is no, then it is your fault when they lose the case because you excluded crucial evidence. If you say yes, then you are implying that the subject is important. Tell them it is up to them. Remind them that this is an adversary proceeding to elicit information and that it is their obligation to select whatever information they think is important.

Preliminaries

The arbitrator first becomes involved in a case when notice of appointment is received. Sometimes it is a formal notice from an appointing agency such as the AAA, the FMCS, or a state agency, or simply a joint letter from the parties. Often one of the parties simply telephones to inquire when you will be available for a hearing. The scope of the conversation should be limited to arranging the details of the time and place of the hearing.

The arbitrator must try not to get sucked into any discussion of the merits of the case during the conversation. If it happens, then one should decline to hear the case. As you know, an arbitrator cannot advertise, but one of the best advertisements still is to let the parties know you are not too anxious to get a case. You do just this when you disqualify yourself after hearing a discussion of one side of a case. This is the professional way to handle this kind of situation and has the advantage of raising your standing in the estimation of the parties.

If you take a case after talking to one side about the merits, you should tell the other side, or carry it on your conscience. You may be misleading the side that spoke to you into thinking it has you in its pocket. Obviously, the mere identification of the issue such as, "This is a case involving discharge for theft," or, "We have an arbitrability issue," does not compromise your position and would not require disqualification. Indeed, the notice of appointment from the neutral agencies will often contain a brief statement of the issues. Sometimes this gives you some idea how long the case will take.

The next step is to provide dates. If you receive a telephone call, you can have the party calling you clear it with the other side. If it is a notice from an agency, you will have to call the agency or write to advise as to available dates. If it is the American Arbitration Association (AAA), the agency normally will contact the parties and set up the hearing. If you receive a joint letter, the safest thing is to write a joint letter back to the parties, and suggest a couple of dates.

Your credibility in your first few cases is very important. It is probably safest to remain a little standoffish. Ask the parties to select a location for the hearing. Put the burden on them. If they specifically ask you to find a hearing room, a hotel or motel usually is acceptable. If expense is important to the parties, the Federal Mediation and Conciliation Service (FMCS) often has hearing space available. In small towns, courtrooms are often used.

Sometimes the parties send you the grievance form, the contract, and perhaps even a prehearing brief. Some arbitrators spend considerable time reading through these materials. My view is the less you know about a case before the hearing starts, the better. In fact, one side may send you material unbeknownst to the other side, which may have valid objections to your receipt of such materials. It is better not to look at such offerings and be able to state at the hearing that you have not been prejudiced by them. In any event, there is nothing the parties like better than to tell you about their case. They are going to tell it all to you at the hearing, even if you study the advance material in detail.

Be on time at the hearing, even a little early if possible. I was once late to a hearing. I knew both sides intimately, both lawyers, and they felt so embarrassed for me. The case involved a discharge for being tardy.

It is a nice touch when you arrive at the hearing to introduce yourself to the people who are there, especially if you are a little bit early. Take the time to say hello to each person present. A quick handshake will help establish a good rapport. When you sit down, pass around an attendance sheet with columns for employer and union. It is like a schoolteacher's seating chart. This will enable you to get to know the names and spellings and the titles of the people present. You will then be able to call them by name.

I also ask the parties to identify the person to whom the decision and the statement should be sent, to give me the correct addresses, and to indicate how many copies they would like. When you get home you need to know the correct spelling of names and similar information.

If the parties do not seem too familiar with the arbitration process, you could tell them that you are used to an informal procedure, that you are not rigid about adhering to the rules of evidence but you will apply them properly. Make it clear that you know how to weigh evidence.

You might wish to tell the parties that you will be happy to accommodate to any procedure they might prefer. They may have their own way of doing things. Other things being equal, it is nice to select the procedure with which they are comfortable.

Procedural Considerations

Ex Parte Hearings

Once in awhile you will have a case where one side does not come to the hearing. You will be pressured by the side that is present to go forward with an ex parte hearing. Its representative may say, "Mr. Arbitrator, the other side is not here. We are. They had notice. Let's proceed." If you do, one side will put in any kind of a case it wants, with no rebuttal by the side not present. If there is any plausibility at all, the case is won without your having to evaluate more than one set of statements.

But there really is a professional burden for the arbitrator to be right in the decision. You can wobble through an ex parte hearing, but it is always better to have both sides present. You can get people on the phone and try to schedule another date, or if the other side has a procedural objection, there is also the possibility of appearing specially without conceding jurisdiction to the arbitrator. In any event, try to avoid holding an ex parte hearing. It will seldom happen that the absent side will absolutely refuse to appear, although there are times when you will have to proceed with only one party present.

If you do this, there is still a professional burden on the arbitrator to be correct in the decision. You can throw out a question once in a while and elicit some facts on points not raised, but you have to be careful not to give the appearance of favoring the other side.

Outside Observers

What about the attendance of outside observers? I have had cases where the grievant's whole family comes to the hearing. If these observers are all there on behalf of one side, then that party can deputize them representatives for their side.

A bigger problem is the grievant who is having a dispute with the union and brings his own lawyer. The company might ask, "What is that outsider doing here?" or the union might say, "This person does not represent us."

In the last analysis, it is the parties to the contract, the union and the employer, who have hired you, and you usually should accommodate to their procedural agreements. Of course, you can try your mediation skills by suggesting to the parties that they let the person sit in and not say anything. You might even suggest that if he or she is excluded, the grievant client may even sue before another forum. If you cannot accomplish a mutual agreement, you probably should exclude the outside spokesperson.

There is another kind of third party, employees who are members of a different union in a different bargaining unit in the same plant. For example, you may have a question about the machinists' right to work on a particular machine in a large plant. The patternmakers, who are in a separate unit in the same plant, come in to say that you have no right to assign that work because it belongs to them.

Here, too, you should try to get the parties to let the patternmakers sit in on the hearing. But, if they will not agree, you probably will have to exclude them. If you do exclude the patternmakers, they will still be ghosts in the chairs, and you will still be aware, at least in the back of your mind, that there is another interested party. One or both of the parties should call the second union as a witness, but they may not. If they do not, just remember the decision you have to write is between the machinists and the company. You cannot write the patternmakers into the award, but you can recognize that there is a problem in how work is assigned in that plant.

Oaths

You do not have to worry about whether you have the legal authority to swear in witnesses. If you are asked to swear the witnesses, just assume that you have the authority. You ask the witnesses to raise their right hands and say, "Do you solemnly swear to tell the truth, the whole truth, and nothing but the truth?" They say, "I do," and sit down. If the parties ask me whether I want the witnesses sworn, I tell them it is up to them. If only one side wants them sworn, I swear them in. Sometimes you come across a witness who refuses to swear. I tell such a witness that he or she can affirm to tell the truth.

Sequestering Witnesses
If either side requests the separation of witnesses so they will
not hear each other's testimony, it has the right to have this
request granted, except for sequestering of the grievant. In a
discipline case there is a basic principle of fair play at stake.
The grievant is the accused, and he or she has the right to be
faced by the accuser.

Since each side can have advisers or experts, there may be
a problem if any of these persons is also to be a witness. In such
cases, suggest that that person be called first, perhaps even out
of order, so that the testimony can be completed early and the
adviser can remain in the hearing room. A problem could arise
if the adviser testifies, then stays in the hearing room, and then
is called as a rebuttal witness. Be prepared for that one.

Separation of witnesses is called for only where there is a
real question of credibility. In my experience, this is true in
only a few cases. But the procedure does give the arbitrator a
good opportunity to determine credibility when there is a
string of witnesses, perhaps each saying something different
about the same incident.

Opening

The Issue
The first question you may have to deal with is the statement of
the issue to be determined. Usually, the parties stipulate to it
before you ask. If they have a problem, you can always fall back
on the statement of the issue as it was understood in the grievance procedure. If the parties cannot agree even on the issue, do
not get involved in an argument. Just leave the room, and give
them time to fight it out. Let them do their work. Most arbitrators will not proceed without the issue being defined. If they
continue to fail to agree on a statement of the issue, you can say,
"I have enough of a problem determining which party is right
on the issue without having to also determine what the issue is.
That is your obligation." Failing agreement at that point you
usually can use the written grievance as a fallback position.

Who Goes First?
If both sides are present and they have agreed on an issue, who
presents its case first? In the early days, the AAA rules said that

the party who filed the case always went first, that is, the moving party. But then the General Motors Corporation saw the obvious—"the grievant in a discipline case is presumed innocent until proven guilty." Why should he or she have to defend himself by starting first? It was quite a job to explain this in some instances. But when I was in Michigan, it was quite helpful to say to an employer, "Well, General Motors decided to do it this way, and I guess you can too."

At any rate, if you look at the grievance or the submission and see that it is not a disciplinary case, you can suggest that the union go first. If it is a discipline case, you would normally expect the employer go forward. If they are old hands, they will probably just pitch in. On the other hand, there may be a big squabble. If you are not careful, you can get into nasty procedural issues about who goes first.

Perhaps the union claims that this demotion is a discipline case, and the company insists the demotion was due to a personnel cutback. Then you have to make a ruling because somebody has to start. Make your ruling. If the other party complains, note that it will have its own turn in good time. Point out that you just want to get on with the hearing and that the burden of going forward is different from the burden of proof. In those circumstances, it really does not matter who goes first.

Opening Statements
Opening statements tend to be argumentative and may precipitate objections from the other side. The arbitrator can smooth ruffled feathers by noting that what was presented is not evidence, that it is a presentation of what the speaker will attempt to prove. In that way, you also alert the speaker that his or her opening statement does not count as evidence.

Objections

Do not forget that if one side objects, you should not rule on the matter until you ask the other side to comment. Let both parties comment. Even if they do not resolve the problem, the time consumed by the discussion gives you a chance to think about how you will rule.

Objections can present tough problems. One time while I

was serving in an umpireship, I ruled to exclude some information on subcontracting, and the union president said that was the last straw. I was through as far as he was concerned, and he terminated the proceeding.

In ruling on objections you often do not know how important the matter is to the parties. Sometimes you can get away with saying, "I'll take it for what it's worth." If there are a lot of objections, you have a right to get a little impatient. You may want to lecture a bit about evidence and point out that you welcome objections and emphasize that you know what weight to apply. You can note that one of the purposes of objections is to save a jury from its own ignorance. Here, you can point out that an arbitrator is supposed to be able to discern what is relevant and what is not.

Sometimes material that you allow imposes a heavy burden on the other side to respond, such as in a claim of surprise. The other party simply may not be prepared. In such a case, I would grant a recess, even several days, for the opposing side to prepare an answer.

Rulings on evidence should be guided by common sense. You have to know what hearsay is—what somebody told somebody—and that that does not have much weight. If someone objects to hearsay, you can either rule on it or, if the claim has already been heard, you can state that it carries little or no weight. Sometimes I am inclined to tell the parties that I will rule on relevance in my decision. But the wise advocate will demand a ruling at the time, and he or she is entitled to it.

An important goal of arbitration is to let the parties have their problem heard and resolved without excessive technicalities. The relationship between the parties in cases where sticky problems arise over objections should be no worse when the arbitrator leaves them than they were before the hearing. If you get too involved in procedural hassles, you may come out smelling like a rose, but the parties may be incensed at each other. That is not the purpose of the procedure. If possible, you should leave them feeling better about each other.

Closing
The side that started, the moving party, goes first with closing arguments. If the parties wish to follow a different procedure,

let them. Then, if the first party wants to respond to the second party's closing argument, I let them. It cannot go on for very long.

I rarely ask for posthearing briefs. It is up to the parties. I ask them what their pleasure is. One side may say it wants to file a brief. In these circumstances, it usually works out that the other also will opt to file; however, you do not have to require it to do so. It can argue orally if it wishes.

Make it clear that you do not expect anything terribly formal in the way of a brief. A good procedure is to require that briefs be postmarked on a mutually acceptable date and that they be exchanged by the parties. Grant them up to thirty days to file briefs. In some cases, they send two copies to you, and you exchange them. In others, they do the cross-filing. In AAA cases, the association does the exchanging.

Questions

My rule on note-taking is, take more than necessary. In about one-third or one-half of all cases, you may have a court stenographer present, but they can make errors.

In my early days as an arbitrator, I remember going back over one particular case and finding that I did not have enough information. Now, I always have too much information. It is a nice feeling. With great care, I fill in the gaps in the parties' evidence by asking a few questions. This does not create a problem if you are careful not to appear to be aiding one side. Remember, the burden is on you to be right without asking questions that will make or break someone's case. Ask a question once in a while if the record needs fleshing out. But do so with care.

The case belongs to the parties, yet you have to have the facts. If you feel that you do not know something as you are taking notes, you can make a marginal note, and then during direct examination and cross-examination and redirect examination and so on, you can cross off some of your questions as the answers come in. You may have questions left. You do not have to ask them. But if you feel that you do not have all the information you need about the case, ask the questions very carefully. You may thus seem to be making the case for one side or the other, but you cannot give that impression when you ask the question.

There may be reasons unknown to you why you should not probe into certain areas. You must take into consideration whether or not both parties are represented by counsel. You must recognize that you cannot get yourself into the position of bypassing the lawyer or even the lay spokesperson and thus being perceived as trying to undercut.

Decorum

With few exceptions, the hearings are orderly, even when there are a large number of witnesses present. Once in a while things get out of hand with catcalls or jeers. If that or worse occurs, I am ruthless about adjourning, recessing, or even canceling the hearing. Disorderly conduct cannot be tolerated. It frequently is educational for a number of people to be present; however, they should not be allowed to disrupt the hearing or to intimidate witnesses. I have had large numbers of people present at hearings, even off-shift people, but they generally have been very respectful and usually have been most interested in the proceedings.

In 95 percent of the cases, the parties are well trained and know the procedure. I make it clear that I want all the facts possible and try not to disadvantage anybody on a technicality. I do not have to ask for better decorum very often. It is almost always recognized that the hearing must have dignity. I usually close the hearing by asking, "Does anyone have anything else to say?" That leaves the parties with a good feeling, that everyone has had his or her chance. The purpose of that wrap-up question is to make sure there has been a full and fair hearing. If you ask that question expressly, it may defuse later legal challenges on that score. It will be in the record.

Conduct of the Arbitrator

Go to the hearing by yourself. Eat lunch by yourself or with the court reporter. Never ride in the company plane. If you have had any prior employment dealings with either party, disclose them before the hearing. I had a daughter who worked one summer for the U.S. Post Office. I mentioned even that to the parties prior to a postal service hearing. If it is more serious, you should notify the parties in writing before the hearing date or perhaps even decline appointment to the case.

If you think that you may get a sticky procedural question you cannot answer, do not be afraid to ask another arbitrator. You can phone another arbitrator and ask, "How should I deal with this kind of problem?" You will get some good advice. Then use your own best judgment.

I emphasize that you are in charge of the hearing. Try not to be a demagogue, but be thoughtful, dignified, sympathetic. Treat all witnesses with consideration. Thank them by name after they have completed their testimony. Do not let witnesses get pushed around. Just be a decent human being, and you cannot go wrong on the procedural part of the hearing.

4

Selected Problems of Procedure and Evidence

Edgar A. Jones, Jr.

EVIDENTIARY MATTERS in arbitration should be considered in light of the purpose of the hearing. There are a variety of possible purposes as well as levels of formality in the proceedings. Sometimes hearings are so informal as to be no more than a few people sitting around a table, talking when they feel there is a point to be made. Some might view that as a problem, but if you feel comfortable with that format, it is not a problem for you. The hearing format depends in large measure on your personality and your views about the best way to make an intelligent disposition of the matter. The arbitrator should seek to fit the situation to the people themselves, looking toward a final resolution of their dispute. In that respect, what the arbitrator does disposes of both the procedural and substantive issues confronted.

I thought it would be helpful to give you an idea of the types of cases that may come up before you in the grist of a year. The Federal Mediation and Conciliation Service (FMCS) fiscal 1974 report discloses that of the 4,490 cases they had awarded 41.0 percent were discipline cases, including discharge, 15.0 percent were seniority cases; 12.5 percent were arbitrability questions in the scope of the agreement; 11.0 percent were job evaluation; 10.0 percent were overtime cases; and 1.0 percent involved jurisdictional disputes.

The number of arbitrator's awards challenged in court is less than two hundred out of more than twenty-five thousand (perhaps as many as forty thousand) awards issued each year. The authority of the arbitrator to make final and binding awards is thus pretty extensive. It can be unsettling to think about the reach of that authority when you are there to wind up a matter of enormous importance to the people present. That places a burden on you to be as open to the needs of the parties as you can. Saul Wallen, a marvelous human being and an extremely capable fellow, observed that there is no best or right way to approach labor arbitration, that the system must be adapted to the basic characteristics of the industrial relations environment in which it must operate. William Simkin, an arbitrator and former director of the FMCS, said that one of the fundamental purposes of an arbitration hearing is to let people get things off their chests, regardless of the decision. The arbitration proceeding is an opportunity for an outsider to act as a sort of father confessor to the parties by letting them get rid of their troubles, air them out in the open. Simkin makes the argument that you should not adhere to the rules of evidence, that you have to make up your own mind about what is pertinent in a case.

My view is that you do have to use the rules of evidence. There is just no other way to do it. You do not have to call them the rules of evidence, but you have to have a way of sorting out information and evaluating what is happening. It cannot be denied that a large part of what goes on in hearings is people getting things off their chests, and this, of course, bears on your attitude toward evidentiary problems as they arise. The arbitrator's basic problem is to find out as much as possible about what really happened.

Ideally, in going through the progressive steps of the grievance procedure, the parties have listened to each other and know pretty much what arguments and evidence will be presented during the hearing.

Swearing Witnesses and Compelling Attendance

I learned early on to swear the witnesses, put them under oath. It does not make a bit of difference whether or not you have authority to do it in a particular jurisdiction. Tell them to stand up and put them under oath. In my third or fourth case, I was about halfway into a three-day hearing when people started charging each other with lying. So I had them all stand up and put them under oath. I have done it ever since. I believe it changes what goes on in a hearing. It gives the proceedings a little bit of solemnity and causes people to say and not to say things they might not have otherwise. What happens in litigation happens in arbitration as well: the lawyer or business agent or industrial relations manager interviews a "client" and gets one story, but when the witness is under oath, it is another story.

There are about thirty states where we have arbitration statutes; and there is the U.S. Arbitration Act. There is some dispute among the several circuits whether the arbitration act is applicable to labor arbitration. But the Court of Appeals for the Second Circuit, which I think has a sort of leadership function relative to developments in this area, has taken the position that the act does apply to labor arbitration. So, to the extent that the parties may be involved in interstate commerce, you do have the power under the act to subpoena and to put people under oath. But, regardless of whether you have legal authority, it will make a difference to the witnesses. They will feel a little bit awed that they are testifying under oath. That is one legalism that I firmly espouse.

Personal Counsel and Observers

In recent years there has been an increasing number of cases where employees want to have their own counsel present. How do you handle that? It is a very sensitive matter for the parties. The union and the employer do not want to lose control of their hearing, and there is great risk of that if you let in a lawyer who is not knowledgeable about labor arbitration. Most such personal counsel are not. Your decision will have to be governed by your perception of how the parties feel about it. I have had cases where the parties just did not care, and they let the attorney sit in and even ask questions. Most of the time, however, that is not the case. One or both of the parties are not receptive to the idea, and you have to work out a compromise. Let the lawyer sit in but not participate. If he wants to counsel his client who is the grievant, that is OK; but he should not intervene in the proceedings unless the parties agree.

An arbitration hearing holds all kinds of surprises. You may come to it with a structured idea of how it should proceed. But you have to flow with what is happening. It is your responsibility to keep things in order. I had a case where there was a claim of racial discrimination: the problem was to apply the collective bargaining agreement in light of a consent decree. We were in a big room and just after we were seated, in came about eight or ten people, leaders of the black community. These were not just people off the street; they had worked hard to secure the decree and wanted to keep an eye on the proceedings: a state senator, several members of the state Fair Employment Practice Committee, several lawyers, all responsible and influential people. The union got very upset and walked out, saying they would not stay with the "outsiders" present. I tried to work it out and ruled they could stay. I concluded with, "Why don't you just go sit in the back of the room there?" The senator came right back at me with, "Well, we're used to that, you know." Although it upset the union people, I felt they had to be there in that case. They came to support the grievant, and he wanted them present.

Another time I walked into a hearing for a teacher case, and there were thirty people lining the walls. They had come to support the grievant, again from the black community—parents, ministers, neighbors. Some of them appeared as witnesses. I let the others stay under the agreement that they would not participate.

Sometimes there is a question of unfair representation where outside counsel are retained because of fear that the union and the company are in collusion to deprive employees of rights under the contract or under the law. In such a situation, a lawyer can threaten to file a class action suit against the union and the employer if his or her clients feel they have been deprived of their rights by both parties to the collective bargaining agreement. In one case I had, there were about three hundred workers sitting on a claim worth about a million dollars. We spent two days just determining procedure. I was trying to arrange an arbitration where this grievant and others in the same situation could have some sort of party status. Of course, the union and the employer are the parties to the contract, and the employees are sort of third-party beneficiaries. They are not parties. It is one thing to let the employee-grievant have his or her own lawyer to represent the grievant and the union; but it is quite another to make such outside complainants technical parties to the proceedings so that they are bound by it. But it can be done, as the Ninth Circuit held in *Michaelson's Food Services*, 545 F.2d 1248 (1976).

Applicability of Rules of Evidence

As arbitrator, the hearing is your own little world: legal rules, procedures, and evidence are not legally required. You are not controlled by the rules of evidence, but you will soon find out that you cannot do without them. There is a certain residuum of common sense involved, although even in the courts there has been a marked tendency to move away from the rigidities of exclusionary rules of evidence.

My practice is to encourage people to make objections. It serves as a red flag in the record. I tell them I may not rule on every objection and I seldom exclude things, but they should still make objections. You will learn very quickly that you have usually not heard enough of the issue to make exclusionary rulings. If someone says something is really not relevant, you cannot tell whether this is so until you have heard the whole case. The only effective grounds for vacating an arbitrator's award is exclusion of evidence material to the case.

You have heard the terms irrelevant, immaterial, and incompetent. Materiality, I think, is the most important. It concerns the degree of the import of disputed evidence in the deciding of a particular case. It is probably a ruling you will not be able to make in the course of the hearing: it is something best decided after the hearing when you weigh the evidence to determine what elements are vital to your decision making. Sometimes materiality is obvious if someone tries to introduce evidence that is clearly not germane and is not going to help you at all. In such a case you can say, "I don't see much point to that." But to make a ruling excluding evidence during a hearing is something you should avoid except in the most extreme circumstances. The objective is to gather material for your consideration, rather than to erect artificial barriers to submission of information.

I try to tell people what I am thinking as the hearing goes along. From time to time, I review where we are, what the parties' positions are, so that if I am not on target, they will educate me. You do not need to be embarrassed. You are supposed to be ignorant; you do not know what happened or what is important. It is essential for the parties to know whether you are grasping the significance of what they are talking about. I never feel I have lost face by saying, "I don't understand this." I want to know *now*, not when I am back in my office trying to decipher my notes.

As to the relevance of evidence, there are times when you will have to make rulings to exclude areas of examination that on the face were not related to the submission. Otherwise, you may be sitting there for days. You probably have not heard enough by the time of the objection to determine if something is, indeed, irrelevant. What I am likely to tell the parties is, "Make the objection and I'll make a note of it. I'll reserve my ruling on it, this is not a good time to do it. Then I'll rule when I feel I can."

On incompetent evidence, we are frequently confronted with efforts to introduce hearsay evidence, either by testimony or document, describing what occurred without the person who said or wrote it being present for cross-examination. The arbitrator usually has to rule on unreliable evidence and not just allow it, saying he will consider it later. This is particularly true of hearsay, when you know that it is not worthy of any consideration either now or later. For the parties presenting the case, it is very frustrating to make an objection, have no response, and then have the challenged hearsay keep pouring in.

An arbitrator has to distinguish situations where a ruling is needed and be decisive. If you do not make a ruling, you leave the parties at sea because the other side must then undertake the burden of proof on items that should not have been allowed.

Problems such as hearsay may be resolved easily when there are lawyers on both sides. It is difficult when one side is not represented by an attorney. You may face a situation where an objection is raised to hearsay testimony and the lay person on the other side simply does not understand what is objectionable and why and is angry at the challenge to his or her position. In such cases it may be important to admit the material even though it is objectionable hearsay, in order to prevent the lay person from feeling harassed.

That situation is also tough for the lawyer who raises the objection and sits there, knowing you are hearing all this objectionable stuff and there is nothing to be done about it. People with legal educations are all products of the same background: there are no regional variations in legal training, techniques, modes of analysis. It can be very frustrating to have a non-lawyer on the other side. The arbitrator must be sensitive to avoiding a put-down. You can tell the nonlawyer that there are other ways to get the evidence or testimony in, or explain why the material is objectionable. I think it is important to explain when evidence runs afoul of the rules of evidence. If you let hearsay come pouring in, you are not doing nonlawyers a favor because they will not realize the weaknesses in their case and you will shock them with your decision. At the same time, you are requiring the other party to develop a response to hearsay, thinking you are going to rely on it. You have a responsibility to advise the parties what you will be relying on when you make your decision.

Nevertheless, there are common situations where you do not rock the boat. You let them man the oars. A lot of parties follow the practice of not calling one bargaining unit member to testify against another. Both sides give summaries of what they understand happened. I let them do that: I am not going to tell them how to present their case. There are plant situations where, if the union were to call George as a witness, all hell would break loose—not at the hearing but later out in the plant. So they do not call George, and the company does not call George, and I sit there and bite my tongue. I will not intervene. The parties have a continuing relationship and are more sensitive than I am. Maybe they could win the case by calling in George, but it might harm future dealings. The parties present the play: they write the script, and they do the casting. I am not an arbitrator who says, "Bring George in here." I have sat in on cases where George's name is on everyone's tongue but he is never called. I am reluctant to get into the act unless there appears to be a serious deprivation of due process and it is the only way to shake them up a bit, such as when I feel poor old George is being purposefully and unfairly left out; then it is, "What about George?"

Submission Agreement

I try to get the parties' agreement on the submission at the start of the hearing. It serves the function of a legal pleading. It makes the parties think about a narrow issue for me to decide. Many parties have a long institutionalized relationship and have no problem deciding on the issue to be determined. But for some who are new to arbitration, it helps to focus their attention on the subject to be arbitrated and tends to exclude extraneous material. In about half of my cases, the parties have not even thought about how to phrase the issue. Frequently one party will try to frame the issue with when-did-you-stop-beating-your-wife language. Then I intervene.

My practice is to write out the question to be arbitrated, and ask them to sign it. In reality you do not need a submission agreement. You derive your authority from the arbitration clause of their collective bargaining agreement. Nevertheless, it is prudent to have the agreed-upon statement of the issue. Whether or not the signatures have any legal significance, it is important at the outset of the hearing to compel the parties to think about what the issue is. Its greatest usefulness is to focus the parties, defining what it is they want you to decide.

Exhibits

The second procedural device I use is to try to get the parties to put the exhibits in immediately, so that we do not have to go through the legal procedures of establishing foundation for their introduction, identifying them, explaining how the witness was aware of the exhibit, and so forth. All that can be bypassed by the initial introduction of exhibits and saves about an hour in a hearing. I usually ask, "What documents will you be putting into evidence?" Sometimes they are unwilling because they want to preserve the element of surprise and introduce the exhibits in sequence. Most of the time, however, the documents will come in very quickly.

Stipulations

The third procedure I use at the start of the hearing is to get the parties to stipulate to as many of the facts as they can. It compresses time for all concerned to get agreement on as many undisputed items as possible. I frequently try to initiate this in telephone calls to the parties while setting up the hearing date, by suggesting that they get together and stipulate to as many facts as they can. This is easier to do when the parties and their advocates have a continuing relationship. Ad hoc advocates often are not knowledgeable about stipulations, distrust each other, and have not done this before. But sometimes you can lead them to it.

You have to beware that the unsophisticated spokesperson does not agree to things that he or she does not believe are true. You have to be sure that both parties know and agree that the facts stipulated are true and did occur. I have saved days of hearing doing this, particularly where the stipulations cover background and tangential material. That permits a better focus on the disputed matters.

Leading Questions

Leading questions do not trouble me. They tell you what the parties are trying to get across. If I feel I can get it across to the questioner without shattering him or her, I will say, "You know, when you ask questions like that, all I'm getting is argument. It is your position, not evidence." I may then intervene to ask the question myself.

One time I had a case with an industrial relations director who had come up through the ranks from the union, and he was asking all kinds of leading questions of witnesses in a discharge case. I badgered him a little because he was warping the case. I was concerned. The minute I said he was leading the witnesses and that I was just getting argument and no evidence, he collapsed, sat back in his chair, folded his hands, and said, "I have no further questions." His face got red. He felt I had attacked him. It took me almost an hour to get back to where he felt that the proceeding in that room was fair. But he literally could not ask a direct question. It is not just the union business agents and company personnel managers who have this problem. Lawyers have it too, especially those who spend a lot of time in arbitration where rules of evidence are not strictly enforced. They get a little sloppy. Since that incident I rarely raise objections to questioning like that.

It is a different story, however, when the other side objects to leading questions. I am likely to suggest to the objector that it would be more helpful if we just let the witness tell his story. In cases where it is crucial to know precisely what happened and I have a lead-the-witness question, I will ease into the questioning myself.

Nonetheless, a lot of cases are not really jarred by leading questions. They can save a lot of time that would have been consumed by endless efforts at direct questioning. It is only when I really need to know a witness's unvarnished, unprompted perception of events that I intervene. But I try to do it with some finesse so that the person doing the inept questioning does not realize what I am doing.

You have to be careful of excessive intervention even if the presentation of the case seems inept. You may be tempted to help out the blundering counsel, but you must realize that people present cases in a certain way for different reasons. The arbitrator is an audience of one, and I prefer to let the parties present the play. I have found that what appears to be chaos may eventually fall into place. If you bide your time, play the audience, and let them proceed from act one to act two, eventually you will have seen the whole play. You should intervene only when you are convinced that somebody cannot perform. There has to be an empathy factor for there to be confidence in the arbitrator and the system. You do not want to put anyone down. It is tricky when you are dealing with inexperienced or uneducated people who may be insecure. If you intervene too abrasively, they may just shut up, and you will never get all the facts.

Voir Dire

Voir dire is a very useful device to assure that a witness knows what he is talking about, what the basis is for a document and for the witness talking about it. It is a permissible procedure for the other side to raise while a document is being introduced; it permits a sort of cross-examination on the background of the witness relative to this item, out of sequence. Once the voir dire is concluded, and the other side has asked all its questions about the exhibit, he will agree to let it in or will object to it. If he objects, the arbitrator has to rule on its admissibility.

Sometimes the objecting party may try to expand beyond the strict limits of inquiry as to authenticity of a document and to use voir dire as an early cross-examination. The arbitrator should say, "You might consider saving that for cross-examination." Voir dire is limited to inquiry to set up possible objections on admissibility.

The Grievant as the Company's First Witness

Sometimes the employer in a discipline case calls the grievant as its first witness. The union objects, saying the employer should put on a prima facie case without the grievant's contribution. The employer insists, and the arbitrator is asked to rule on it. I usually say no to the employer in such a situation. I want the employer to prove the case using its own witnesses. There are some parties who do it all the time with no objection from the union, and I will go along silently so long as I see no problem. But when the objection is raised and I am asked to rule on it, I do. In one aircraft company where I had been an arbitrator for fifteen years, the company kept calling the grievant as its first witness in discipline cases. The union never made an objection until one day a union rep said, "I don't think that's fair." I sustained his objection; but it took fifteen years for me to have to make that ruling.

It really is not a fair procedure. It amounts to moving cross-examination of the grievant up front. As a matter of orderly procedure, I would rather hear the company say what they saw, what they heard, and why they did what they did. Then in due course, you can cross-examine the grievant. It is not as if there is something new to be disclosed. The parties know what has happened. They have been living with the case through the grievance hearings before it gets to arbitration. That is why the traditional argument in favor of such testimony, to avoid perjury or influence by other witnesses, makes no sense.

A distinction is usually made between calling the grievant first and the union calling a supervisor as its first witness in a contract interpretation case in which it goes first. The latter tactic is used to get more informed substantive background about the operation or the events and is not related to any claim regarding perjury.

Hallway Conferences

Frequently during the hearing issues arise that you would like to discuss with counsel outside the presence of the grievant and witnesses. You have to be careful when you do this to respect the relationship between clients and their counsel.

Usually the arbitrator says, "I would like to speak to counsel out in my chambers," pointing to the hall. Such a meeting might be used to learn what the thrust of a particular point is, to see if embarrassing legal issues are avoidable, to encourage the parties to attempt a settlement of the case, or to get an unduly zealous or abrasive advocate to calm down. It can also be used to clarify the arbitrator's understanding of a particular point. You have to be careful that such sessions are not viewed with suspicion by the constituents. In some cases, counsel may say that they cannot discuss the case without the grievant present. The arbitrator has to respect that, and so does the other side. Such a session may put the lawyers in a difficult position but may be useful means of exploring problem areas. The arbitrator should generally not play mediator in those hallway chambers unless the parties indicate that they want him to do so, although some would dispute me here.

Sequestration

Sometimes at the start of the hearing, the parties try to get the arbitrator to order segregation of witnesses from the hearing so that they will not hear the testimony of other witnesses and their testimony will not be influenced by what they could have heard. Sometimes counsel will even ask for exclusion of a grievant—in one case I had an employer attempt to exclude eleven of them from the hearing room. But grievants are entitled to stay in the room and not be sequestered. They have a legal right to face their accusers: they are like complainants in civil litigation, entitled to be present while their cause is being pressed.

The idea that people are going to change their testimony or commit perjury in response to earlier testimony is very naïve. They have already fixed their stories, if they are going to be fixed. Do not forget, they have been hearing and rehearing the facts of the case inside and outside the grievance procedure in each of its prior steps.

Transcripts and Note-Taking

Different arbitrators take different kinds of notes: some are very detailed and some are not. The level of detail may depend in part on whether there is a court stenographer present, a matter that is usually up to the parties, although there are regions where the use of transcripts is routine and some arbitrators will not proceed without a stenographer. Generally, though, the arbitrator leaves it up to the parties whether or not to have a transcript. This is partly due to the fact that he or she does not know in advance what the case is about or whether it will be complicated and require careful review of the exact testimony of witnesses.

Some arbitrators make tape recordings of their hearings. I did this three or four times, but the burden of having to listen to hours and hours of repeated testimony forced me back into reliance on my own notes. It is hard to index the tape to find what you want. Sometimes it is boring enough to sit through a hearing once, let alone twice! On top of that, you have to charge the parties for listening to it all over again. If the parties want to tape the proceedings, I have no objections, and 99 percent of the time the other side has none.

I try to take down the substance of all the testimony as it is offered, certainly not verbatim except when the exact words are crucial. Then when I get home, I have a pretty reliable record of what happened. It is much faster—and cheaper for the parties—to be able to go quickly through your handwritten notes than to listen again to the entire hearing on tape. Even with a transcript, there is a lot of semantic filler that is recorded. I would guess the water content might be as high as 99 percent, with relatively few facts coming in. I write down only what I think is factual.

As to the accuracy of note-taking, you develop a certain amount of self-assurance that you have done your best to hear and record what has been said. There is always the possibility that you might have missed something; but even then, court reporters may make errors in transcribing their notes or in getting down exactly what has been said.

If the parties agree on a transcript, I am agreeable. But what if one side requests it and the other objects? Under AAA rules, any party can demand a stenographic record. One party may not believe it needs it, or it cannot afford it. The other side may insist it needs one to assist in writing its brief. I will say that I will not accept a copy of the transcript unless the one side provides a copy to the other. I will then take my own notes. More often than not, the one side agrees to provide a copy to the other or to share its copy, and I also get one for myself. Any material the arbitrator sees, both sides should also have an opportunity to inspect.

As to the official record of the hearing, even if I am taking notes or there is a court reporter present, I tell the parties there is no record of the proceedings except what I later express in my written findings. Maybe because I am so heavy-handed about it, I have not had any problems.

Credibility

Once a witness has been sworn, we assume he or she will testify truthfully. Some advocates try to exploit that by reminding a witness ominously during examination, "Remember, you're under oath." I always interrupt at that point and say, "He took the oath" very sternly. I take a dim view of people impugning other people's honesty and integrity during the course of a hearing. We have a duty to protect the witnesses from harassment.

Sometimes the exchange between the two counsel will become very heated and personal. The minute something like that starts to happen, I take a break, get away from the room. It is not lost on the parties what is going on. I do not have to say to the management attorney, "What is going on here?," particularly if he or she is badgering a witness. In one case where this nonetheless continued, I announced that we were going to recess for a half hour and if the conduct continued after that, we would recess for another half hour. That managed to bring the offender back into line. If things get out of hand, take a recess.

The core problem of credibility is that, no matter how insistent may be the conventional wisdom about a trier observing demeanor, it is simply impossible to tell by observation if someone is lying under oath. You cannot tell by looking at and listening to the person. A trial judge in Chicago once compiled a list of tests to see if a witness is telling the truth: does he perspire; lick his lips; fidget in his seat; is he shifty-eyed? From my experience as an arbitrator, I can tell you that shifty-eyed people often tell the truth, while the most honest-looking people will lead you by the nose right down the primrose path. It is going to happen to *you,* too. The only way you can hope to cope with this is by careful attention to circumstantial evidence: the old saw that direct evidence is the best evidence is not necessarily true. The best evidence is that which snares the truth in a web of circumstance.[1]

You are kidding yourself if you believe that you can tell which witnesses are telling the truth. I have needled some very prestigious arbitrators about this. One fellow topped me very well with, "I may not know who is telling the truth, but I sure know whom I believe." I have sat in hearings and assuredly known whom I believed, only to my distress to discover that what was said was not so.

In one particular case early in my career, a very earnest, calm young man got on the stand and said that he had been sick in bed, unable to phone in, so he should not be viewed as a voluntary quit. Then the company called a rebuttal witness, a retired policeman who had investigated and discovered that the witness was working for another employer at the time. He was

---

1. For a more extensive discussion of arbitral evidentiary problems, see Jones 1966 and 1968.

collecting sick pay while working at another job. Of course, all the time the ex-officer is testifying, I am watching the grievant like a hawk. If I had to pick out a credible witness, I'm thinking, it would have to be *this* character! Then by golly he went back on the witness chair and convinced me again! He had an explanation, an improbable one, true, but what delivery! I really believed him! Such demeanor! But that good old arbitral nerve twitched a bit even so (and I actually felt embarrassed at my instinctive instant of cynicism!) So I said to the union representative, "Well, it's about 4:30 now. I suggest we recess for today and you go check out the story." I really wanted this guy to win! I had acquired a vested interest in him. I believed him and then believed him again. A few days later, the union called to tell me they were withdrawing the grievance. The grievant had been lying. He had conned me twice! So, be careful. Don't think you can always tell who is telling the truth.

Whenever I can avoid making credibility determinations, I do. I once had a case involving a shouting match between a shop steward and a personnel manager during the course of discussing a grievance in the manager's office. The employee allegedly had directed an obscenity angrily to the manager, leading him to respond just as angrily, "You're fired! " There was a simple dispute over whether that obscenity was ever uttered, a matter of credibility of the two witnesses. But the credibility issue was not crucial, because even if he had uttered the profanity, it was not a ground for termination. So I did not rule on the credibility issue.

Many people claim that issues of credibility can be resolved by using the concept of burden of proof. All that signifies is that the arbitrator as the trier of fact has to be convinced of something. But if you find yourself not convinced after considerable reflection, then the burden of proof may become a device to duck out on further reflection, to make findings where you lack conviction, to quit the task of thought prematurely. These considerations are all in contest while you are making up your mind.

Lie Detector Tests

There has for years been a growing trend in the use of lie detector (polygraph) tests. These are machines that, at their most sophisticated, measure such physical functions as eye movement, pupil size, muscle tension, brain waves, skin temperature, blood volume, breathing rate. Some even think, particularly the commercial polygraph operators, that the polygraph is to modern factfinders what the microscope is to biologists, that it can reliably disclose deception when it occurs by revealing the physiological underpinnings of psychological behavior. But unfortunately we must still cope with the imperfections of human perception and recollection. The greatest flaw of a "lie detector" of any sort is that it cannot reliably help us resolve confrontations of credibility. Since you cannot reliably test the significance of nervousness, you still do not know if a witness has it within him, regardless of his intent, to be honest or dishonest. We still have to assess the extent and accuracy of people's perceptions of events and of their recollection of what they earlier had perceived. It is not going to help very much to put someone on the stand, attach this sophisticated machinery to him, and find out whether or not he intends to tell the truth. When you look through a microscope, you can observe cells and their behavior. But with a polygraph, you cannot accurately test perception or recollection. You may see proof of nervousness, but it may not be caused by the same thing that you are concerned about.

People thirst for certainty. If you have a lie detector that costs a lot of money and has lights that go dot-dot-dot and a wheel with a tape that goes around, it *has* to be reliable. After all, it is *science!* It is claimed as *the* device to root out perjury. My impressionistic judgment is that I have rarely been in the presence of a perjurer in an arbitration hearing. But I have often been in the presence of people who either did not perceive things or cannot recall them in any reliable way. I believe that the majority of people who testify before me do their best to tell the truth, sometimes at great personal cost, psychologically and economically. But I cannot document that belief any better than can one who believes that most witnesses are ready, willing, and able to lie under oath. The sad reality is that there is no reliable method—demonstrably *not* the lie detector and its operator—to determine whether the nervous arousal the polygraph records signifies deception, merely present anxiety about the whole situation, guilt feelings over past conduct, or even wholly unrelated thoughts.

What I *know*, however, is that the lie detector remains an unscientific snare and a popular delusion, as it has been for the past fifty years during which it has almost universally been rejected by courts and labor arbitrators. Fortunately, research has recently become available that demonstrates conclusively that the rejection of its probative value has been well based. Unfortunately, it continues to be promoted among employers and law-enforcement officials with ignorant fervor by persons who, with only a literal handful of exceptions, lack the psychological education to know better. It is a machine that is capable of measuring only nervous arousal; it is utterly incapable of disclosing whether that arousal signifies truthfulness or deception.[2]

Retention of Jurisdiction

There are all kinds of questions lurking behind a reinstatement with back pay. Frequently the parties cannot agree on how to compute it. There is always some question about whether there is to be a set off of interim earnings and what interim earnings are involved. If an employee had been moonlighting for years before termination, and continues that moonlighting during the period of termination, may those earnings be deducted in determining the amount of back pay? Also, how are unemployment insurance payments to be treated? This varies from one state to another.

In one case where an arbitrator in a theft case had rein-

---

2. The scientific invalidity of polygraphing has been demonstrated in Lykken (1980). Lykken documents that (1) innocent persons have little better than a fifty-fifty chance of having their innocence confirmed by submitting to polygraph testing; which is to say, for an innocent person to submit voluntarily to the polygraph is to run the substantial risk of being falsely identified and penalized as guilty of whatever misconduct is being investigated; and (2) guilty but knowledgeable or coached persons can with minimal effort (involving diversionary physical tricks or depressive narcotics) fool the polygraph operator into thinking them truthful.

For a comprehensive study of how labor arbitrators and courts have historically and currently coped with lie-detector "proof" (practically all have rejected it), see Jones (1978). See also the findings and discussion in the arbitration between Clark County, Nevada, and the International Association of Firefighters, 82-1 ARB par. 8097 (Edgar Jones, 1981).

stated forty-six employees without retaining jurisdiction, the employer took more than one year to investigate and determine the appropriate back pay; it would not settle one claim until it had settled all claims. What apparently held up payment was one person's sick leave claim. But the arbitrator could do nothing because he was legally regardable as *functus officio;* he had not retained jurisdiction nor had one or the other of the parties asked him to do so.

Problems like that can be readily avoided by the arbitrator retaining jurisdiction to deal with possible problems in administering the award. I have used the following language as part of my awards: "This hearing shall remain open and the jurisdiction of the undersigned arbitrator shall continue to dispose of any problems that may be encountered by the parties in the administration of this award." Legally, this is not a "reopener." It allows the hearing to remain open. Legally, we are in recess and can resume on request. It is not designed to allow relitigation of the merits but solely to resolve problems that may arise in the administration of the award. This device saves the parties time and money. I have had dozens of cases such as this; often a phone call from the parties, and five or six words from me, resolve what might have taken another arbitration. I tell them, you should pay that, or you should deduct this, or whatever. Because of the retention of jurisdiction clause in the award, their problem is readily solved. The language is for a limited purpose and is not vulnerable to charges of violating the doctrine of *functus officio.*

Multiparty Proceedings

Sometimes you may confront a grievance in which the company has assigned work to one employee that arguably should have gone to another employee in some other bargaining unit. This is a jurisdictional dispute over who is entitled to the work. The majority of arbitrators would probably take the position that they are there at the request of the company and the one union, to resolve a dispute under those parties' collective bargaining argeement. Although they may believe the other union should be involved, they will not require its joinder. These arbitrators believe they lack the power to compel people to engage in multiparty proceedings. But I believe I cannot solve the problem between the parties unless I get the views of the other union. I have held in such cases that the dispute is not arbitrable unless the first union will sanction the joinder of the second union. (For an example of how this works, see *Stardust Hotel*, 50 *Lab. Arb.* 1186 (Edgar Jones, 1968); also see *Michaelson's Food Services*, 61 *Lab. Arb.* 1195 (Edgar Jones, 1973), enforced in part and denied enforcement in part, 545 F. 2d 1248 (9th Cir. 1976). This is a workable way to resolve such disputes.

Although the procedure is the parties' and may vary from one agreement to another, it is very flexible and can be adapted to fit each unique situation. The parties who are confronted by a problem that will not be resolved in any other way should welcome such an innovation to resolve their dispute. In the area of jurisdictional disputes, to issue a bilateral award is a futility. Either make a joinder available or find the proceedings to be not arbitrable.

5

Due Process
and Fair Procedure

Robben W. Fleming

THE QUESTIONS of due process and procedural regularity will not trouble you in every arbitration case. I had arbitrated for about ten years before I ever thought much about them. That is partly because, in most arbitrations, evidence does not present the types of problems it does in the courtroom. My generation of arbitrators learned most of what we know in the War Labor Board days. We thought we had some particular sensitivity to the industrial relations problems of both employers and unions. We hoped we had some sympathy with the problems of both of them, but we were very aware of the fact that the company and the union had a continuing relationship and were going to have to get along after the arbitration. In making awards in arbitration cases, we were not just deciding a dispute that the parties could walk away from and forget. They had to live with the results. That tempered many of the things we did. While many of us, particularly those of us who were lawyers, were troubled about due process and procedural regularity, in nine out of ten cases such problems did not arise.

Then at one meeting of the National Academy of Arbitrators (NAA) Bill Wirtz gave a paper pointing out that we had not sufficiently thought through the fairness of the procedure, for example, a seniority case in which a favorable ruling for a grievant meant that someone else, who was not represented, was bound to be hurt by this decision. Some rationalized that the company was in most cases defending its choice, i.e., the missing person, and probably giving this person better representation than he or she would have. But the fact remained that the affected individual was not there and that there were times when his interests were not necessarily parallel to those of the company. Bill, who had been our conscience on a lot of issues, started Ben Aaron and me thinking, and the three of us sent out a questionnaire to NAA members and had a group of regional meetings at which we discussed the issues.

Cases for the Cooperative Arbitrator

Let us consider a couple of cases as examples. Take the case where you as arbitrator have worked well with both sides over the years, and one of the spokespersons calls you and says: "I've got the other side's spokesperson on the phone and we have a messy discharge case between us. We tell you right off the bat that the fellow ought to be discharged, but we can't handle the case internally because it is a political situation. We agree he ought to be discharged. It's the only answer for the problem. We can't agree upon it publicly, though. Now, what we would like you to do is hear the case. We will see to it that it is adequately presented. There will be no railroading, and all the evidence will be put in. But we know—in terms of our relationship—what the result has to be because that man must go because he is such a disruptive influence in the plant, a real troublemaker."

Now what would you do? You have several possible options. One is to say, "No, I won't hear it." Another is to say, "I will hear it. But I will tell you in advance that I will decide it on the merits, and if I don't agree with you, I will not sustain the discharge." The third is to say "OK, I have confidence in you and that you would not agree that a person is to be terminated unless you both believe it is in the best interests of the company and the union. I will cooperate."

Suppose you take the second option and go hear the case. Despite your sense that you have been given all the pertinent evidence and have asked the questions on the matters on which you are unclear, and despite your belief that you have a complete understanding when you leave the hearing, there may be facts of which you are never made aware. Suppose the evidence in that case omits any reference to the fact that no terminations have ever been given for this offense in the past, but only letters of warning. Suppose that vital information is never introduced in the record, or that the examination of past records that would have established the fact was never conducted. And suppose further that you say to the union rep, "Have you examined the records to see whether there are any other cases of this kind in the past?" and he says no. Would you then ask him to? If he has not done so yet, it would require a search. Would you then ask him to go search the company records and come back and tell you whether in similar cases there have always been terminations? Or would you decide it is up to the parties to present their own cases, that if the union did not think it was important, it is not your business to present their case for them? No matter how great your personal integrity, if the case is not as well prepared as it could have been, you will miss something that an alert advocate for the party would have thought about and would have presented. After all, you know nothing about that case until you get to the hearing. We have all had the experience after a case is over of going over it and saying, "I wish I had thought while I was there to ask such and such."

Since most arbitrators do not reconvene a hearing to ask something that they thought was insignificant during the hearing, they have to rely on the integrity of the spokespersons to present their most complete case in an effort to prevail. So it is possible that some important element of the case will not be presented because the parties are so strongly convinced that a man deserves to be discharged that they say, perhaps subconsciously to themselves, "We can't build a record here suggesting that the other side was wrong in this. We have asked the arbitrator to take care of it. The least we can do is build a record that supports the conclusion on which we have already agreed."

Doesn't that worry you? Even if you feel you have the integrity to go into such a case uncommitted, you do know that the parties are in agreement, and that the presentations will be designed to support the conclusion they have already reached because they do not want the record to be at odds with the conclusion.

Some may take the position that they will hold the hearing with the provision that they reserve the right to decide differently, because if they do not the parties will select another arbitrator who will gladly sell the employee down the river without any reservations at all—"If I went, he would at least have a partial chance." That is the rationalization that all of us have used from time to time. "If I don't do it, somebody else will."

Take a different type of case. Right after World War II the textile industry in New England was very hard put to stay in business because of a trend to move to newer, more technologically competitive plants in the South. Fewer employees would be needed because of the improved equipment. Companies and unions negotiating new contracts in the New England area had real difficulties. Workers in other industries were getting large increases, while textile workers were being told that they would not get more money because any raise might force the company to close its New England doors and move to the more appealing South. The workers naturally wanted the same increases as workers in the more successful industries, but the companies believed they were unable to grant these kinds of increases. The union leadership very often understood that the company really could not stay in New England if it had to meet the workers' demands. So the spokespersons would call their old friend the arbitrator and say, "Look, we have a very difficult problem. We cannot resolve our new contract in terms of wages because it is totally impossible for the union to accept by vote of the membership any bargain which we leaders might agree upon. The company cannot afford an offer that would be accepted without having to move this textile industry out of New England. We have to have an interest arbitration, even though you arbitrators say that the parties know more about the business and ought to reach their own agreements. Now we will agree on what the wage increase has got to be. We will see that it is properly documented, and you award it. You won't have to worry about whether it is a proper increase because we will tell you privately it is. We know this industry. We have worked in it. It will be a fair increase from both of our viewpoints. It is not one the membership will accept, but they will commit themselves to arbitrating the issue. Will you come and do it?"

Now what do you say? Again you have several options. One, you can say, "No, I'll have no part in a situation like that." Two, you can say, "Yes, I agree. I've always said you people know more about your business than I do, and I have no question about your honesty or integrity or that someone is selling out one of the parties." Furthermore, you believe the figure they will give you will be the right amount for an increase, but that they cannot sell it to their membership. Three, assume that you are convinced as a matter of your own judgment that any settlement the membership could be induced to agree upon is probably too high for the industry in New England and will have the effect of running the industry out of New England.

Do you say, "OK, I understand you, and I trust you. If that is your problem, I'll come and do it"? Or do you say "No, I will have no part of it," or do you once again take the middle course "OK, but you understand that I will go along with your plan, but only if the record supports your position"?

You must recognize that if you take option one, the same union leadership that has asked you to do this will almost certainly feel compelled afterwards to condemn you for it, because the union is an organization in which the leadership must be elected. They are giving you a case that by definition is one they cannot sell to their membership. You can hardly expect them after you do this to stand up and cheer you for it, so you must understand you will be condemned.

There is, of course, a difference between the grievance discharge under the contract and the wage determination in an interest arbitration. In the first case it is an individual who may be prejudiced by the result, while in the second it is the collective membership of the union that will be hurt or helped, depending upon your point of view. It is perhaps easier on the conscience to participate in the second case if you respect the integrity of the company and union, because you may have independent knowledge of the difficulty the industry is having in its fight to survive in obsolete plants.

Is there a right answer to difficult questions like these? Perhaps the best advice is to be conscious of the problem and to struggle with one's own conscience about the right path to pursue.

Surprises

About the so-called surprise issue, let me describe two quite different kinds of situations, one of which might not seem a surprise to you but is often viewed as such by the parties. The first case involves a discharge where the evidence is one man's word against another's—no witnesses. The first question is, Did the individual commit the alleged act or not? and the second question, of course, is, If he or she did, was it worthy of the discharge? The case goes all the way through the grievance procedure with one side alleging the grievant was caught smoking in the refinery, and the other side asserting that it just was not so. The relationship between the parties is not particularly good. They are not interested in admonitions about the good working relationship between them. Their philosophy of arbitration views it as an adversary proceeding in which both parties take advantage of the situation as best they can. At the hearing, the company announces that it has a witness to the incident whom it did not find before the grievance hearing and did not produce at the arbitration because it knew that this was a kind of case where the union would never agree to the termination of the individual. The union meanwhile had made a statement that if the man was smoking he should have been terminated because of the danger of smoking to the plant and other employees. The company claimed the bad relationship was the union's fault rather than its own. Therefore, the company knew it was going to have to go to arbitration, and thought it would just put its chips on the table in arbitration. When the witness was announced, the union, of course, shouted "Surprise!" in outrage that they had gone through the entire grievance procedure with no witness being produced. What do you do about this situation?

  The other kind of surprise arises after the hearing is concluded, and you have studied the record and are ready to make your decision when you suddenly discover a clause in the contract that you think is dispositive of the case, but which was never argued by either party. You read it and puzzle over it more and more, and the more you read it the more you think the answer is perfectly clear, that it comes under the clause in the contract. You do not know why it was never cited by either party, but the whole contract is in evidence before you for you to examine. Or perhaps, as you examine the record you suddenly construct a new theory about the case that had not been argued but that is perfectly supportable on the record. You do not have to go outside the record for any facts. It is just that this is a new theory of the case.

Assume you make a decision on one of those two cases and assume that the parties are outraged because you have either invented an entirely new theory, even if a valid one, or you have found a new clause in the contract that they have not mentioned. What do you do with this sort of case?

Turning to the first, what do you do if the parties suddenly produce a new surprise witness at the hearing? Someone who has been saved up for the hearing? Will you let the witness appear? Will you say it is too late, that he or she should have been produced earlier at the grievance hearing steps? Are you concerned, if you don't allow this witness, by the possibility that his or her testimony may be very strong and unshaken on cross-examination and may provide the critical evidence in the case? You may be excluding the only witness to what is in fact a very dangerous and hazardous situation, which could have caused a terrible explosion and loss of a great many lives.

Some arbitrators would offer to withdraw from the case to avoid charges of prejudices, to start the process over and allow the grievance procedure to be at least a little more equitable, and to provide the union an opportunity to prepare with full knowledge of what they face in arbitration. Some arbitrators would exclude the evidence on the grounds that it should have been presented earlier in the grievance procedure. The arbitrator's answer might depend on whether there is an umpireship or ad hoc relationship and on whether the witness was newly discovered as distinguished from known and held back until the hearing. Most arbitrators would at least give the union an opportunity for a recess or for another hearing. If the union insisted on going forward, say on the grounds that the international rep did not have another free day for six months, then most arbitrators would proceed, even though they might not feel it proper to do so. Some arbitrators would decline to proceed on the grounds that if the hearing proceeded the grievant would be getting a bad break because the union was not fully prepared to respond to the new witness, or to argue the case. Is that the parties' problem, the individual's problem, or the arbitrator's problem?

Do you feel an obligation to make sure the grievant gets the fairest advocacy, or do you believe the grievance belongs to the union and they make the decision as to what the disposition of the grievance should be, that the individual is not really a critical part of the case?

Some arbitrators might take the parties out into the hall and suggest they might want to take the case back to the grievance procedure, and if the union does not accept the opportunity for a recess, go forward with the case. Would you impose the extra cost on the company for the surprise and causing the recess? Even if there were a contract clause splitting the cost of arbitration?

Is this any of the arbitrator's business at all? Should you tell the parties what you consider to constitute good practices or is that none of your business? Should an arbitrator say this seems to me to be a pretty stupid way of going at this, or not raise that issue? Do you put it in the opinion that you view it as a pretty lousy way of going at this? If you put it in your opinion, you must remember that that is not the question the parties asked you to answer. They asked you only to resolve the grievance itself. If it is their practice to do it this way, is it your business to moralize about the preferred industrial relations practice? Indeed, if you felt it appropriate in the opinion to comment adversely on the use of a surprise witness, should you go the next step and suggest to the parties that other kinds of legal action might be available after arbitration to challenge the fairness of the proceeding ? Or should you learn to live with the parties in the way they have learned to live with each other and express your disapproval only by a recitation of the way in which the issue came up?

Actually the case is quite interesting for a number of reasons. First of all, most arbitrators are probably going to be offended by the way the parties have gone at the case, coming into a hearing and trying to surprise the other side. Most believe it would be a much sounder industrial relations practice for the parties to level with each other in the grievance procedure, and that if they had done so in this case, it could have been settled without the need to go to arbitration.

But even if most arbitrators are going to have a negative reaction to this tactic, what do they do in the opinion? You probably are not going to surprise them any if you tell them that you regard that as a lousy practice. They have almost certainly been told that by a good many people, and they are likely to respond, "Mind your own business. We did not ask you that question. All we asked you was to hear this particular grievance."

The second question is, of course, If you produce a surprise witness of that kind all of a sudden, can the case be fairly heard now that one party is not really fully prepared? Can that be cured by a decision by the surprised party to go ahead? Even if there are other reasons, such as time limitations and commitments elsewhere, that caused them to decide to go ahead even though they are not fully prepared? Is that fair to the individual grievant who is involved? Where there is a hostile relationship, is a witness who is suddenly discovered likely to be reliable?

You have a number of different factors to consider. What do you say in your opinion? Do you just address yourself to the question of whether or not there was smoking? If you decide that question affirmatively, the answer to your other question is easy because everybody has already told you that if the employee was smoking discharge was warranted.

Where there is a dangerous practice involved, such as smoking in a refinery, it may well be that a potential witness cannot be put aside. If so, there are really only two options: to recess the case, thereby giving the union time to investigate the whereabouts of the witness at earlier grievance conferences, or to go ahead, especially if the union does not object, and rely on cross-examination, perhaps supplemented by your own questions, to establish the reliability of the witness. Which of these approaches you take may be dictated by the circumstances, and by your sense of fairness.

On the issue of the new theory you discover after the close of the hearing, should you decide on the basis of that theory or not? Many arbitrators try to avoid raising such new theories because of the effect it might have on the losing party. But of course that is not unknown in the courts. Judges suddenly derive whole new theories that were not really argued by counsel. There is nothing illegal about it, even though it might tarnish your acceptability. Anyone who arbitrates has to understand that acceptability cannot always be preserved. Some arbitrators might utilize their new theory, see where it leads, and then write their opinion from the facts without detailing that new theory. But if you do that, why bother with the new theory in the first place?

Similarly, when an arbitrator finds a contract provision that the parties have not referred to, he or she is not privy to the history of that provision and has no insight as to how the parties view that provision. Is there some presumption that if the parties did not argue that provision, it was not because they did not know it was there, it was because they did not feel it applied? If you were sure the provision you found was controlling, would it have been fair to them to reconvene the hearing and say, "It seems to me as I study this case that this provision of the contract really is important, even though neither of you argued it? I need to know why." Do any of you have any concern about writing the parties a letter and saying you believe this provision applies? Here again, if you do consider the new theory, do you give the parties a chance to consult on it? If you come to the same conclusion by other contract provisions and ignore any reference to the provision, aren't you worrying about acceptability, which we agreed we never should worry about? Does whether or not acceptability makes a difference depend on whether the arbitrator is very busy or just starting? Should it? If that becomes a standard, does it mean that someone can afford to try a new theory only if he or she has lots of business?

The central question here is whether it is fair to the parties to spin a new theory or to rely upon a clause they have not argued. Is it fair in the sense that you do not know why they did not argue that clause? It is not an unknown phenomenon to find a clause in a contract that, for historical reasons, both the parties feel strongly has nothing to do with the case, and that is the reason they did not argue it. Is it fair to them if you suddenly rely on that clause and you give them no opportunity to tell you why it does not apply or that they overlooked telling you what they think it has to do with the case? But is it a function of an arbitrator to spin a completely new theory of the case? However sound it may be and however desirable it may be in the long run, should this theory be used without giving the parties an opportunity to see what he is going to do?

Or should the proceeding be reconvened? Should you write to the parties and say, "It seems to me such and such is true in this case—I would like to have your comments on it, or to reconvene at your option so that I can learn if what I am suggesting has anything to do with this case." Do you owe them that? Is that really the point of this case? Since courts do it, there is not a question of whether there is due process if you do not do it. Are we different from the courts in their spinning out of new theories because the court is establishing precedent for the general public rather than for just the immediate parties to a dispute?

An arbitrator is merely trying to make sure that two private parties have a dialogue between themselves about their relationship, and a new theory should more properly be presented to them so that they would have a chance to argue it out before it is resolved by the arbitrator's opinion. Furthermore, the court decision is appealable to appellate divisions (except for new theories by the Supreme Court), while the arbitrator's usually is not.

Most of us who have spent a good many years arbitrating are no more confident that we know the answers than we were when we started. These are troublesome questions, and I am sure that many of us answer them variously throughout our careers.

Think about these questions. Be aware of the problems, even if insecure about the answers. The important thing is to be conscious of these various interests, and how you will reconcile them as you face these issues.

Substantive Issues

6

Management Rights and Union-Concerted Action

Charles C. Killingsworth

WHEN I STARTED arbitrating some thirty years ago, between Bethlehem Steel Company and the steelworkers, management rights were considerably more controversial than they are now. In approximately 50 percent of the cases, management rights were the major issue; they were a peripheral issue in another 25 percent of the cases. At present I would say that management rights are a real issue in only 5 to 10 percent of the cases presented in the steel industry. The basic issues were decided years ago. There has evolved a body of common law. These decisions deal with very important issues. Once the decisions are rendered (and particularly if you get several different arbitrators ruling the same way), it becomes pointless to arbitrate the same question over and over again.

Yet in a number of areas, management rights still are a big issue. In the public sector, for instance, as state and local governments are becoming more and more involved in collective bargaining, by statute or reality, management wants a foolproof management rights clause in their legislation and agreements. Sometimes in the legislation, that expression of management rights may be written in such a fashion that if applied literally there would be very little left to bargain about. In teachers disputes, management rights are quite frequently a major issue. The intensity and the heat engendered by a management rights clause are directly related to the stage of development of a collective bargaining relationship.

There is an interesting intellectual problem involved in the issue of management rights. The pristine version of reserved management rights holds that management goes into the bargaining room possessed of all rights in the labor management relationship and that the collective bargaining process is one by which management decides which rights, if any, it is going to limit or give up. Thus, whatever rights management does not explicitly limit or give up, it retains. It therefore follows that on any subject about which the collective bargaining agreement is silent, it is obvious that the arbitrator must conclude that management retains unfettered discretion with regard to that subject. This was the viewpoint that had been expressed many times in Bethlehem Steel arbitration cases and that was presented to the National Academy of Arbitrators by James C. Phelps in the 1956 proceedings. Arthur Goldberg, then general counsel for the United Steelworkers of America, found that view thoroughly offensive, of course (Goldberg 1956). He pleaded a theory of past practice and status quo in that debate.

My view is that the pristine view of management rights is based on a mistaken assumption as to the status of management and labor in the absence of a collective bargaining agreement. This question of status overlaps both legal and economic areas. A realistic analysis of the relationship is that both management and labor have a kind of uncertain and contingent control over working conditions. It is probably technically accurate to say that an employer with a union in the plant recognized as the bargaining agent does have the legal right to offer whatever wages it sees fit to offer in the absence of a collective bargaining agreement. Similarly, that employer has an unfettered control over what it offers in the way of working conditions. But if the analysis stops there, you get a misleading picture of the situation.

By analogy, when I put my house on the market I have the legal right to ask any price for that house that I wish. (One of my neighbors put his house on the market a couple of years ago with an asking price of $250,000. He did not get it, but he had the legal right to ask for that amount.) Before any sale can take place, I have to find a buyer who is willing to deal, and the terms of the final transaction may represent a considerable compromise between the original asking price and the original offering price. The buyer as well has some control over the price at which my house is sold. The case of a management and union without a collective bargaining agreement is similar. Management has the right to offer whatever it wishes. The union, on the behalf of the employees, has the right to demand whatever it wishes. Each has something the other wants. The employer can withhold jobs, and the employees can withhold services. Of course, the bargaining process is one in which each tries to bluff the other. Each tries to accommodate its needs and the needs of the other party, so the collective bargaining agreement is the result of this give-and-take. It is highly unrealistic to assume that one party comes into the bargaining with a monopoly on power and sits back and decides what little pieces of power it is going to hold on to or hand across the table. The union and the employees have power also, and the collective bargaining process is one of accommodation of sometimes sharply conflicting interests, which also may turn out to be mutual interests.

Interpretation of Silence

The arbitrator must be aware of the power relationships when he or she undertakes to determine the meaning of silence in a collective bargaining agreement—assuming there is silence in the agreement. In some cases, as in article 9 of the GE-IUE agreement, the parties can arrange to take the whole problem from the hands of the arbitrator by agreeing to language such as, "This agreement sets out expressly all the restrictions and obligations assumed by the respective parties and no implied restrictions or obligations are in this agreement or were assumed by the parties in entering into this agreement."

But the vast majority of agreements that I have seen have no such clause. One I am familiar with, the Firestone-United Rubber Workers agreement, uses the following language: "The management of the plants including the direction of the working forces and all other functions normally incident to such responsibility is vested in the company . . ." If the provision ended with a period there, very little would be left to bargain about, beyond those issues the company opted to discuss. But the provision goes on, ". . . and will be exercised in a manner consistent with the terms of this agreement and the applicable local plant supplementary agreement."

The big problem comes in determining, of course, whether there are implied obligations in the collective bargaining agreement, and if so, what they are. The Supreme Court decisions in the Steelworkers Trilogy strongly support the view that where there is silence in a collective bargaining agreement, the silence can have more than one meaning. Obviously, if the agreement is perfectly clear, at least to the arbitrator, and there is a violation, you do not have to look to any implied obligations or implied rights. If the contract grants employees the right to have a union representative attend a meeting called by the employee's supervisor, that supervisor cannot, under the agreement, refuse the employee that right to a union representative. If union representation is refused, there is a clear-cut violation of the agreement.

But on some matters there may be a complete silence. Take a case of an incentive operation where there are production standards while the production equipment is in operation. When there is a machine breakdown, the employee is not able to do production work but must work on unmeasured tasks. There has never been a standard for such activities, but the employee is required to exert "reasonable effort" at the work he is doing during the machine breakdown while he is on day work, to which the incentive system does not apply. All of a sudden the company engineers come up with a production standard for such downtime. The union objects to the imposition of the new standard, claiming it is the responsibility of the company to see that the employee adheres to the reasonable effort standard, that the contract covers what will happen to the employee if he or she fails to put forth such effort, and that this is an initial step toward adopting a standard for *all* work. The employer responds that they have had a real problem with employees goofing off when there was a breakdown and just making a semblance of a reasonable effort. Both sides referred to the minutes of past negotiations to show that its position on the introduction of standards for this kind of activity was or was not justified. The question presented to the arbitrator was, can specific quantitative production standards be used as the sole measure of reasonable effort in an incentive plant where the union had not agreed to these standards?

The arbitrator held that the long history of the bargaining between these parties, plus the total absence of any reference in the collective bargaining agreement to the methods for determining such "off-standard standards," and all the other details which were provided for the determination of incentive standards, convinced him that the silence of the agreement with regard to what they called day work standards was persuasive evidence that there was no justification to introduce the day work standards. Thus, although the employer was within its rights in policing the day work of the employee to ensure a reasonable effort, it could not impose and enforce a unilateral production standard as if it were a day work standard the parties had negotiated.

A couple of years later at another new plant of the same employer, management had placed the plant operations entirely on day work standards before unionization. When the union came in, it did not like the day work standards and tried to bargain them out. The company stood firm, and the union agreed to day work standards in this plant.

Thus there were two different results within the same company in different locations. In one case the union won on the basis of the parties' negotiating history, in which the employer had through negotiations surrendered its right to impose such standards in the plant involved. In the other plant, the employer had held fast, and the union had agreed to those standards, in a sense acquiescing to the employer's insistence on continuing the management right it had exercised before unionization.

No-Strike Clauses

What are the implications of management rights in the no-strike-no-lockout clauses? In broad versus narrow provisions? The majority of agreements in the steel industry, rubber industry, and many others have an unlimited, unqualified no-strike clause. The statement simply is there shall be no interruption of work: "There shall be no authorized strike for the life of this agreement"—period. It is an absolute and complete prohibition on strikes. Sometimes it even goes further to specify no slowdown, no interference with production, and so on. This is a blanket prohibition of collective action designed to influence grievance handling or to win some concession that is not covered in the agreement. Under this kind of blanket prohibition, there is not much of a problem of interpretation for the arbitrator. There are other industries that have more limited no-strike-no-lockout clauses. In the automobile industry, for instance, the companies have strikable issues, issues on which after a certain procedure is followed a strike during the life of the agreement is completely legal; such strikes occur with some frequency. Thus, since the parties have very clearly and explicitly excluded production standards as being not arbitrable, and since they have explicitly stated that the union retains the right to strike over production standards after a certain procedure has been followed, strikes on that issue are allowed. The union will, according to the company, call a strike on a strikable issue in order to get a concession on something else, and when the company makes the concession, then the strike issue is very quickly settled. There is a problem when there is a blanket no-strike clause but some limitation on arbitration. There are issues that the union may not strike over, but they cannot grieve or arbitrate them either. What happens then? An arbitrator held that the no-strike ban covered strikes for any reason since the parties had not specifically authorized any type of strike. Even though the union had a just complaint, the arbitrator found that the appropriate recourse for the union was to take the issue to negotiations, rather than to strike or submit it to arbitration.

Wildcat Strikes

As a practical matter, one of the greatest values of a collective bargaining agreement to an employer is the protection against strikes of all kinds and particularly wildcat strikes. I have been in the middle of an arbitration hearing at a steel plant when someone has come in and said there is a wildcat strike; whereupon the employer representative says, "This hearing must terminate right now because we have a wildcat strike, and the contract says that anytime there is an illegal stoppage in any plant the grievance procedure—including arbitration—is suspended for the duration of that wildcat strike." It is a pretty effective way of putting pressure on the wildcatters to go back to work. The people who want their cases heard are denied that hearing as long as the wildcat continues. In this case, we took a recess for the rest of the afternoon and resumed the next morning after the wildcat was ended.

There are other clauses in other industries that are not quite so restrictive. They will say, for example, that any grievance that becomes the cause or the subject of a wildcat strike shall not be discussed by the parties until the wildcat ends. Of course, when a wildcat occurs even without a grievance being filed, which is not at all unusual, then both the company and the union can go to the wildcatters and say to them, "Look fellows, you are losing money—go back to work, file a grievance, and we will expedite it through the grievance procedure and up to arbitration if necessary. But go back to work." That kind of appeal is frequently effective.

Some people question whether an arbitrator can really conduct a hearing when there is a strike going on, with crowds and yelling. Can he or she decide the case impartially? The answer may vary according to the arbitrator's ability to withstand external pressure. If you are likely to be greatly influenced by that kind of threat—or the claim that if you decide a case one way the union will be destroyed or the company will be forced to go out of business—maybe you should seek other employment.

7
Discipline and Discharge

Jean T. McKelvey

WE TEND to take just cause clauses for granted, at least in the private sector, forgetting that they were the subject of bitter controversy in the early days of collective bargaining. The first textbook used at Cornell's New York State School of Industrial and Labor Relations in the mid 1940s was entitled *Management at the Bargaining Table* (Hill and Hook 1945). Most of that book was devoted to the proposition that the worst blunder management could make at the bargaining table was to agree to incorporate in the contract a substantive provision limiting its right to discipline or discharge employees except for just cause.

The reason this was a subject of dispute should be obvious. Important and vital interests were at stake for both parties. From the employer's point of view, the right to discipline was an inherent management prerogative, a sovereign right, which by retaining the unchallengeable authority of management to establish and enforce the rules necessary for the conduct of an efficient enterprise was essential to the control of production. On the other side, the union had an equally strong concern for protecting its members' interest in job security by limiting the employer's asserted right to discipline or discharge at will. Out of this conflict over competing institutional interests there gradually emerged the compromise with which we are now familiar; namely, that management may establish reasonable rules governing employee conduct, but that discipline or discharge for their violation can be imposed only for just or proper cause, with the determination of the reasonableness of the rules and the existence of just cause left to the grievance procedure, which culminates in binding arbitration. Today more than 95 percent of the collective bargaining agreements in the private sector contain such express clauses with final and binding arbitration as the last step of the grievance procedure.

The public sector, however, is still experiencing the controversy over the inclusion of just cause clauses with arbitration as their terminal step that characterized the private sector three decades ago—those who are ignorant of history are condemned to repeat it. Many public employers today, especially in local governments and school districts, resist the inclusion of such clauses in their negotiated agreements, although I predict that it will not be too long before just cause clauses will be prevalent in the public sector as well. Finally, in the federal sector, the initial insistence by management, supported by the early executive orders, on limiting grievance arbitration to "advisory" arbitration and leaving adverse actions to the processes of statutory appeals, may well give way to contractual procedures similar to those in the private sector, as the Federal Service Impasses Panel proceeds to order the adoption of such clauses on a case-by-case basis.

Even in the absence of express contract provisions limiting management's right to discipline and discharge at will, many arbitrators have found that such limitations can be implied, their reasoning being that an agreement covering seniority rights, wages, hours, and other conditions of employment is not worth the paper it is written on unless there is an implied protection for employees from arbitrary and discriminatory discharge.

The Concept of Just Cause

What is just cause? Unlike other substantive areas of contract construction involving the interpretation and application of contract language to such matters as seniority, wage rates, hours, and overtime and fringe benefit entitlement, the determination of just cause involves a value judgment on the part of the arbitrator. I hope you have noted and pondered Lawrence Stessin's definition of just cause: "what a reasonable person, mindful of the habits and customs of industrial life and standards of justice and fair dealing, would decide" (Stessin 1973). Such a decision, Stessin elaborates, involves the use of common sense and a knowledge of industrial standards governing employee deportment as well as of the common understanding governing the relationship of the particular parties.

It should be obvious that these standards of common sense, reasonableness, and fair dealing, are slippery and elusive, wholly lacking in objectivity and concreteness. To illustrate, let me use an extreme but true instance of an arbitrator using his own subjective value system to decide an issue of just cause for discharge. The incident occurred at a company-sponsored picnic for employees of a paper plant in Rochester, New York. After the picnic, one of the female employees accepted a ride home from two of her male co-workers. Upon arrival she was so brutally raped by both of them that she had to be hospitalized. The following week the police entered the plant with warrants for the arrest of the two men. The employer then fired the men as well as the victim. The case of all three discharges went to arbitration. The arbitrator, selected by mutual agreement of the parties, was a Protestant minister, prominent in the community. His brief opinion found all three guilty of immoral conduct. What was most novel, however, was his remedy. He condemned them all and sentenced them "to fry in Hell forever." The union, which had agreed to the clergyman's designation as arbitrator in the belief that he would show mercy because of his calling, then sought my advice as to how the award could be set aside. I suggested that it file a motion in State Supreme Court to nullify the award on the ground that the arbitrator had exceeded his jurisdiction.

Although this is an extreme example of how subjective judgments and value systems enter into arbitral decisions concerning just cause, it poses an important question. If an arbitrator's own concept of fair play controls his or her decision, why would either labor or management agree to entrust outsiders with authority to review and judge disciplinary actions? After all, management could retain its unfettered discretion to discipline and discharge at will, and the union could retain its right to protest by striking. Fortunately, however, once just cause clauses were adopted, arbitrators began to develop certain principles and criteria to apply to just cause cases, thereby creating a body of common law that served to reduce some of the elements of unpredictability and surprise that might otherwise have made the process of arbitral review unacceptable to both parties.

General Arbitral Criteria

Although collective bargaining agreements, the past practices of the parties, and the particular facts of disciplinary incidents vary from case to case, arbitrators in general analyze each case in terms of the following considerations: (1) Was the alleged misconduct proved to the complete satisfaction of the arbitrator? (2) If so, was it of such a nature as to warrant disciplinary action? (3) If the misconduct is proved, was it the result of provocation or other extenuating circumstances that might mitigate the guilt of the grievant? (4) Is there evidence that discrimination motivated the disciplinary action? (5) Was the misconduct of such a nature that it affected the employer-employee relationship, or was it a matter more appropriately the concern of the civil authorities? (6) Did the employer adhere to principles of corrective or progressive discipline?

At a minimum, keep these considerations in mind when you write opinions and awards.

Incompetence and Undependability

A cardinal principle in just cause determinations is the concept of progressive or corrective discipline. Although some collective bargaining agreements expressly mandate that discipline must be progressive, not punitive in nature, many if not most are still silent on this matter. Nevertheless, the great body of disciplinary arbitration opinions implies an obligation on the part of the employer to follow principles of corrective discipline before resorting to the ultimate sanction of discharge. This implied obligation emerged from the early awards of arbitrators. It was based on notions of fairness and on the assumption that, if suitably warned or punished by penalties of gradually increasing severity, employees would be motivated to improve their conduct or behavior, thereby preserving their own jobs and saving their employer the expense of hiring and training replacements. Corrective discipline was viewed as a policy mutually beneficial to both employees and the enterprise. But although this concept is now accepted as part of the common law of arbitration, its application raises some troublesome questions. This is especially true in cases involving incompetence or inefficiency in performing a job. One must distinguish here between mere negligence or carelessness, which usually are amenable to corrective discipline, and innate incompetency due to mental, emotional, or physical disabilities. Before applying a mechanical rule of corrective discipline, arbitrators must first determine what kinds of behavioral problems are truly corrigible and what kinds are beyond the individual's own control.

These determinations are not easy to make. A few examples may indicate the problem. An employee never or rarely performs an assigned task properly. Is the employee a deliberate malingerer? If so, progressive discipline is appropriate. Or is the employee inherently incapable of doing the work? If so, transfer or demotion may be appropriate, but seniority or other contractual provisions may bar such a solution. Termination or discharge without prior warnings or penalties may then be justified, but it may be impossible to determine the cause of incompetence without initial recourse to progressive discipline.

Or take the instance of an employee whose frequent or prolonged absences disrupt the entire operation of the enterprise. Chronic absenteeism is most commonly subject to the application of progressive discipline, by management as well as by arbitrators. But suppose the employee is suffering from a recurrent and progressively disabling illness, such as hypertension or cancer. Clearly, progressive discipline is inappropriate in this situation, since the absences are not willful and are truly beyond the employee's control. I submit that an arbitrator has little choice except to sustain an employer's decision to terminate the employee, unless the contract contains provisions for a long-term medical leave of absence or early retirement.

Insubordination

One of the most frequent offenses with which employeees are charged is that of insubordination, usually defined as a refusal promptly to obey an order issued by a supervisor. This offense is viewed by management as a challenge to its right to exercise authority and is reinforced by the dictum that an industrial plant is not a debating society. The general rule applied by arbitrators is that an employee must obey first and grieve the order later, instead of resorting to self-help. Of course the order must be clearly stated and given as a direction, not a suggestion. But there are exceptions to this rule. As one arbitrator remarked, in reversing the discharge of an employee who refused to work in subzero temperatures and went home without permission when the plant's heating unit failed, "Resort to the grievance procedure is not an antidote for pneumonia." Moreover, because of OSHA, we can expect more such cases of temporary job abandonment under working conditons that involve an actual or perceived threat to employee health or safety.

Another category is that of verbal insubordination. Few arbitrators today would find that a brief argument between a worker and a supervisor over a job assignment would rise to the offense of insubordination. Similarly, a worker's comment to a foreman who told him to perform a particular task, "why me?" would not constitute an act of insubordination, since it would be judged as a mere verbal or visceral reaction to an order. But abusive language directed at a supervisor is more apt to be treated as insubordination, especially when it is threatening or obscene and uttered in the presence of other employees, thereby undermining the status and authority of the supervisor. But here, too, arbitrators make exceptions according to the facts of the case and their findings of credibility. For example, did the supervisor's language provoke the response? Can the words themselves be viewed as the customary language of the shop? Has management itself used or condoned such shop talk in the past without resorting to disciplinary action?

On a related point, arbitrators generally agree that the use of intemperate language or verbal epithets by a steward or committeeman in a grievance meeting cannot be viewed as an offense of insubordination since the parties are meeting as equals and not in a subordinate-superior relationship.

Misconduct

The types of industrial misconduct are legion. Space permits the discussion of only a few of what are regarded as serious offenses, recurrent or typical instances of misconduct, or those which present troublesome issues of fact, credibility, and remedy. Let us consider the following: theft, absenteeism, fighting, alcoholism and drug abuse, and off-the-job conduct.

Theft and Dishonesty

To the employer, as to society, theft is viewed as a criminal offense for which the appropriate industrial penalty is summary discharge. Yet an early study of arbitral awards in this area revealed that in over two-thirds of the cases, management discharges were either reversed or replaced by a lesser penalty (Holly 1957). What accounts for this apparent arbitral leniency? Of prime importance is the fact that most arbitrators employ a stringent standard of proof in cases of alleged theft of company property, using the same standard applied in criminal proceedings, namely, proof beyond a reasonable doubt.

Needless to say, this is heavy burden for the employer to shoulder. When an employee is caught with the goods, in his or her locker, in a handbag or briefcase, in a car or even at home, the employee's defenses (and I have heard all of them) are usually among the following: "The material was scrap"; "I was framed by someone else who put it in my locker, car, or home"; "I borrowed the tools overnight"; "The tools were mine"; "I carried the stuff off by mistake"; "I intended to return it later in the day." Although these defenses are frequently incredible, they are often sufficient to create the doubts in the arbitrator's mind as to the employee's guilt or intentions that lead to a reversal of the penalty. If the employer's action is based on mere suspicion, circumstantial evidence, hearsay, entrapment, or the results of a lie detector test, it is almost certain that the employer will not prevail. To judge by their published opinions, some arbitrators, despite their positive findings of guilt, are reluctant to brand a long-term employee with a good record as a thief because of the social and economic stigma involved. They therefore cast about to find mitigating reasons for reversing or reducing the penalty. I do not commend this bleeding heart approach to you. It does a great disservice to the integrity of arbitration as an institution.

Falsification of employment records is another type of alleged dishonesty that finds its way to the arbitration forum. In this area, there is substantial agreement among arbitrators that if the falsification is of a minor nature or only a factual mistake of no significance, if the falsification is not discovered within a reasonable period of time (six months to a year after hire), and if it can be shown that the employer suffered no harm from ignorance of the falsification, just cause for disciplinary action will not be found. On the other hand, if the employee falsified his training, experience and prior employment record, arbitrators are more apt to view this as a disciplinary offense, if not grounds for discharge.

Absenteeism and Tardiness
Cases involving absenteeism and tardiness are numerous. This is an area where little common law has been established and where criteria for judgment are largely undefined, making generalization difficult, if not impossible. Not only do individual employees differ in their attitudes toward punctuality and regular attendance at work, but the requirements of the industry and the occupation in which they are engaged also vary from those where occasional absences can be tolerated to those, like the airlines, where dependability is essential to the operation of the enterprise. Moreover, the reasons for absenteeism cover a wide range between willful or deliberate abstention from work and prolonged absences due to severe illness or injury. Finally, there is great variation among the absenteeism control policies of different employers, ranging from a practice of condonation to one administering a strict point system of penalties, which leaves almost no discretion to the arbitrator once the offense has been established and no extenuating circumstances have been found.

Absenteeism is also an area in which it is essential for the arbitrator to make findings of fact and judgments as to credibility. All arbitrators have been presented with bizarre reasons for tardiness and absenteeism, some of which turn out to be true, while others, we must conclude, are sheer fabrications, especially when skillful cross-examination trips the grievant into contradictory explanations or admissions against interest. Judgments concerning medical evidence are particularly troublesome in this area. All I can advise on this point is that you develop a healthy skepticism toward doctors' certificates, especially when they are undated, unsigned, or vague as to diagnosis, treatment, or prognosis.

Finally, I should remind you that while progressive discipline is often warranted in cases of absenteeism or tardiness, there are situations in which corrective discipline is wholly inappropriate.

Fighting and Altercations
Overt acts of physical assault in the plant or on the work site usually lead to summary discharge, which, in the absence of provocation or other extenuating circumstances, is rarely reversed by an arbitrator. The danger of injury to others or of damage to equipment that such behavior threatens is usually sufficient to warrant peremptory discharge without prior recourse to corrective discipline. Some arbitrators, however, take a more lenient view of altercations between workers, as distinguished from assaults on supervisors; they judge the former as more suitable for the application of progressive discipline, but treat the latter as a capital offense. In my opinion, such a distinction is wholly unwarranted, for co-workers as well as supervisors need protection from acts of unprovoked aggressors.

One of the most difficult problems of proof in this area, however, is that of provocation. Racial, sexist, or religious slurs, although verbal, are now increasingly regarded as acts of provocation, in some instances leading arbitrators to substitute lesser penalties than those imposed by management. In one of my recent cases, a seventy-year-old employee was terminated for beating up his foreman. The foreman testified that he told the employee to move some pallets, and the man refused. The foreman remarked, "I'll be an SOB," and the employee knocked him to the floor. The employee, who wore two hearing aids, testified that he heard the foreman call him "You SOB," to which he responded with his fists. Was this an act of provocation that should have mitigated the penalty?

A related problem is that of assessing an argument of self-defense, in other words, determining the aggressor. Many arbitrators are reluctant to sustain management when it either decides or enforces a rule that all participants in a fight must be discharged, without first trying to determine who started it. Should management engage in indiscriminate firing, it is then the arbitrator's responsibility to make the determination on the basis of the evidence and the testimony adduced at the hearing. Only if the aggressor cannot be determined is equal treatment of all participants justifiable.

Alcoholism and Drug Abuse

Although alcoholism is not a new problem for arbitrators, drug and substance abuse has only recently begun to appear on arbitration dockets. Like absenteeism, there is little arbitral common law applicable to these cases, both because of the variety of factual situations under which these incidents arise and because of differences in the nature of the job and the safety requirements of the particular operation. Thus when an assembly line worker reports for work under the influence, he or she may be sent home or disciplined without untoward effects, whereas as airline pilot or flight attendant, a bus or truck driver, or a crane operator who is proved to be an alcoholic or a drug abuser (or both) will undoubtedly be discharged.

The basic disagreement among arbitrators is whether discharge is appropriate for this type of offense. At one end of the spectrum are those arbitrators who see no difference between such employees and those found guilty of other serious offenses such as fighting, for whom peremptory discharge is the proper penalty. At the other end of the spectrum are those arbitrators who view alcoholism and drug abuse as illnesses that require treatment, not punishment. In between these poles are those arbitrators who steer a middle course, giving the employee a chance to rehabilitate himself or herself by entering a treatment program or by conditioning reinstatement upon regular attendance at such programs. Others place the employee on a medical leave of absence of definite or indefinite duration.

As employee assistance programs begin to proliferate, I predict that arbitrators will increasingly be asked to decide the conditions under which employees may or should be referred to such programs and, in the case of recidivists, when a last-chance or sudden-death rule should be applied. Given the present ambiguous state of the art concerning alcoholism and drug abuse, I can suggest only that you become as familiar as you can with the growing body of medical literature on the subject (much of which you will receive in evidence at hearings on this subject) and make up your mind as to the appropriate remedy in a particular case. Whether you were right or wrong may be subsequently revealed if you retain jurisdiction over the matter, or if you are able to obtain information on what happened later. Did the employee achieve rehabilitation? If not, should you have been able to predict his or her failure? Only in this way can you test and evaluate your own judgments as you, like others, steer your way through uncharted waters.

Off-Duty Misconduct
Many incidents of misconduct—drinking, fighting, theft—occur off company premises, in parking lots, bars, or at sports events. Should these incidents result in disciplinary action, arbitrators generally ask themselves two questions: Was the misconduct a matter of public knowledge and of such a nature as to bring disrepute upon the enterprise or its products and services? Was the misconduct work-related in some form? For example, was the fight between the employee and the supervisor a continuation of a dispute that started in the plant? Did the employee's drinking violate the type of work rule common in the airlines industry that mandates abstinence for a specified time period before a flight?

A more serious problem is that of an employee whose off-duty misconduct leads to arrest, indictment, or conviction. Can evidence thereof be introduced at the arbitration hearing? If it is introduced as evidence that the misconduct occurred, I would consider it nonprobative, in the absence of corroboration, since the evidentiary rules applicable to criminal proceedings may be different from those used by arbitrators. The same standards as those for judging off-duty misconduct should still be used to determine whether the offense was work-related.

But if the employee is unavailable for work because of incarceration, a different question arises. Many arbitrators have found that a short-term jail sentence excuses an employee from being terminated as a quit because of a failure to report for work within the period stipulated by the contract. At the other extreme, a life or long-term sentence would obviously render an employee unavailable for employment and hence subject to termination, although he or she could hardly be termed a voluntary quit.

Special Procedural Problems

There are some general principles or normative rules usually followed by arbitrators in discipline and discharge cases:

1. The burden is on the employer to prove that the discipline or discharge was for just or proper cause. If the employer sustains this burden, the burden then shifts to the union to show that the penalty was improper.

2. In cases involving charges of misconduct of a criminal nature or of moral turpitude, the standard of proof applied by most arbitrators is that of proof beyond a reasonable doubt. In instances of lesser offenses, the standard may be either the preponderance of the evidence or clear and convincing proof. I would remind you, however, of a caveat of a distinguished arbitrator, Benjamin Aaron: legal standards of proof have no place in arbitration and the only standard that should be applied is that of convincing the arbitrator as to the truth of the matter.

3. The reasons known to the employer at the time of discipline or discharge must be sufficient to justify the action taken. Incidents occurring subsequent to the action are normally not admissible as evidence of guilt.

4. Decisions of unemployment insurance hearing or appeal officers are usually not admissible as evidence of misconduct or innocence, since the standards for defining misconduct in these forums are different from those used by arbitrators. But if these decisions are introduced to impeach the testimony of witnesses at the arbitration hearing, including the grievant, they may be admitted.

Another procedural problem peculiar to disciplinary cases concerns the grievant's prior disciplinary record. May it be introduced into evidence? On this question, I would urge you to be familiar with those sections of the contract dealing with prior records. Many agreements contain specific provisions proscribing any reference to prior records beyond a specified period or beyond a period when the slate has been wiped clean. Although counsel may call your attention to such restrictions, it is your responsibility to read them before making a ruling solely on the basis of oral arguments.

Many contracts today provide that an employee's past record may not be used to prove the occurrence of the instant offense, but may be evaluated to judge the propriety of the penalty. A good record over a long period of time is one of the most important mitigating factors that may warrant a reduction in the penalty imposed by the employer. Even in those instances where the contract is silent, you may want to apply this principle.

Whether you can, in fact, modify a penalty, however, may also depend upon the contract. Some agreements provide that the arbitrator is limited to a finding of guilt or innocence only. If the grievant is found guilty, the penalty stands; if not, the grievant obtains full recovery. These contracts, which reflect initial distrust of the arbitration process, often present the arbitrator with a Hobson's choice, somewhat akin to final-offer arbitration of interest disputes. Fortunately, they are becoming fewer. Other contracts limit the possibility of recovery to a specified period of time, customarily the date upon which the grievance was filed. Still others, the vast majority in my experience, give the arbitrators free scope to determine the remedy. But this latitude, while more desirable from the arbitrator's point of view than the very restrictive clauses, also presents some troubling problems. Suppose, as is frequently the case, that you determine the grievant's discharge is not for just cause, but that some penalty is warranted for the offense. You decide to substitute a suspension. How do you determine the length of the suspension? In the absence of a price list of progressive penalties set forth in the contract or in the plant rule book and in the absence of any evidence of past practice as to how similar offenses have been treated, you are forced to make a somewhat arbitrary judgment or to order, as many arbitrators have done, reinstatement without back pay. If the suspension period is a long one, this remedy may be unfair to the employee. If it is a very short period, it may be unfair to the employer since it amounts to only a slap on the wrist for the errant employee. In either case, this remedy may create disparate treatment among employees, depending upon the existence of such fortuitous circumstances as the time it takes to process a grievance, hold a hearing, and render the award. Many arbitrators, while conceding that this is only a form of rough justice, either frankly admit that they cannot construct a more rational remedy or defend the penalty on the ground that it satisfies both parties since the employer is relieved of financial obligations and the employee gets his or her job back. I find this kind of compromise inherently wrong in many situations.

Should you decide to reinstate the grievant and to make him or her whole, further questions arise. Do you intend to include fringe benefits? If so, do you specify them in the award or simply state "benefits to which the grievant would otherwise have been entitled?" What do you do about outside earnings during the period when the grievant was not employed at his or her regular job? Normally, they are deducted, but who determines what they were? What do you do about earnings from a second job which the grievant held both during his or her regular employment and while suspended or discharged? Do you deduct any unemployment insurance the grievant may have received? To answer this question you should become familiar with the unemployment insurance laws of the state in which the incident occurred. Should you award interest on the amount owed to the employee? If so, why and at what rate?

These are only a few questions that may seem minor and inconsequential but may cause one or the other party to return to you seeking clarification of the award. Unless you have retained jurisdiction or secured a commitment from the parties that they can compute back pay, if necessary, without assistance (a somewhat dangerous commitment to secure, since it may tip off the parties as to your eventual decision), you cannot clarify an award unless both parties ask you to do so. I urge you to be careful in the way you word your remedy. Make it as clear and unambiguous as you can.

Discipline and discharge cases are among the most difficult to decide. The facts are often complicated; credibility is difficult to evaluate; emotions may run high at the hearing; and the misconduct itself may be sordid or shocking even to one who professes sophistication. Do not be misled by parties who assure you at the outset of a hearing that "this is a simple case." There is no such thing as a simple case.

8

Job Classification, Overtime, and Holiday Pay

Jack Stieber

IN THE UNITED STATES wages are not usually set by arbitration, except for those rare instances when the parties have agreed to interest arbitration as a means of resolving impasses over new contract disputes. But during the life of a contract some issues of wage determination may arise. For instance, in a contract running two or three years, there will undoubtedly be some provision for wage increases that are deferred until later in the contract period, to be given at a specified time in a specified manner. When there are disputes between the parties on the amount, timing, or application of the agreed-upon deferred wage increases, those disputes are normally referred to the grievance procedure and ultimately, if not resolved, to grievance arbitration. This is also true of cost-of-living escalators, even though parties should be able to write such provisions in a manner that would make their implementation automatic. Problems should not arise if the language is carefully drafted. But problems do arise when there are differences of opinion as to the parties' intentions. Perhaps they did not properly specify which consumer price index they were going to use, or perhaps the Department of Labor shifted from one base to another base or changed the items covered by the index. Or the question might be how to calculate the cost-of-living adjustment.

New and Changed Jobs

The issues that arise more frequently in arbitration, however, are wage adjustments related to technological and operational changes. These are important because a primary interest and an important objective of management is to remain competitive. A company will naturally be alert to and want to take advantage of technological changes that will help it in its business, increase its profits, or protect it against innovations introduced by competitors. Quite apart from technological change, an issue may arise from a change in organizational structure, or a different way of staffing operations that will require some reorganization of the work force. This may affect job content and wage rates on the job. Experienced negotiators are aware of these potential problems and will provide for them in their contracts. Agreements often give management the right initially to set the rates for new or changed jobs. Even in the absence of such specific provisions, arbitrators have often held that management has the right to set the rate, subject to the grievance procedure. Under some agreements, arbitrators have required management to bargain over new rates.

But even if the parties are required to bargain over new rates, what happens if in their negotiations they cannot agree on the rate for the new or the changed job? There may also be a distinction in some contracts between new jobs and changed jobs. What is a new job? What is a changed job? Rarely will you find a definition to answer this question to your own satisfaction, let alone to the satisfaction of both the parties, because if there were such a definition in the contract, the grievance would probably not have come to arbitration.

What is the difference between a changed job and a new job? How many changes does the employer have to make in a job before it becomes new? When does a single change in a job make that job a new job? These can be important considerations because the contract may treat these phenomena differently. Under an incentive system, there may be a provision, as in the steel industry contracts, for the same earnings opportunity under a changed job as under the old job; the earnings opportunity must be continued for a period of time. The question then arises: Is there any relationship between the effort required for the job and the earnings opportunity? If the contract is not specific on this, is it justifiable to permit earnings opportunity to decrease because the amount of effort required on the job is now less? Conversely, should the earnings opportunity increase if the job calls for greater effort? Answers to these questions will depend upon the contractual provisions.

Another question may arise: Does a change in job content require a change in the wage rate? Again, the answer depends on what the parties have negotiated in their agreement. If the parties have a job evaluation system with various factors of the job being assigned certain point values, a large enough increase in the number of points assigned to a particular factor of the job triggers an increase in the point total, and since compensation is usually determined by a range of total points, this might result in a wage increase for that job change. Under the steel industry job evaluation system, for instance, a point change of less than 1.0 does not call for a change in the wage rate.

You can see why, under the steel industry approach, there may be disputes over whether a job was a new job or a changed job. It may be in the union's interest to call the job a new job because this might result in a higher job class than if there were a reevaluation of one element that might not bring a large enough increase to achieve a change in job class. In other situations it might be beneficial for the union to take the position that there was a job change rather than a new job. For example, if the job carried a rather loose incentive, the union would prefer to keep that incentive rather than to call it a new job with a new incentive that might have a tighter standard.

All these variables, well known to workers, union representatives, and management industrial engineers, lead to arbitration cases in which the arbitrator is asked to set the proper wage rate for the job. A few cases provide some examples. In one, the issue was whether a new job had been created or whether there had only been a redistribution of the work load in an existing job, specifically, "Is the floor inspector classification a new job for which the company is required to negotiate a proper base rate in accordance with Par. 22 of the parties' agreement?" That paragraph read, "When new jobs are created or jobs are combined then the company and the union will meet and negotiate a proper base rate for the jobs." The union was pressing for negotiations on this particular rate. It asked the arbitrator to order the company to negotiate a wage increase that properly reflected the value of the increase in mental and manual skill, physical skill and effort, responsibility for records and product, and increased requirements demanded by the company under the new system. The company argued that the agreement was not applicable because a new job was not created. It defined a new job as the creation of a classification and a wage rate, both of which never existed, or as the introduction of changes in an existing classification that so substantially altered the physical and technical skills and ability required for the job that the existing hourly rate became obsolete. The company went on to argue that, if anything, the change in the job involved less physical work and fatigue than before, with no change in technical skill. The arbitrator would not credit the union's contention that the institution of a check sheet on the job represented a clerical duty so difficult for the type of person usually employed as a floor inspector as to amount to the creation of a new job. He found that the company had successfully refuted all claims regarding significant changes in job content except the use of the inspector's check sheet, which did not substantially change the job content.

In another case, the issue was, Did the company violate the agreement by establishing the new classification of tool room machinist? Here, the employer argued that a new job had been created. The union contended that the changes were just a rewrite of an existing job that paid a higher rate than the company wanted to set for the new job. The contract provision said, "When a new job classification is established, the company will submit to the union a temporary job description and will establish a temporary rate therefore. Thirty days after the job has been in effect, the company and the union will review the job description and rate to see that it conforms to actual practice. If the original rate is set too low, correction will be made retroactively."

The union claimed that the job was not really new, that it duplicated the duties of the toolmaker classification, and therefore the company was required to bargain over it. The arbitrator said that in order to sustain the union position, he would have to find that the tool room machinist classification duplicated the toolmaker classification to such an extent that it did not qualify as a new job under the quoted provision of the parties' agreement. He ruled that the descriptions of the two classifications did not warrant such a finding and therefore the company had not violated the agreement. But if, the arbitrator said, after thirty days work on the new job, it turned out that there was considerable duplication between the two jobs, the company would be obligated to bargain over the question.

In this kind of case, both sides usually call expert witnesses. A toolmaker, who was in the bargaining unit, testified that, in his opinion, this job would duplicate the duties of a toolmaker to the extent of 90 percent. For the other side, management engineers testified that, in their judgment, duplication between the two jobs would not exceed 50 percent. The arbitrator, who may not have understood the difference between a toolmaker and a machinist, had to decide this dispute. In cases like this, the parties would be well advised not to rely on arbitration. They should realize that the arbitrator is less likely to reach an intelligent decision than they are if they work it out themselves. Yet, all too often, the parties cannot agree, and they prefer any decision to no decision. As arbitrator, you may be the one who will be called upon to provide the decision.

In a third case of this genre, the parties could not agree on the proper classification of a job in the absence of a job evaluation system. Many small, and sometimes even fairly large, plants have no formal system of job evaluation. Frequently, there are not even written job descriptions. Yet the parties must reach an agreement on the content and compensation of new jobs. The issue in this case was, Is the job of Shipping and Receiving Clerk A as presently constituted in line with existing rate structure of the plant, giving due consideration to the work content and skill or ability involved?

The parties' collective bargaining agreement said,

> In the event the company establishes a new job classification or substantially changes an existing one during the term of this agreement the company will notify the shop committee of the new and changed duties and the new or changed rate. If the union has any objections concerning the new or changed rate the company and the

union will meet and negotiate over such questions. If agreement on such rate is not arrived at within 10 days of such notification to the union the rate may be placed into effect by the company immediately. And the union may within 30 days submit the question to arbitration. The arbitrator shall be limited to determining whether or not the rate placed into effect by the company is in line with the existing rate structure of the plant giving due consideration to the work content and skill or ability involved but he may not change the job description or job content.

As arbitrator, I heard both sides explain why this job was different, how other jobs paying more or less than the new job related to it, and where this job should be slotted in the wage structure. There was no job evaluation plan in the plant, although the factors that they talked about seemed to indicate that they were using criteria and standards that are usually included in a job evaluation system. The hearing lasted all day.

These cases are hard to decide. It often helps to see the job, as well as related jobs, being performed. The arbitrator may suggest to the parties that he or she view the job, accompanied by a union and management representative. This may not be possible if it is a new job that is not yet in operation or operates on a different shift. But even looking at the job environment and asking questions of some of the operators about the equipment involved and the physical setup may better prepare the arbitrator to make a judgment.

One of the primary reasons that the parties often opt for a permanent umpire rather than an *ad hoc* arbitrator is to permit the arbitrator to become knowledgeable about their plant. The designated neutral becomes familiar with the operations of the plant or industry and with the interrelationships among various jobs. When disputes of this type arise, the arbitrator is better equipped to resolve wage rate problems, whether there is a formal job evaluation system or not.

Parties who do not have a permanent umpire but believe they have a technical issue may agree to select an industrial engineer as their arbitrator, or an individual with experience in the industry. The designating agencies, upon request, will try to accommodate the parties by providing lists of individuals with competency in specific areas.

Or the parties may nonetheless prefer to follow the regular selection process in selecting arbitrators for technical wage cases; or they may not realize that it is a technical case until they get into the hearing. When the arbitrator tries to explain that he or she is not an industrial engineer, or not especially qualified to hear the case, the parties often say that it does not matter. Indeed, their reason for selecting a nonexpert in the field may be that they want someone with less knowledge than they have so that they can more easily persuade the arbitrator to their point of view.

Job Evaluation Plans

While job evaluation plans are often tailored by the parties or the employer to the particular needs and jobs of the enterprise, there are common elements to all job evaluation plans. A typical plan has a number of factors that represent elements into which all jobs can be broken down. Different systems evaluate from six to as many as ten, twelve, and fifteen factors on each job. Typical factors are manual skill, mental skill, physical effort, surroundings, hazards, responsibility for safety of others, responsibility for safety of equipment, training, and educational background. Each of these factors is allotted a certain number of possible points. Each factor has several levels and points for each level. For example, under mental skill there might be six levels from A to F, each with a brief description. Level A may read: "Perform simple repetitive routine tasks, simple sorting, make changes in routine only, closely directed." This would be the base level. The highest level in the factor, the F level worth, say three and a half points, may require the individual to analyze and plan complex nonrepetitive tasks to be performed by a skilled worker. Benchmark jobs, those used as examples of jobs calling for different degrees of skill, are helpful to the arbitrator because they provide a basis for comparison on the various factors. Disputes that arise in these cases often involve disagreements on the factor level or the grade to be assigned changed jobs. If some new duties are introduced into a job, do they move it from level B to level C or even higher, or are the new duties insignificant or a duplication of existing duties and thus not worthy of an increase in the points assigned?

Remember that job evaluation refers to evaluation of the

job, not the person performing it. It makes no difference how much education the incumbent has beyond the level of education that is called for on the particular job. If all this job requires is a high school diploma, the fact that the occupant has a Ph.D. does not make him or her worth more to the employer in that job. This may be very difficult for the employee to accept or understand. Experience or training beyond the requirements of the disputed job is treated in the same way. If all that is required to do the job is three months of experience and the individual has been doing that work for three years, he or she may be overqualified for the job, but the extra experience does not justify a change in the job evaluation or a higher wage rate for the job.

There are some jobs for which the individual's personal qualifications are considered because they call upon the job occupant to perform a variety of tasks involving different skills. Therefore the more strings to the employee's bow, the more valuable he or she is to the plant. This applies particularly to craft jobs for which the experience and the personal qualifications of the individual will be considered in setting the wage rate.

Because of the complexity and technical aspects of some job evaluation cases, it is natural for the arbitrator who is not an industrial engineer to feel inadequate. It is perfectly appropriate in such cases to tell the parties that you need outside help and request permission to secure it. You might want to hire a consulting engineer or somebody else who is qualified to go in and report back with findings that are relevant and important in arriving at your decision. Most parties will not take exception to that and will grant the permission, especially if the case involves a large number of jobs and could affect the entire wage structure of the plant.

Job evaluation systems are of two types, those negotiated by the parties, as in the steel industry, and those unilaterally introduced by the employer. If the system is written into the contract the parties cannot argue over the equity of the system because they have already agreed to it. If, on the other hand, the plan has been unilaterally introduced by the employer and the union has had nothing to do with the institution of the system, the union can argue not only about the particular factor or points in dispute but also about the equity of the system itself. The union can say it never agreed to use that system, that it is unjust, unreasonable, and inappropriate to this kind of operation in the plant. In such a case, the arbitrator has to decide whether to follow the company's job evaluation system or to make the decision on some other basis.

Some contracts, as in steel, permit a change in job classification if the underlying conditions of the job have changed, but do not permit a change simply because management decides that it can improve upon its original manning arrangement and reorganizes.

Our free enterprise system places a high value on efficiency and on the company's responsibility to operate at a profit and be competitive. Often a decision will turn on whether or not it is necessary for the company to make a particular job change in order to remain competitive. Unless there is contract language that expressly provides for other considerations, an arbitrator will usually consider the necessity of the judgment that is made by the company in terms of its ability to operate efficiently and the rationality of the job evaluation plan.

The arbitrator's function is to assess such management actions. The arbitrator may find that the effect of the change on the employees is excessive, that it will not bring greater efficiency, or that it will not increase production. The extent to which an arbitrator might overrule a company action depends upon that person's confidence in his or her knowledge and ability to make a judgment contrary to testimony by the company experts. Different arbitrators have different degrees of competence in different areas. An arbitrator might not hesitate to rule against management on a discipline case where a penalty of a month's suspension or discharge is at issue. The same arbitrator, however, may hesitate to question management's judgment when a company says, "For us to compete in the market, we must be able to introduce X machine, which will cost us $250,000, and in order to make that machine operate efficiently we must run it twenty-four hours a day. If we run it twenty-four hours a day, we must make certain changes in our work schedules and perhaps in our manning. None of the changes we contemplate are contrary to the agreement." Indeed, management will usually point out that the management rights clause clearly gives the employer the right to manage the work force, hire, fire, discharge for just cause, set work schedules, and operate the plant efficiently, as long as its actions are not contrary to other provisions of the collective bargaining agreement.

In such a case the arbitrator has to weigh whether what the employer has done is consistent with its authority under the parties' collective bargaining agreement. If the contract is clear and unambiguous that management is to make all of the decisions in a particular area, then you have to decide as the parties have agreed. But when defining efficiency and making a judgment whether certain actions management took will produce greater efficiency, you, as arbitrator, have to weigh the different union and management views.

Arbitrators are concerned about the effect of job changes on the bargaining unit, whether they result in layoffs and how they affect seniority rights of individuals. If the parties start off with a unit of a hundred employees and, as a result of job changes or combinations, the size of the unit is significantly reduced, some arbitrators might rule that such changes threaten the viability of the entire bargaining unit and therefore are not consistent with the collective bargaining relationship or the recognition clause of the agreement.

Arbitrators must be careful to avoid making judgments regarding matters that are not specified in the agreement, such as job satisfaction, for example. An arbitrator has no license to bar a job change because the affected employee finds the job as presently constituted more interesting and satisfying than it would be after the change. If the union wants to have job satisfaction considered in job changes or to freeze the number of employees in a crew or in the plant, it must succeed in having this written into the agreement. Arbitrators must keep in mind that they are creatures of the parties. They are there because the parties provided for them to be there, and the parties have circumscribed the function that they want arbitrators to perform by the language in their agreement.

Management's right to establish, eliminate, or combine jobs may be expressly covered by the agreement. But even in the absence of specific contract language giving management that right, it may be considered a management right initially, subject to the grievance procedure. Management's ability to remain competitive, especially as related to technological change, changing demand for the product, and other economic considerations may be relevant in this regard.

Premium Pay for Overtime

Overtime disputes often involve the right of management to require overtime work on the one hand or the right of an employee to insist on overtime work to which he or she has not been assigned, on the other. Employees often want overtime work because of the premium pay attached to it. On other occasions, employees prefer not to work overtime even though management wants them to do so.

The allocation of such overtime is usually a management right unless the contract provides otherwise. If the contract is silent on the subject of overtime, then obviously management is entitled to decide whom to assign to overtime work. Even when there is contract language on the allocation of overtime, disputes may arise. If the contract provides that overtime work is to be distributed equally among employees, questions may arise about the period over which the distribution is to be equalized or the group among which the equalization is to occur. If there is no specified time period, the arbitrator may have to decide whether overtime should be equalized by the week, by the month, by the quarter, or by the year. Such a decision may involve a question of judgment, and unless there is some help from language in the agreement, the arbitrator may have to rely on the logic of the situation. To require equalization of overtime every day or every week would probably be ridiculous, particularly in a plant where overtime does not occur frequently; on the other hand, to say that overtime shall be equalized over the period of a three-year contract may also be extreme. So the arbitrator looks to past practice for guidance. Sometimes the contract will use such language as, "Overtime will be equalized as far as practicable," or "Overtime shall be assigned in the following way except in emergencies . . ." or "Provided the individuals have the ability to do the job, overtime will be assigned in the following manner." Each of these clauses involves questions that may end up in arbitration. You may wonder why the parties were not more specific. The answer often is that they may have found it difficult to agree on more specific language in their negotiations and preferred to leave disputes to be resolved on a case-by-case basis either by themselves or in arbitration.

In resolving such issues, the standard is reasonableness. Management must act reasonably, even if the contract is silent on the issue. The arbitrator asks, "Was this a reasonable action that a prudent management might take, or was it an extreme kind of action that would only be justified by unusual circumstances?"

In overtime disputes, arbitrators may consider a number of questions. Did the company have the right under the contract to require overtime? Did the company comply with the overtime provisions of the agreement and rules pertaining to procedures? Assuming justification under the first two questions, should the company have excused the grievant? Was the grievant's reason for not wanting to do overtime so clearly justifiable and reasonable, or one that had been accepted in the past by management, that the company, despite its right to assign overtime, should have acceded to the request? If overtime is properly assigned, can the company discipline the individual for refusing it? Is discipline specifically provided for in the agreement, or is it a reasonable management action to prevent such behavior in the future? Finally, was the degree of discipline reasonable, given all the circumstances of the case?

Self-Help

One of the other interesting aspects of overtime work is that this is one of the few areas where self-help may be justified. Self-help occurs when an individual believes that he or she is not being treated in accordance with the agreement and decides not to obey a management directive. There are few areas where self-help will be sustained by abitrators. One of them is in safety and health, where it is widely accepted that an employee may refuse to perform a task that he or she believes with good reason will cause him or her injury, rather than do the job first and grieve later.

Generally, the rule against self-help is justified on the ground that the arbitrator has the authority to set the matter right through remedy powers. In most cases, the arbitrator can fashion a remedy that will make the grievant whole for any loss suffered as a result of management's violating the contract. Grievances involving health and safety are logical exceptions to that rule. Some arbitrators might also regard refusal of overtime work as an exception under certain circumstances. They would rule so on the ground that, if the overtime assignment is later found to have been made in violation of the contract, there may not be a suitable make-whole remedy. For example, a man is told at 11:30 p.m. that he is going to have to work for another three, five or eight hours after the end of his shift at midnight to get a certain job done. He believes that, under the contract, he should have been given more notice or that he is not the right person to be assigned the work. The question is, Should he do the work and file a grievance, or would he be justified in leaving at midnight because he had an important engagement? Some arbitrators have reasoned that if he does the overtime work and later is sustained in arbitration, the damage to him cannot be rectified by additional compensation or some other remedy. He was prevented from keeping his important commitment because of management's contract violation. Sanctioning self-help in such a situation may be particularly justifiable if it is shown in arbitration that the employer was indisputably wrong and must have been aware it was acting in violation of the contract when making the assignment. Under normal circumstances, an arbitrator would expect the individual to work the overtime and grieve later. If it is later found that the employer was guilty of a deliberate contract violation, the arbitrator can rectify matters by penalizing management in such a way as to discourage future violations of this kind.

Holiday Pay

There are few provisions in an agreement as open to ambiguous interpretation as those dealing with pay for holidays worked. Here are some examples.

It is not unusual for a contract to require that in order to be entitled to holiday pay an individual must work both the day before and the day after the holiday. The purpose is to discourage stretching a holiday into a little vacation, e.g., where a holiday falls on a Tuesday, taking Monday off and stretching the weekend into four days.

In writing such a provision the parties have to be careful. For example, a provision says that an individual must work *his* or *her* last scheduled day before and *his* or *her* first scheduled day after a holiday, as opposed to *the* last scheduled day before and *the* first scheduled day after a holiday. *His* last scheduled day may mean that an individual is entitled to be paid for a holiday that falls during a period when he was laid off for a week and not scheduled to work the day before that holiday. Or the employee may not have been scheduled to work the day after the holiday. Management might argue that the intention was to refer to the scheduled workday of the entire plant and that it was not intended to grant holiday pay to individuals on layoff. But the language is, to say the least, ambiguous.

A problem might also arise under an agreement that says an individual must work the last *regularly* scheduled day before and the first *regularly* scheduled day after a holiday to be entitled to holiday pay. A dispute might center on whether or not an individual must also work scheduled overtime on the day before the holiday. If the wording is "regularly scheduled day," the inference might be that it refers to the regular workday, namely eight hours, whereas if the word regularly is omitted, management might argue that all scheduled work, including overtime, was intended.

Some agreements are so poorly drafted as to say that to be entitled to holiday pay, the employee must work the day before *or* after a holiday, when they really meant the days before *and* after a holiday. Somehow the parties did not recognize what the wording in the agreement conveyed. An employer may have a pretty hard time convincing an arbitrator that the use of *or* instead of *and* was just a slip of the pen if a grievance arises over this issue.

When confronted with sloppy contract language you can enlist a number of aids to ascertain the true intent of the parties. There may be testimony by witnesses as to what was said during negotiations regarding the contract language.

There are a number of problems with such testimony. You will often have union and employer witnesses, both of whom were present at negotiations, who will testify to different things having been said at negotiations. It may turn out that there was no discussion at all regarding the meaning of the disputed provision. There may be a question as to the credibility of witnesses offering conflicting testimony. For example, if one witness produces notes, which he testifies he took at the meeting on the day that the language was negotiated, and the other witness cannot recollect whether or not it was discussed and has no notes as to what took place at the meeting, the arbitrator may consider the first witness to be more credible.

Some holiday pay disputes involve absence during part of a day or tardiness on one or both of the days surrounding a holiday. Do partial days of work meet the requirements of working days before and after the holiday? Is an employee entitled to holiday pay during a layoff? There are also disputes over pay for holidays that fall during vacations, sick leave, leave of absence, weekends, and so forth. How about holiday pay during a strike? In one case, I held that employees who were waiting to be called back to work following the settlement of a strike were entitled to holiday pay because they were no longer on strike, 46 *Lab. Arb.* 967. The issue was whether the employees who had not yet been called back to work were actually on layoff, since recall of employees after the strike was made according to the layoff provisions of the contract.

In addition to contract language and testimony, there are other tools to determine the parties' intent. One is past practice, the way in which they have interpreted the contract in the past. This may be the best indicator of what they understood the contract to mean.

Another device to determine intent is to look to other provisions of the agreement that may apply tangentially to the disputed provision. Arbitrators are generally loath to browse through the collective bargaining agreement unless specific provisions have been brought up at the hearing. If you are a permanent arbitrator and you are dealing with sophisticated parties who have made it clear that they do not want you to consider provisions that have not been cited in a particular proceeding, you should honor their wishes. But in an ad hoc arbitration, you may find another provision in the contract that the parties had not realized had a bearing on the disputed provision. If you find such a provision to be consistent with one interpretation but not with another, you may consider it in deciding the meaning of the disputed language.

Finally, while contract language will usually be given its ordinary meaning, it is well to keep in mind arbitrator Harry Platt's admonition: "Experience teaches that contracting parties are not always absolutely precise, nor can they be expected to be, in their Agreement formulations. Not infrequently, words and phrases are unthinkingly included which, if construed according to their literal meaning would produce results in opposition to the main purpose and object of a provision. . . . In such a case, there can be no doubt as to the right of an interpreter to modify and mitigate—in effect excise—the unpremeditated unintended language in order to prevent an absurd result and to give effect to the true intention of the parties," *Evening News Association,* 50 *Lab. Arb.* 239, at 245.

9

Seniority Systems in Collective Bargaining

Harry T. Edwards

[T]here has been increasing acceptance of the principle that a worker's job rights should be related to his length of service. Common-sense ideas of equity suggest that a man who has devoted more years to the company deserves more of the company in return. Seniority is objective, relatively easy to measure and apply, and easy to defend before workers and outside arbitrators (Reynolds 1974, p. 508).

MORE THAN twenty-five years ago, Jay Kramer, in a paper delivered to the National Academy of Arbitrators, analogized seniority rights to property rights (Kramer 1956, p. 41). Because Kramer's analysis straightforwardly sets forth a useful conceptual framework, it is offered here as a starting point for a discussion of seniority systems in collective bargaining:

> I would suggest to you that seniority is job security. Thus, as generally understood, can it not be said, at least provocatively and to stimulate discussion and analysis, that seniority rights are the wage earner's equivalent of the right which we all call the right to private property? But private property is not an absolute right. It is limited in various ways, and so, too, with seniority rights. If seniority is, then, the wage earner's "private property," as the term is generally understood, is it then unrestricted, unqualified, and unendangered? Does it really mean job security? Is length of service the equivalent of money in the bank or an ownership in fee simple? Hardly so; and just as the private property of real estate may be subject to zoning restrictions, so seniority too is generally zoned off in departmental, occupational, or other groupings less than company-wide.

Just as our private property may be large at one moment and then subject to contraction or diminution by governmental taxation, so too is seniority a mountain of support for "layoff" purposes and a mere hillock of protection as against "bumping." . . . Private property may be lessened in capital gains fashion or by the greater inroads of ordinary income tax, dependent upon the nature of the transaction involved. So also with seniority. It may be greater in retaining one's job and mean much less if promotion is involved and "ability" or "adaptability" or "competence" come into play. Finally, just as the non-wage earner's private property or, if you will, the wage earner's private property in his "non-industrial life" is subject to elimination by "eminent domain" and "condemnation" or business failure, so too may seniority be eliminated by merger or technological displacement—both factors hardly within the control of the individual wage earner. Indeed, the union shop steward's greater seniority is terminable in the same way as the jurist who is elected for a stated term.

It is therefore hardly inaccurate to say that, while collective bargaining strives to make jobs meaningful and satisfying through seniority rights or, if you will, job security, seniority may, under differing circumstances, mean either more or less than the possession of private property, outside the wage-earning group; although to the worker seniority rights, it is submitted, is [sic] normally viewed by him as an absolute private property right (Kramer 1956, pp. 41–42).

As a simple proposition, seniority is nothing more than accumulated time. Thus, someone who has been with a company for eighteen years has more seniority with the company than someone with only five years' service. In the context of collective bargaining, however, seniority often means much more. Time on the job is used to determine work, pay, and benefit entitlements. Thus the notion of seniority as a property right.

By way of introduction, the most critical point to be made is that for the most part, *seniority is strictly a creation of the parties in a collective bargaining relationship; seniority does not exist in the abstract.* Viewed as such, it becomes clear that "seniority is a *grant;* it is not a common law right. Hence the definition of seniority rights must depend on the language of the particular agreement" (Hill 1956, pp. 44–45).[1]

---

1. As noted in Slichter, Healy, and Livernash (1960, p. 104), "[i]n any given collective bargaining relationship . . . the word ["seniority"] acquires special meanings through the language of the agreement, through practices followed in the daily administration of the contract, and not uncommonly through arbitration decisions."

This paper is a modest attempt to generalize about seniority systems that have been produced pursuant to collective bargaining in the private sector. Although many aspects of the subject defy generalization, it is nevertheless important for any arbitrator or practitioner in collective bargaining to understand the basic applications of seniority and the factors that may cause the parties to a bargaining relationship to opt in favor of one approach over another.[2]

The Pros and Cons of Worker Seniority Systems

In collective bargaining, seniority is viewed by employers, unions, and workers as an objective reward for experience. In particular, seniority is used as a factor in promotions and other job placements, job assignments in lieu of layoff, benefit entitlements and payments (e.g., vacations), and wage payments (e.g., longevity pay), and as a potential mitigating factor in disciplinary actions. Although questions are frequently raised among labor relations scholars and practitioners as to whether seniority is a disincentive in the workplace, commentators universally acknowledge its significance. Most importantly, "there has been a [long-standing] belief among both managements and employees that for many purposes the long-service workers are entitled to greater security and superior benefits as a matter of equity" (Slichter, Healy, and Livernash 1960, p. 104; see also Reynolds 1974, pp. 508–16).

There are a number of perceived advantages of seniority: it arguably decreases worker turnover, which in turn may cause an employer to be more selective in hiring; it improves worker morale—and may even ward off grievances—insofar as it guarantees application of an objective criterion in employment decisions; it avoids favoritism, arbitrary discrimination, and excess subjectivity in employment decisions; it allows older workers,

---

2. No effort has been made in this paper to deal with seniority systems produced by collective bargaining in the public sector. The basic principles of seniority are the same in both sectors, and it is no doubt true that many seniority systems in the public sector mirror those in the private sector. However, the public sector is a more complicated subject because of the vast differences in state laws governing collective bargaining and because of the possible application of civil service laws.

who otherwise might be less employable, a measure of job security; it serves to spread the burden of unemployment to some extent among old and young, skilled and unskilled workers; and it rewards long service, experience, and loyalty.

On the other side of the coin, those opposed to seniority argue that: it tends to discriminate against younger (potentially more efficient) workers; it tends to create an older work force; it may force management to lay off critically important skilled personnel in a work reduction; it improperly presumes a positive correlation between skill and experience; it destroys worker ambition to excel because job benefits are keyed more to seniority than to performance; it produces numerous grievances due to ambiguous contract provisions; and it decreases worker mobility.

> The craft worker moves horizontally in the craft area, and the industrial worker vertically in the seniority area. Interoccupational movement is reduced for the former and employer-to-employer movement for the latter. Job rights protect but they also confine. Reduction of insecurity also brings reduction of independence. . . . The more secure are the "in", the greater the penalty for being an "out" (Kerr 1954, pp. 92–110).[3]

Many of these arguments pro and con seniority are unverified, but they do serve to highlight the importance of the subject. "It is doubtful whether any concept has been as influential, pervasive, and troublesome in collective bargaining as that of seniority" (Slichter, Healy, and Livernash 1960, p. 104; see generally, Rothschild, Merrifield, and Edwards 1979, pp. 583–630).

The Definition of Seniority

In considering seniority systems, it is important to distinguish between the measurement of seniority and its application. An employee's seniority may be measured by reference to his or

---

3. Reynolds (1974, p. 514), however, argues that
labor mobility can be too high as well as too low. It is not desirable that everyone in the labor force shuttle about constantly from job to job. Efficient operation of the market requires only a mobile minority, which may be made up largely of new entrants to the labor force plus the unemployed. For the bulk of the labor force, stability has advantages in terms of productive efficiency as well as personal satisfaction. Thus, even if it could be shown that seniority reduces labor mobility, one could not conclude that this result is necessarily harmful.

Figure 1. Different Types of Seniority

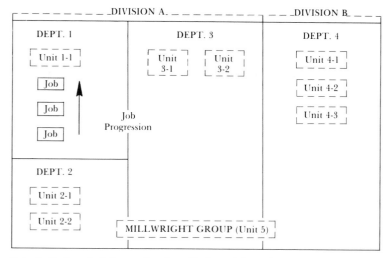

Note: In the hypothetical example reflected in figure 1, it may be assumed that all promotions and layoffs are determined by *department seniority* (with "ability to do the work" as a factor). The contract might also provide that persons within a *unit* have first preference to jobs within their unit (i.e., over other persons within the department).

The Millwright Group is an example of an occupational group within which employees work across several departments. The employees, however, only exercise seniority rights within their occupational unit.

The example might be varied to allow bumping (during layoffs) between *divisions*, instead of just departments.

Benefit entitlements and amounts might be determined solely with reference to an employee's *plant seniority* (last date of hire), without regard to his department, unit or job seniority.

It should be stressed that this is merely a hypothetical model; the model might be changed in any way deemed to be satisfactory to the parties to a collective bargaining agreement.

her time with the company, or in a particular plant, division, department, classification or occupational group (see figure 1). Under some systems, seniority is not applied in the same unit in which it is measured. Thus, for example, parties may agree that the senior employee in job A fills any vacancy in job B, with seniority determined by reference to the employee's length of time in the department.

Another variation in seniority usage will occur where the

parties agree to different measures of seniority for different purposes. For instance, *plantwide seniority* (from last date of hire) may be used for vacation benefit entitlement and amount (see Slichter, Healy, and Livernash 1960, pp. 109–10); *departmental seniority* may be used for purposes of promotions and layoffs within the department; and *job seniority* may be used to enforce shift preference rights among employees on a particular job. Generally, the measure and application of seniority varies with the type of industry, the complexity of the work operation and the levels of occupational skills within the company. Figure 1 depicts several types of seniority as well as the units within which they may be applied.

Last date of hire has become the most widely used, although not the exclusive, measure of seniority. A plantwide system of seniority, employing last date of hire, has several advantages over departmental, unit, or job seniority systems. The use of a single date is administratively simpler for both the company and the union. More importantly, date-of-hire seniority does not require employees to forsake seniority when they transfer from one department or division to another.[4]

Date of hire for purposes of determining seniority may not have the same meaning under all employment contracts. Normally, seniority is established only after an employee completes a prescribed probationary period. The length of probation may run anywhere from thirty to ninety days or more. An issue that may arise in counting days is whether calendar or work days are intended. Since the employer often retains the right to terminate an employee without cause during the probationary period, it becomes extremely important to the parties to know precisely when the probationary period has ended. Another important question that may arise is whether at the end of the

---

4. Before the enactment of Title VII of the Civil Rights Act of 1964, many companies had segregated seniority systems under which race or sex determined departmental or line-of-progression assignment. Transfer from a "black" department to a "white" department required a black employee to forfeit accumulated seniority and begin at the bottom of the list in the new department. Although the Supreme Court, in *International Brotherhood of Teamsters* v. *United States*, 431 U.S. 324, 355 n.41 (1977), made it clear that departmental seniority was not a per se violation of Title VII, *Teamsters* and the cases preceding it signaled the need for unions and employees to reexamine their systems for possible discriminatory effects.

probationary period the seniority date commences from that point, or whether it relates back to the employee's date of hire. Answers to these questions ideally should be provided by the parties in their agreement; but often the language of the contract is obscure, and it may be incumbent on the arbitrator to search the bargaining history or the parties' practices to determine contractual intent.

The Application of Seniority

There are four principal applications of seniority: job security, benefit qualification, benefit amount, and as a mitigating factor in discipline cases. Each application is distinct and should not be confused with the others. *Job security seniority,* otherwise known as "competitive status seniority" (Slichter, Healy, and Livernash 1960, pp. 106–9), embodies the principle that employees with the greatest amount of time on the job should have some priority to available work during promotions, layoffs, recalls, transfers, overtime, shift assignments, and the like.

Benefit qualification seniority principally fixes a minimum standard of experience on the job for various benefit entitlements. An example might be a provision stating that "employees with at least one year of service shall be entitled to vacation pay"; this establishes a minimum service requirement for vacation benefits. Other areas that may be covered by benefit qualification seniority are holiday pay, jury duty pay, longevity pay, sick leave, severance pay, merit pay, pensions, etc.

Benefit amount seniority determines the precise amount of benefits earned as a function of seniority. For example, employees with one year of service may earn one week of vacation with pay, while those with two to eight years may earn two weeks, and those with ten or more years may earn three weeks, and so on.

Last, seniority is frequently considered as a *mitigating factor in discipline cases.* This application was thoughtfully described by the late Arthur Ross, a highly regarded student of collective bargaining and himself an arbitrator:

> In deciding whether to sustain or to reverse a disciplinary discharge, we consider numerous circumstances which really have little or nothing to do with guilt, innocence, mitigation, extenuation, or other criteria of criminal law. One of these circumstances is senior-

ity. Long service creates a presumption that the employee is capable of satisfactory performance, so that stronger evidence is needed before the contrary is established. Moreover, the senior employee has developed a greater equity in his job, which is thought of as a species of property right. He has more to lose when he is terminated and finds it more difficult to get readjusted. We therefore tend to feel that an employer must be willing to put up with more from a long-service employee (1964, p. 149).

Seniority as a Criterion in "Job Security" Cases

In any *job security* case, there is always a threshold question to be considered: to what extent, if any, does seniority apply? It is possible for a company and union simply to provide in an agreement that, "in selecting employees for promotions, demotions, layoffs and recalls, the company shall apply the principle of seniority." However, such a provision would be hopelessly ambiguous, because it fails to indicate the work areas in which seniority is to apply and, more importantly, it fails to define the extent of the application of seniority. There are a number of different approaches that the parties may take to delimit seniority applications; only a few will be mentioned merely to highlight the issue at hand.

Straight seniority. This, obviously, is the simplest use of seniority. It guarantees that the most senior person in the affected unit will be selected without regard to other comparative factors.

Senior qualified. This approach assumes that, so long as senior persons are minimally qualified to perform the available work, seniority will control in job selections. Where the work is of a semi-skilled or low-skilled nature, the senior qualified standard is virtually the same as a straight seniority approach.

Relatively equal test. Perhaps the most common standard for the application of seniority in promotions and layoffs is the relatively equal test, or some variation thereof. Under this type of a contract provision, seniority is a determining factor only if the qualifications of the competing candidates for the job are roughly equal.

The wording of these "relative ability" clauses varies. The contract may provide that seniority shall govern unless there is a marked difference in ability, or unless a junior employee has greater ability. Some clauses provide that seniority shall govern if ability (or other qualifying factors such as physical fitness, competence, etc.) is *relatively equal,* or *substantially equal,* or simply *equal.* Even in the latter regard, however, it has been held that the term "equal" does not mean exact equality, but only substantial equality. . . . Where the junior employee is substantially superior in ability, however, he may be given preference over a senior employee (Elkouri and Elkouri 1973, p. 569; emphasis in original; footnotes omitted).

Arbitrators continue to differ on the nature of the evidence required and the burden of proof in seniority cases involving an application of the relatively equal test. Some arbitrators hold that a union challenging management's determination must sustain the burden of proving "discrimination, caprice, arbitrariness, or bad faith on the part of the employer or that the employer's evaluation of abilities was clearly wrong." Other arbitrators have required the employer to prove, "by specific and understandable evidence which relates to capacity for the job in question, that the junior man is the abler." In a final group of cases, arbitrators have ruled that the employer must show not only "greater ability in the junior man . . . but also . . . the absence of discrimination and arbitrariness and the presence of good faith" (Elkouri and Elkouri 1973, pp. 573, 574).

It should be noted that any arbitral standard that relies on the employer's "good faith" may effectively ignore the contractual standard that has been agreed upon by the parties. Thus, it should not matter that management acted in complete honesty, and with good faith, in selecting a junior employee over a senior one if the two employees are in fact relatively equal in fitness and ability.

Quite apart from the burden of proof issue, the relatively equal standard also presents difficult problems concerning the nature of proof required to measure fitness and ability. One question is whether *ability* refers to actual ability or potential ability to perform the job. Another question concerns whether prior experience on the job should be considered in any determination of ability (e.g., if a junior employee has worked on the job in the past as a result of temporary transfers, should this count in his favor?). Still another question involves the breadth of the concept of ability (i.e., does it include factors such as reliability and aptitude to perform higher level jobs, or should it be confined to a measure of the person's current skills to perform the job at hand?). In many instances, the parties answer these questions with specific contract language indicating the factors that are relevant in any determination of fitness and ability.

Best qualified. This approach preserves for management the right to select the person(s) best able to perform the job without regard to length of service. Only ability (and whatever it is intended to mean under the parties' agreement) may be considered under this standard.

Management choice. Subject to possible claims of bad faith, discrimination or violation of some external legal standard, this approach preserves for management something close to unfettered discretion to promote and layoff employees. Except in special job categories, however, it is rare nowadays to find a management choice clause in a collective bargaining agreement.

Three Variations of Seniority Usages in "Job Security" Cases

In any possible application of seniority in a "job security" case (i.e., one involving promotions, layoffs, recalls, etc.), there are at least three additional factors that may be relevant to an arbitrator. One is any contractual requirement of a trial period. If the parties have agreed, for example, that "ability" to perform the job means ability after a reasonable trial period, then the arbitrator must consider this in weighing competing claims. Also, if a trial period is included in the measure of ability, then it will be more difficult for a company to justify the promotion of a junior employee under a relatively equal standard.

An arbitrator must consider further whether employees who are vying to move to another job are entitled to a training period in the new job. This, too, would substantially alter the measure of ability if a senior employee was required only to show that he or she was qualified to train on the open job (as opposed to being qualified to perform the job).

Finally, an arbitrator may be forced to consider job progression charts that modify the application of seniority by providing that employees must serve for a specified time in a given job before becoming eligible to move up to higher level jobs. Thus, a senior qualified employee who, on any other objective measure, is the best able to perform an open job, may not be eligible to bid on a promotion if he or she has inadequate service in the present job. (This approach is analogous to an apprenticeship system and it appears in many different versions under different collective bargaining agreements.)

Special Problems Involving Seniority and Layoffs

The application of the seniority principles during layoffs is generally understood to mean "last hired, first fired." Nevertheless, it is important to recall that seniority does not always apply comparably in all kinds of job movements. Thus, for example, seniority may be a more weighty factor in job movements downward than in promotion situations. If the employing enterprise has a relatively narrow upward path of jobs and employees at the upper end of the job progression generally are able to perform the work in jobs below them, the parties may rely on seniority alone for regressions and layoffs. In other words, there is a convenient presumption that employees in the upper level jobs can always perform lower level work. However, absent a narrow job path, reliance by the parties on seniority alone for downward moves (as opposed to some type of mixed seniority and ability standard for promotions) can present problems. This is so because an employee who has gained a higher level position under a mixed standard is not necessarily able to perform all jobs of a lower rank. Parties will normally consider these realities in adopting a seniority system for regressions and layoffs.

A critical threshold question with respect to seniority and layoffs has to do with the definition of a layoff. Subject to specific contract variations, it is often true that a layoff does not include periods of time less than one day. In many cases, one-day reductions are covered by report-in pay provisions. Also, layoffs typically do not include strikes. It is not clear, however, whether temporary shutdowns, vacation shutdowns, or inventory shutdowns are layoffs for purposes of seniority application; these latter cases often involve situations in which employers prefer to retain select numbers of employees on bases other than seniority. Whether or not a layoff is involved will depend upon the precise terms of the contract.

Problems may also arise when an employer proposes to

schedule all employees on a short workweek (to share the work) rather than laying off a portion of the work force. "In the absence of a specific contract provision regarding the right of management to reduce the workweek in lieu of making layoffs, arbitrators have gone both ways on the issue" (Elkouri and Elkouri 1973, p. 484).

After discerning that a layoff exists, an arbitrator typically must determine whether the layoff was accomplished in accordance with the agreement. Most contracts mandate layoffs in reverse order of seniority and some grant senior employees the right to avoid layoff by bumping into another job. Bumping rights are exercised in a number of different ways. Employees generally cannot bump up because a layoff provision is not designed to permit an employee to improve his or her job status; normally such upward moves must be attained through the normal bidding, transfer, or promotion provisions of the agreement. Many contracts permit employees to move from one unit to another in a layoff situation. Some contracts even allow chain bumping where, for example, employee X in unit A may be able to move to unit B by bumping employee Y, who in turn may bump employee Z in unit C, and so on. Chain bumping presents a myriad of problems from the company's perspective, especially where there are broad job units and movement under the contract is on the basis of plantwide seniority.

Where seniority is a factor in layoffs, it normally will be a factor during recalls of workers from layoff. Many of the same issues arise in both contexts. Typically, employees retain recall rights for only a limited period of time and only to specified categories of jobs. Also, employees sometimes are foreclosed from securing a "promotion" to a higher job during a recall. However, many contracts require employees to accept a recall, albeit in a job in a lower position than the employee held at layoff. As with layoffs, all these matters are subject to the specific terms of the agreement.

Seniority and Principles
of Equal Employment Opportunity

The Legal Ban against Employment Discrimination

In any discussion of seniority, especially in the context of layoffs and recalls, it is impossible to ignore the problem of employment discrimination.[5] When Congress passed Title VII of the Civil Rights Act of 1964, 42 U.S.C. §§ 2000e et seq. (1976), it plainly recognized that employment discrimination against blacks, other minorities, and women was a critical problem in the United States. For a time, the legislative ban against racial discrimination in employment was effectively enforced. For example, in 1971, in the landmark opinion in *Griggs* v. *Duke Power Co.* the Supreme Court stated,

> The objective . . . of Title VII is . . . to . . . remove barriers that have operated in the past to favor an identifiable group of white employees over other employees. Under the Act, practices, procedures, or tests neutral on their face, and even neutral in terms of intent, cannot be maintained if they operate to "freeze" the status quo of prior discriminatory employment practices (401 U.S. 424, 429–30).

The Court also pointed out that "Congress directed the thrust of the Act to the *consequences* of employment practices, not simply the motivation" (at 432). This expansive reading of Title VII enabled the federal courts to define broadly discrimination against blacks and other minorities to include both *disparate treatment* and *disparate impact*.[6] Remedial concepts were also developed by the courts to require employers and unions to modify discriminatory seniority programs, provide for back pay and retroactive seniority for victims of unlawful discrimination and allow for preferential remedies, including quotas, to deal with cases of proven past discrimination.[7] In addition, Executive Order 11,246 (3 C.F.R. 169 (1974)) was adopted to prohibit employment discrimination and require "affirmative

---

5. Much of what appears in this section is taken from Edwards (1977a and 1980).

6. See, e.g., *Gregory* v. *Litton Syss., Inc.*, 472 F.2d 631, 632 (9th Cir. 1972). *Disparate treatment* and *disparate impact* were given fuller definition by the Supreme Court in *International Bhd. of Teamsters* v. *United States*, 431 U.S. 324, 335–36 n. 15 (1977), and *Furnco Constr. Corp.* v. *Waters*, 438 U.S. 567, 577–78 (1978).

7. On modifying discriminatory seniority programs, see, e.g., *Patterson* v. *American Tobacco Co.*, 535 F.2d 257, 267 (4th Cir.), *cert. denied*, 429 U.S. 920 (1976); *United States* v. *N.L. Indus., Inc.*, 479 F.2d 354, 380 (8th Cir. 1973); *Local 189, United Papermakers & Paperworkers* v. *United States*, 416 F.2d 980, 985 (5th Cir. 1969). On back pay, *Albemarle Paper Co.* v. *Moody*, 422 U.S. 405, 421 (1975). On retroactive seniority, *Franks* v. *Bowman Transp. Co.*, 424 U.S. 747, 762–66 (1976); *Meadows* v. *Ford Motor Co.*, 510 F.2d 939, 949 (6th Cir. 1975). On preferential remedies, *EEOC* v. *Local 638, Sheet Metal Workers' Int'l Ass'n*, 532 F.2d 821, 830 (2d Cir. 1976). See generally, Edwards and Zaretsky (1975).

action" among federal contractors;[8] the federal courts construed the Civil Rights Act of 1866 (42 U.S.C. § 1981 (1976)) to provide remedies for private acts of employment discrimination (apart from those available under Title VII);[9] and the Civil Rights Act of 1871 (42 U.S.C. § 1983 (1976)), which proscribes any deprivation of constitutional rights under color of state authority, was construed by the courts to provide a remedy for employment discrimination on account of race, sex, or national origin in the public sector.[10]

These developments reflected a clear understanding on the part of the executive and judicial branches of government that, in dealing with employment discrimination cases, the goal of equal opportunity could not be implemented effectively solely through neutral employment practices. It became obvious that even if all employers hired, paid, and promoted employees on a nondiscriminatory basis following the passage of Title VII, it would still be decades before blacks and other minorities reached a status in the job market comparable to that of white males. Therefore, judicial and executive remedies were created to require employers and unions to take positive, affirmative action to overcome the present effects of past discrimination and to ensure equal opportunity in employment.

The Current Picture: Title VII and Seniority Systems

For a time, the broadened legislative mandate of Title VII, plus strong judicial enforcement of civil rights laws, especially when coupled with the affirmative action obligation imposed upon government contractors under Executive Order 11,246, produced some significant improvements in employment opportunities for blacks, other minorities, and women. However, these employment gains were short-lived. During the periods of high unemployment after 1973, blacks and other minorities, as the last hired, were usually the first laid off. Therefore, even where affirmative action had worked to secure temporary gains for minority persons in the employment market, these gains were

---

8. For a good discussion of the history of contract compliance under presidential executive orders, see Murphy, Getman, and Jones (1979), pp. 431–47.

9. See *Johnson v. Railway Express Agency,* 421 U.S. 454, 459–60 (1975).

10. See *Johnson v. Branch,* 364 F.2d 177, 181–82 (4th Cir. 1966).

often lost due to layoffs in periods of high unemployment. The problem was compounded by the fact that, as the employment market tightened during periods of unemployment, it became more difficult for blacks and other minorities to move into formerly segregated areas of employment; it was also clear that the competition for jobs in recessionary markets helped to heighten racial tensions between the minority and nonminority communities in the United States. Whereas the concept of affirmative action was a by-product of the civil rights movement of the 1960s, the notion of reverse discrimination was given birth during the 1970s when nonminorities began to perceive that they were disadvantaged by efforts designed to ensure equal opportunities for minorities.

At about the same time that the employment market softened during the 1970s, the Supreme Court issued a series of decisions that appeared to confine and narrow the relief available for employment discrimination under the Civil Rights Act. At least until 1976, *Griggs* was the guiding light for judicial enforcement of the proscription against discrimination in employment in cases arising under Title VII, section 1981 and section 1983. However, several significant opinions issued in 1976 and thereafter signaled a change in judicial thinking.

In 1976, in *Franks* v. *Bowman Transportation Co.* (424 U.S. 747 (1976)), the Supreme Court ruled in favor of retroactive seniority for identified victims of racially discriminatory hiring practices. However, the Court in *Franks* indicated that the disputed seniority system, although responsible for locking minorities into lower paid positions, was not the source of discrimination. Therefore, the victims of past discrimination were limited to an award of retroactive seniority to the date of their individual employment applications. The Court recognized the incompleteness of this remedy, because "most discriminatees even under an award of retroactive seniority status will still remain subordinated in the hierarchy to a position inferior to that of a greater total number of employees than would have been the case in the absence of discrimination" (at 776–77). Nevertheless, the Court was inclined to balance the rights of discriminatees against the legitimate expectations of nonminority workers who had achieved job status under the existing seniority plan.

In 1977, the Supreme Court, building on the principles established in *Franks*, decided *International Brotherhood of Teamsters* v. *United States* (431 U.S. 324 (1977)). At issue in *Teamsters* was section 703(h) of Title VII, 42 U.S.C. 2000e-2(h) (1970), which provides that application of different standards of compensation to employees pursuant to a bona fide seniority system does not constitute an unlawful employment practice. This section had been interpreted in an unbroken line of decisions by eight circuit courts of appeals to stand for the principle that Title VII does not immunize seniority systems that perpetuate the effects of prior discrimination.[11] These courts primarily based their rulings on the oft-cited district court opinion in *Quarles* v. *Philip Morris, Inc.*, 279 F. Supp. 505 (E.D. Va. 1968). In *Quarles*, the district court determined that a "departmental seniority system that has its genesis in racial discrimination is not a *bona fide* seniority system" under Title VII (at 517).[12] In rejecting this line of reasoning, the Supreme Court in *Teamsters* held that "an otherwise neutral, legitimate seniority system does not become unlawful under Title VII simply because it may perpetuate pre-Act discrimination" (431 U.S. at 353–54).

The facts in *Teamsters* highlight the impact of the decision. The Court found that the employer was guilty of "systematic and purposeful employment discrimination" by limiting blacks and Spanish-surnamed persons to less desirable jobs as "servicemen" or "local city drivers," while reserving most of the better over-the-road "line driver" truck driving jobs for whites (431 U.S. at 342 and n.23). This discrimination was reinforced by a seniority system that created separate lines of seniority for line drivers and city drivers and provided that any city driver who transferred to a line driver position had to forfeit all his or her prior seniority and start at the bottom of the line driver seniority list (at 343–44). On the basis of this showing of discrimination, the court of appeals, relying on *Quarles*, ruled that all of the minority incumbent employees were entitled to bid for future line driver jobs on the basis of their company senior-

---

11. See cases listed in Justice Marshall's dissent in *Teamsters*, 431 U.S. at 378 n.2, 379 n.3.
12. See also *Local 189, United Papermakers & Paperworkers* v. *United States*, 416 F.2d 980 (5th Cir. 1969).

ity rather than in-job seniority (517 F.2d 299, 317, 319 (5th Cir. 1975)) and that once a class member had filled a job, he or she could use his or her full company seniority—even if it predated the effective date of Title VII—for all purposes, including bidding and layoff (517 F.2d at 317). In vacating the court of appeals decision, Justice Stewart, writing for the majority, attempted to distinguish *Quarles* by observing that *Quarles* was based on the proposition that a seniority system perpetuating pre-Act discrimination could not be a bona fide system if the intent to discriminate existed at the plan's inception (431 U.S. at 346 n.28).

The decision in *Teamsters* upholding a seniority system that perpetuates pre-Act discrimination restricts the ability of parties to obtain relief from such discrimination. This restrictive impact is compounded by the Court's observation in a footnote that "the operation of a seniority system is not unlawful under Title VII even though it perpetuates post-Act discrimination that has not been the subject of a timely charge by the discriminatee" (431 U.S. at 348 n.30). Thus, the Court rather summarily disposed of the question of the legality of the seniority system to the extent that it perpetuates post-Act discrimination. The Court took this holding directly from *United Air Lines, Inc. v. Evans* (431 U.S. 553 (1977)),[13] a case decided on the same day as *Teamsters*. In *Teamsters*, however, the Court expanded on the holding in *Evans* by further observing that:

> [In *Teamsters*] the Government . . . sued to remedy the post-Act discrimination directly, and there is no claim that any relief would be time barred. But this is simply an additional reason not to hold the seniority system unlawful, since such a holding would in no way enlarge the relief to be awarded. Section 703(h) on its face immunizes all bona fide seniority systems, and does not distinguish between the perpetuation of pre- and post-Act discrimination (431 U.S. at 348 n.30 (citations omitted)).

Thus, in *Teamsters*, the Court held that since "the seniority system [at issue] did not have its genesis in racial discrimination, and [since] it was negotiated and . . . maintained free from any illegal purpose," it was protected under section 703(h) even

---

13. In *Evans*, a female flight attendant alleged that the airline's refusal to credit her with seniority from an earlier period of employment was a violation of Title VII when her separation from that employment had been a Title VII violation (431 U.S. at 554–57).

though it perpetuated the effects of pre-Act and post-Act discrimination (at 356).

In 1982, in *American Tobacco Co. v. Patterson* (456 U.S. 63 (1982)), the Court continued the trend established by *Franks* and *Teamsters*. In *Patterson*, the Court held that a seniority system established after the effective date of Title VII was immunized by section 703(h) from disparate impact claims. One commentary has opined that "[b]ecause of the past history of discrimination by unions and employers in making collective bargaining agreements, [*Patterson's*] broad immunity for post-Act seniority systems conflicts with title VII's goal of equal employment opportunity and legitimates systems that have a disparate impact on minorities" (Harvard Law Review 1982, pp. 287–88).

Taken together, *Franks, Teamsters,* and *Patterson* appear to reject the possibility of "fictional seniority" for minority persons who are unidentified victims of proven discrimination, either to give them some preference for future promotions or some special protection against layoffs. As a consequence, newly hired minority persons presumably are required to follow job progression rules established pursuant to existing facially neutral seniority systems. This is so even though it may be shown that a seniority system operates to perpetuate past discrimination by favoring nonminority persons who have the most service and thus are given the first right to bid on higher jobs and the greatest protection against layoffs. Although the concept of reverse discrimination is not specifically discussed in *Teamsters,* the opinion manifests a concern over what are perceived to be the legitimate expectations of nonminority employees who claim job rights under facially neutral seniority systems.

In 1983, the Supreme Court had occasion to consider a matter posing a direct clash between the exercise of seniority rights and the enforcement of a "fictional seniority" remedy, given pursuant to a consent decree, in an employment discrimination case. In *Boston Chapter, NAACP v. Beecher* (679 F.2d 965 (1st Cir.), *cert. granted,* 103 S.Ct. 293 (1982)), the First Circuit held that a Massachusetts civil service law that required layoffs in reverse order of seniority was preempted by a prior consent decree that required the police and fire departments to increase minority hiring. In response to claims that not following the last-hired-first-fired rule would force innocent employees to sacrifice seniority rights, the court of appeals stated:

> While seniority was the normal way to decide who must go first, there is nothing magical about seniority, and here common sense suggests that it should be tempered by other entirely rational considerations so that the racial equity achieved at considerable effort in the past decade not be erased (679 F.2d at 978).

Following the court of appeal's decision, Massachusetts enacted legislation providing the City of Boston with new revenues, requiring reinstatement of all police and fire fighters laid off during the reductions in force. In light of these changed circumstances, the Supreme Court vacated the judgment of the court of appeals and remanded for consideration of mootness (*Boston Firefighters Union, Local 718* v. *Boston Chapter, NAACP,* 103 S.Ct. 2076 (1983) (per curiam)).

The Role of the Arbitrator in Deciding Legal Issues

Arbitrators frequently must consider public laws to resolve private disputes under collective bargaining agreements. However, I do not consider this to be the same as arbitrators deciding cases brought pursuant to public law. On this point, I am inclined to concur in Ted St. Antoine's thoughtful analysis of the arbitrator as a "contract-reader":

> [T]here [are] obviously . . . situation[s] in which the arbitrator is entitled or even mandated to draw upon statutory or decisional sources in fashioning his award. That is when the parties call for it, either expressly or impliedly. If a contract clause . . . plainly tracks certain statutory language, an arbitrator is within his rights in inferring that the parties intended their agreement to be construed in accordance with the statute. Similarly, the parties may explicitly agree that they will abide by the arbitrator's interpretation of a statute whose meaning is in dispute between them. In each of these instances, I would say that technically the arbitrator's award implements the parties' agreement to be bound by his analysis of the statute rather than by the statute itself. . . .
>
> As between the parties themselves, I see no impediment to their agreeing to a final and binding arbitral declaration of their statutory rights and duties. Obviously, if an arbitrator's interpretation of . . . [a Title VII] requirement did not adequately protect the employees, or violated some other basic public policy, a court would not be bound by it. But if the arbitrator imposed more stringent requirements, I would say the award should be enforced. . . .
>
> Whatever damage may be done to the pristine purity of labor

arbitration by this increased responsibility for statutory interpretation, I consider an expanded arbitral jurisdiction inevitable. . . . [R]ecent statutes [such] as Title VII . . . are so interwoven in the fabric of collective bargaining agreements that it is simply impracticable in many cases for arbitrators to deal with contractual provisions without taking into account statutory provisions (St. Antoine 1978, pp. 34–36, footnotes omitted).[14]

In the past, I have often expressed grave reservations about arbitrators deciding public law issues (Edwards 1976a, p.59, 1976b, 1977b). In the light of my experiences on the court, however, I have found that my reservations have been significantly tempered. Like my colleagues, Judge Alvin Rubin and Judge Betty Fletcher, I agree that

[a]s new issues and problems in improving employment conditions arise, and as we deliberate better ways to handle issues now being resolved only in the courts, we must consider seriously the possibility that some problems can best be resolved by giving a wider hand to collective bargaining and to resolution of disputes by arbitration (Rubin 1979, p. 36).

Judge Fletcher went so far as to suggest that, for individual claims,

arbitration in the context we know it . . . is the best tool we have, the best forum for the grievant. And I think arbitrators have it within their power and their grasp to improve the process in order to accomplish the goals of Title VII, in the context of the traditional forum. . . .
    The advantage[ ] of relying on private arbitrators . . . [is] that . . . arbitration provides speedy dispute resolution by persons knowledgeable about the industry and the players, and persons who are skilled in resolving disputes in a way that does not disrupt ongoing relationships (Fletcher 1982, p.228).

Miscellaneous Issues Involving
the Application of Seniority in Collective Bargaining

As can be surmised from the foregoing discussion, there are a wealth of issues concerning the application of seniority in collective bargaining relationships. In addition to the issues already raised, which are among the most important, there are a few additional ones that warrant at least passing mention.

---

14. See also Bloch (1978) and, in contrast to the views of St. Antoine and Bloch, see Feller (1976). For a time, many of my own views were quite similar to certain of the principal themes expressed in Professor Feller's *Golden Age* article.

Filling Job "Vacancies." In many cases involving disputes over the proper application of seniority in promotions and layoffs, an issue arises as to whether there is in fact a job *vacancy* to be filled. A vacancy is generally regarded as a *permanent* opening as declared by the employer; however, to avoid management circumvention of seniority rights, many contracts limit the time that an employee may work on a temporary transfer or otherwise mandate that a job opening be declared permanent after a given length of time.

Posting and bidding are the most popular means of filling vacancies under collective bargaining agreements. There are a multitude of possible variations in the job posting requirement. For example, a company may be required to post a job in only a single department, and only employees in that department may be entitled to bid on the job. Or the employees in the affected department may simply have first right of refusal to openings in the department. Bidding for a job usually must occur within a specified time period, and beyond this time the company can select someone to fill the vacancy pursuant to an agreed upon selection procedure.

Some parties fill vacancies through an application-on-file system. This system tends to limit the number of bids to be considered for a particular vacancy by requiring management to consider only those employees who already have an application on file at the time a position becomes vacant. Another limitation on the number of bids may result if the parties have a rule limiting the number of bids that a person may have on file at any given time.

Superseniority. Under superseniority clauses, individuals—usually union stewards and officers—are granted greater seniority than all other workers in a particular seniority unit regardless of how long they have been in the unit. These clauses are designed to protect union officials against job moves or layoffs that might remove them from their areas of representational responsibility. The National Labor Relations Board has held that superseniority clauses limited to layoff and recall may be justified by a substantial business need of effective administration of the collective bargaining agreement and, therefore, are lawful under the NLRA. A superseniority clause that goes beyond layoff and recall is presumptively discriminatory in favor of union adherents, and the burden of providing a substantial business justification is on the party claiming its legality (*NLRB v. American Can Co.*, 658 F.2d 746 (10th Cir. 1981); *Dairylea Coop., Inc.*, 219 N.L.R.B. 656 (1975), *aff'd sub nom. N.L.R.B. v. Milk Drivers & Dairy Employees, Local 338*, 531 F.2d 1162 (2d Cir. 1976)).

Continuation, Interruption, or Termination of Seniority. Absent some interruption in the employee's normal employment, seniority generally continues for as long as the collective bargaining agreement remains in force. Seniority may even survive an agreement under the National Labor Relations Board's successor doctrine (see generally, Gorman 1976, pp. 575–78). Seniority also may survive termination of the contract in a merger of two companies (see Kennedy 1963, pp. 1–34).

Apart from the successor and merger cases, seniority may be lost or interrupted due to a number of factors. As a general matter, once an employee is hired and is considered to be part of the bargaining unit, seniority will accumulate except where the parties otherwise agree. For instance, in many collective bargaining agreements, the parties specify that seniority is frozen or cancelled after a certain period during a layoff, leave for union business, assignment to management, absence without leave, and when an employee is discharged for cause or voluntarily quits. The contract language is usually very specific in these instances (Rothschild, Merrifield, and Edwards 1979, pp. 611–30).

Conclusion

In *Collective Bargaining and Labor Arbitration*, the authors suggest a checklist of the following principal questions to be considered by parties negotiating a seniority provision:

(1) For what purposes is seniority to be recognized? Reductions in force (layoffs)? Re-employment after layoff? Promotions? Transfers? Shift preferences? Work assignments?

(2) What *kind* of seniority is to be recognized? Company length of service? Plant length of service? Department length of service? Occupational group length of service? Job classification length of service? Some combination of these? May this depend in part on the degree of complexity of the plant and the variety of different occupational skills required in the operation? How does the type of

seniority comply with the anti-discrimination proscriptions of federal law?

(3) To what degree shall seniority be made the controlling factor? Entirely controlling? Controlling if the employee has the necessary job competence? Controlling if relative merit and ability are relatively equal? Not controlling at all, but only a factor to be "considered," along with others?

(4) How shall an employee's seniority standing be determined? Credit, if any, to be given for non-working time (sick leave, layoffs, leave of absence, etc.)? Credit, if any, to be given for time spent outside the bargaining unit (prior to initial agreement, subsequent to initial agreement)? "Super-seniority" for union officers or others?

(5) Under what circumstances shall seniority be lost or forfeited? Resignation? Discharge? Extended layoff or other absence from work? Transfers to jobs outside the bargaining unit? Change in employer status (merger, consolidation, abandonment of facilities, relocation of plant)? (Rothschild, Merrifield, and Edwards 1979, pp. 583–84).

This checklist, although written for the parties, offers some useful clues for arbitrators concerning the proper questions to be answered in cases involving seniority claims under a collective bargaining agreement. The most important thing for an arbitrator to recall, however, is that "[s]eniority rights are not inherent in the employment relationship, but are created most frequently by collective bargaining agreements, as previously indicated through seniority systems" (Rothschild, Merrifield, and Edwards 1979, p. 586).

10

Individual Rights in Arbitration

Clyde W. Summers

MY STARTING premise is that individual employees have rights that the union and employer cannot ignore or barter away, and the arbitrator must adjudicate those rights as an independent arbiter, not as a creature of the union and employer.

It is an uncomfortable but obvious fact that in some cases the union brings to arbitration, the union does not act on behalf of all the employees. Indeed, the union may not, in fact, be acting on behalf of the grievants in the arbitration. Of necessity, the union's position is at times hostile to or divergent from the interest of some employees whose fates are being determined in the arbitration.

Some cases, by their very nature, affect others than the grievant. There may be a forgotten man or woman, or men and women, other than the grievant whose job rights will be determined by the arbitration decision. This is inevitable in cases involving seniority, whether it is a case of layoff, transfer, or rehire. When the union grieves that A's layoff is out of line of seniority, it demands that A be reinstated, with the implicit request that X be laid off in A's stead. The arbitrator, in adjudicating A's rights must also adjudicate X's rights.

Seniority rights are termed relative rights, but they are more accurately described as competing rights, for the rights of employees run against each other. Therefore, when a union brings such a case to arbitration, it argues against the interests of some of its constituents. I do not suggest that this is in any way improper; the union is entitled to argue on behalf of what it believes is the proper application of the agreement. That, however, only underlines the problem that an employee whose job is at stake is not being represented by the union.

The question is, How is this employee's interests to be represented when the union is arguing not for, but against, his or her interests? This presents a fundamental issue of due process: the right of the individual to be heard. The arbitrator who presides over the proceeding, whose legal status and authority flow from federal law and whose decision is enforceable in the federal courts, has a duty to ensure due process. Apart from this moral and legal obligation to protect due process, the arbitrator has a responsibility to the parties, and to himself (or herself), to make a fully informed decision. He cannot do this unless he hears the arguments on behalf of the individual whose interests the union opposes.

The employer is, of course, an adversary party in the proceedings and might be expected to present the arguments supporting the order of layoff the union is opposing. The employer thus supports the interests of those employees who would be adversely affected by the union's grievance. But the employer may be a poor protector of the individual's interests. In many situations, the employer may be quite indifferent as to which employee is to be laid off, but is at most concerned with avoiding liability for back pay. Where the employer does not care who is laid off, there may be no one energetically arguing on behalf of those employees whose present employment is placed in jeopardy by the arbitration proceedings.

The same problem is more sharply focused in promotion cases. If A gets promoted and the union files a grievance on behalf of B, claiming that he or she should have been awarded the promotion, the union grievance is, in effect, against A. If the arbitrator upholds the grievance, A is demoted. Again, the fundamental due process issue is present, and the arbitrator needs to know the merits of A's case in order to make a fair and fully informed decision. In promotion cases, the employer may be a more effective advocate on behalf of the individual than in layoff cases. The employer, in making the promotion, has expressed a preference for A and has an interest in protecting A's promotion. Even so, the employer's interest may not be the same, nor be as strong, as that of the individual employee. The employer may be a less than fully committed advocate on behalf of the employee who is threatened by demotion.

Discipline cases do not present the same inherent conflict of interest, but in some cases the union may be less than a wholehearted advocate. For example, when wildcat strikers are discharged, the union is not always sympathetic or anxious to have the strikers reinstated. The strike may be directed as much against the union leadership for its lack of aggressiveness in getting conditions corrected as against the employer for continuing the conditions. The union may see the wildcat strikers as troublemakers and be glad to see them gone. Apart from these considerations, the union may be reluctant to press too hard lest it appear to have supported the strike or encourage future wildcats.

The union's advocacy may also be less than wholehearted in other discipline cases. The grievant may be disliked by the other members. He may be a thorn in the side of the union leadership. He may be an advocate of unpopular views, or he may be a potential rival for union office. Even when there is no color of improper motive, the union's advocacy may not be enthusiastic because those presenting the grievance may have concluded that the grievant is guilty and that, at most, the discipline is too severe. The grievant may, in fact, not be guilty. There may not have been a thorough investigation, or there may be mitigating circumstances that the union has not taken into account. The union's presentation may be only the performing of last rites—"It is the last thing we can do for him as a union member." The result is that the employee does not get an adequate defense.

I do not mean to suggest that unions generally fail to take meritorious cases to arbitration. The dereliction more often runs in the opposite direction; the union takes palpably worthless cases to arbitration rather than accept responsibility for declaring them worthless. This is particularly true of discharge cases. But there appear, from time to time, those cases in which the union fails or refuses to defend adequately an individual in arbitration.

Duty of Fair Representation

These cases of seniority, promotion, and discipline pose problems of fairness and propriety for an arbitrator, but they also involve an important legal principle. How an arbitrator deals with these cases must take account of that legal principle. The principle is simply stated: a union has a duty to represent all employees fairly, in both the negotiation of contracts and the administration of contracts.

This principle was first articulated by the Supreme Court nearly forty years ago in *Steele* v. *Louisville & Nashville Rd.*, 323 U.S. 192 (1944). The union had negotiated a seniority arrangement that had the effect of placing black employees at the bottom of the seniority list. The Court held that the statute, by conferring on the union the power to represent the employees, imposed on the union the duty to represent all employees "without hostile discrimination, fairly, impartially, and in good faith." Then, said the Court, "Wherever necessary to that end, the union is required to consider requests of non-union members of the craft and expressions of their views with respect to collective bargaining with the employer and to give them notice of and opportunity for hearing on its proposed action." (p. 204)

That case involved discrimination in negotiation of the collective agreement, but, the Court in *Conley* v. *Gibson*, 355 U.S. 41 (1957), held that the principle was equally applicable in administration of the collective agreement. Once the union "undertook to bargain or present grievances for some of the employees it represented, it could not refuse to take similar action in good faith for other employees."

In the intervening years, the rights of the individual under the collective agreement and the duty of the union in processing grievances has been more fully developed and explicitly stated. In the leading case of *Vaca* v. *Sipes*, 386 U.S. 171 (1967), an employee was denied reinstatement after sick leave on the basis that his heart condition made it unsafe for him to work. His doctor said he was able to work; the company doctor said he was not. The union processed his grievance through four steps to no avail. Before deciding whether to go to arbitration, the union sent him to a new doctor to get better evidence.

When this doctor found him unable to work, the union decided not to go to arbitration. The employee sued both the employer and the union. Although the Court ruled against the employee, it articulated three propositions of crucial importance for our purposes.

First, the individual employee has legal rights under the collective agreement. If he is wrongfully discharged, this is a violation not only of the union's rights but of his rights. In the absence of grievance and arbitrator provisions, either the employee or the union may sue the employer for breach of contract, *Smith* v. *Evening News Assn.*, 371 U.S. 195 (1962).

Second, where the grievance and arbitration provisions give the union exclusive control over whether to appeal the grievance, the individual can sue the employer only if the union has unfairly represented him or her. If the union has violated its duty of fair representation, the employee may then sue the employer for breach of contract and the union for breach of its duty of fair representation.

Third, the Court described what was required of the union. The union's action must not be "arbitrary, discriminatory, or in bad faith." The union must "in good faith and in a non-arbitrary manner, make decisions as to the merits of particular grievances." It can not "arbitrarily ignore a meritorious grievance or process it in a perfunctory manner."

This case was crucial, for it solidly established that the individual has rights under the collective agreement, and both the union and the employer may be legally liable if the employee is not represented fairly in the handling of the grievance. The liability is not only for back pay and other damages but may also be for lawyers fees, which may be greater than the back pay.

A second Supreme Court case, more directly relevant to our purposes, is *Hines* v. *Anchor Motor Freight, Inc.*, 424 U.S. 554 (1976). In this case, a truck driver was discharged for falsifying a motel receipt, and this discharge was upheld by the joint area arbitration committee. He claimed that if the union had adequately investigated, it would have discovered that he was innocent and that the falsification was made by the motel clerk. With this evidence, the union would have obtained his reinstatement. He sued both the union and the employer, and both were held liable. The employer argued that the arbitration award should be considered final, particularly as to the employer because it was in no way responsible for the union's failure to investigate. The Court rejected this reasoning. The individual was suing for breach of his contract right against the employer not to be discharged without just cause. The arbitration award was no bar where the union's failure to represent "seriously undermines the integrity of the arbitral process" (at p. 567), . . .

> Congress has put its blessing on private dispute settlement arrangements provided in collective agreements, but it was anticipated, we are sure, that the contractual machinery would operate within some minimum levels of integrity" (at 571).

Another illuminating case is *Holodnak* v. *Avco Corp.*, 381 F. Supp. 191 (D.C. Conn. 1974). Holodnak was discharged for publishing an article in a newspaper charging that the union and employer were acting in collusion to deprive individuals of their rights under the contract and to suppress criticism of plant conditions and union practices. The union processed his grievance to arbitration. The union attorney failed to raise various available defenses or present certain relevant evidence. The union did not argue that Holodnak had the right to speak freely outside the workplace, but argued that he was a naïve man who "really knew not what he was doing" and pled for leniency, not vindication. The arbitrator upheld the discharge. Holodnak brought suit against both Avco and the union. The federal district court found the union had failed to represent Holodnak by failing to press available arguments and present relevant evidence. The court vacated the arbitration award and gave Holodnak back pay, lawyers fees, and punitive damages of $15,000. This was affirmed by the court of appeals, 514 F.2d 285 (2d Cir. 1975), except for the award of punitive damages, which the Supreme Court has since held the individual cannot recover from the union, *I.B.E.W.* v. *Foust*, 422 U.S. 42 (1979).

One more case to fill out the picture: in *Belanger* v. *Matteson*, 346 A.2d 124 (R.I. 1975), two teachers were competing for a promotion in a Rhode Island school system. When one was promoted, the union filed a grievance on behalf of the other, processing it to arbitration. The arbitrator ruled in favor of the union, but the teacher who had thereby been deprived of his promotion brought suit. The court vacated the arbitrator's award, saying that the union had violated its duty of fair representation because the teacher who had been displaced by the award had been neither heard by the arbitrator nor listened to by the union, and the union had advocated one employee's interest without taking into consideration the interests of the other.

The lesson for arbitrators in these cases is quite plain. The arbitration proceeding is not a private proceeding between the union and the employer. Individual rights under the contract are being adjudicated, and the arbitrator has an obligation to those whose rights are being adjudicated. If those whose rights are involved are not fully heard and fairly adjudicated, the award may be vacated and the parties may be liable for damages. When individual rights are involved and the individual is not provided due process, then the courts will give no deference to the arbitrator's award. The arbitrator has a responsibility, not only to the law and to the profession but also to the parties, to ensure that individual rights are fully protected.

Implementing Fairness

The first, and perhaps most important, question in the implementation of these principles is whether the arbitrator should insist that individuals whose interests are involved should have an opportunity to be present and submit evidence and argument. In discipline cases, I follow the stiff-necked rule that I will not proceed unless the grievant is present or I have direct, reliable information that he or she does not want to be present.

On occasion, I have had problems with unions and employers who want to proceed without the grievant. The customary arguments were that "the dispute is between the union and the employer," that "the grievance belongs to the union," and that "the grievant is not a party to the arbitration agreement or the arbitration proceedings." These arguments were always, for me, unpersuasive. The obvious reality was that it was the individual's fate being decided and he or she was entitled to be heard.

At present, such cases seldom arise and are easily corrected.

The arbitrator need only breathe the words "fair representation" and immediate steps will be taken to produce the grievant or explain why he or she is not there. All but the naïve are aware of the risk of fair representation suits, and even if they are willing to run that risk, they lack the brass to ask the arbitrator to be party to challengeable proceedings. For the inexperienced, it is enough to explain that if the arbitration proceeds, the disciplined employee will be in a position to sue both parties for violation of the duty of fair representaton, vacate the award, obtain reinstatement with back pay and sizable lawyers' fees. If, after being informed of these risks, the parties still want to proceed, the arbitrator should withdraw. He or she should be no party to collusion or indifference to individual rights. Though appointed by the parties, he is not their creature. He is acting under legal authority to adjudicate contractual rights that belong to individual employees as well as the union and employer; his decision is given deference and is enforced by the courts. He should act like a judge, not a prostitute.

Having the grievant present serves a practical need: without him or her, you will never know whether you are getting the full story. This is not necessarily because the union is trying to hide something. It is because unions and employers are not always the best investigators and they may not have obtained the full facts. The hearing often produces new and unexpected facts, and only the grievant may be able to explain their relevance or irrelevance. With the grievant present, the arbitrator can ask questions, get answers from the most relevant witness, and thereby make a more reliable decision.

For example, in one case, the employer had dismissed two employees for horseplay. The employer's witnesses testified at length as to the large amount of time the women spent together, and their unusually close friendship—"almost like they were married." One day they got in a shoving match—they said friendly jostling. One fell down, and both were fired. The employer made it clear that one of the reasons for such a severe penalty was its belief, from their constant companionship, that they were lesbians and that was causing disruption in the plant. During the hearing, one of the women was cross-examined about inconsistencies on her application form. When she disclaimed any knowledge of it, she was given the form and told to read it aloud. She refused to do so and when pressed said, to the surprise of both the union and the employer, "I can't read." It then emerged that she relied upon the other woman for all reading, and they were always together because she needed the other one to read all instructions and directions on the job and manage affairs off the job. Out of this dependency had grown a friendship based not on lesbianism but on illiteracy. Without the grievants present, the crucial facts would never have been known, and the decision would have been misdirected.

In another case, one in which the grievant was not present until called when the proceedings began, a man was discharged because he had refused to obey the group leader's orders, grabbed the group leader around the neck from behind, and tried to slug him. This occurred in a foundry near molten metal. These facts were not in dispute. The union's defense was that in other cases, employees were not discharged for fighting in the plant, so discharge in this case was unequal treatment.

When the grievant took the stand he admitted that he had done what he was charged with. But other facts emerged. The grievant had recently been married, and the group leader had told others in the plant that the grievant's bride was crazy, that he had "known her in the nut house." This was true. The group leader had met her when he was a patient in a psychiatric ward. The group leader had also told others in the plant that the grievant's wife was sleeping with the foreman. This was only a part of a pattern of harassment that had continued for several weeks. The grievant had complained to supervision to get the group leader "off his back," but supervision had done nothing. On the day of the incident, the group leader had told the grievant to take some castings in a dim and dusty room to clean them. The grievant said he would take them outside in the open where such work was usually done, whereupon the group leader shouted, "Do as I say or you will be fired." This was the last straw. The grievant grabbed him around the neck and swung—missing him.

These facts were apparently not known to the union, or the union did not recognize their relevance. Most of them were known to management, but management was more anxious to justify its action than to tell the full story. Had the grievant not been called and provided the full story, the decision would have been quite different. The arbitrator needs the grievant to be present and testify if he is to have full understanding of the facts.

A possible cost of insisting that the grievant have an opportunity to be present is that it may delay the hearing. The delay, however, will seldom be more than an hour or two, a trivial price to pay for fair procedure. Even if the grievant's appearance required postponement to another day, I would postpone. Better delayed justice than immediate injustice, and better a later valid award than a later fair representation suit. Claims by the parties of the need or desire for a prompt decision has a hollow ring when the parties have been months in getting to arbitration. If the complaint is the cost of another day of hearing, I would prefer not to be paid than to be party to an unfair procedure.

Two special cases of the grievant's unavailability are worth mentioning. What if the grievant is in jail? The fact that he is in jail is, of course, no proof that he is guilty of anything. He is still entitled to a fair hearing on his contract rights and the employer still has the burden of proof. The solution is relatively easy: hold the proceedings in abeyance until he is able to attend. No back pay will accumulate, and few problems will be caused by waiting. The case may, of course, become moot by the fact that he is in jail. The contract or plant rules may provide that failure to report for work for a particular period automatically results in termination—a questionable provision, in my judgment, if there are provisions for leave of absence. Or a conviction may itself be grounds for termination, as in the federal government.

A more difficult case arises when an employee is awaiting trial on a criminal charge for the same conduct that is the basis for discharge. The grievant may be able to appear at the arbitration hearing but be unable or unwilling to testify for fear that this testimony will be used in the criminal proceedings. In such a case, the arbitration should be postponed until after the trial. The practical need is for the grievant's testimony, and this person should not be inhibited by fear that testimony before the arbitrator will be used against him or her at the trial.

The outcome of criminal prosecution or civil suit should

have little or no weight in the arbitration proceedings. The arbitrator must decide on the basis of evidence before him or her, and that evidence may be substantially different from the evidence represented in court. The jury performs a different function and may not view evidence from the same perspective as the arbitrator. Although plant discipline has been analogized to criminal sanctions and discharge has been described as capital punishment, the functions performed by arbitration and the standards applied are quite different from those of a court. For these reasons, the fact that an employee has been acquitted by a jury, or that the charges have been dismissed by the prosecutor, does not bar a grievant's being subject to discipline or bind the arbitrator to find the person innocent. Furthermore, disciplinary proceedings after acquittal do not constitute double jeopardy.

Fairness in Nondisciplinary Cases

In nondisciplinary cases, the problem is somewhat different, for usually the employee or employees whose rights may not be represented are not the grievant but others. In promotion cases, the question is whether the employee who has been promoted by the employer, and who will be displaced if the union wins, should have an opportunity to appear and be heard. This question more often becomes a real issue in promotion cases than in discipline cases, for the parties more often appear at the arbitration hearing with the grievant but without the promoted employee against whom the grievance is directed.

As in discipline cases, the promoted employee should be given an opportunity to be heard. Here, the union does not even pretend to represent this employee's interests, but is openly hostile. Although the employer may defend its action in promoting the employee, its interests are quite different from those of the employee, and it may be willing to trade or compromise at the employee's expense. The only one in a position to represent fully the promoted employee is that employee. Also, as in discipline cases, the presence of the employee will aid in obtaining a more complete picture and better understanding of the case and thereby rendering a more responsible decision.

The burden imposed on the arbitration process by allowing the promoted employee to participate is minimal, especially as compared with the risks of inviting a fair representation suit. The need to delay the hearing will be more frequent than in discipline cases until the parties become sensitive to the need for notifying the promoted employee of the hearing and his or her right to attend. The arbitrator, by informing the parties of the reasons for having the promoted employee present and by refusing to proceed until he or she is given that opportunity, will sensitize the parties so that delays will be avoided in the future.

Seniority cases may have the character of a grievance being directed against an employee or group of employees. For example, an employee filed a grievance that he was put in the wrong place on the seniority list. As the case got underway, the real problem became apparent: he and a number of others claimed that a former supervisor who had been returned to the bargaining unit had been placed on the seniority list in accordance with his original date of hire. The effect was to give him seniority credit for the dozen years he had worked as a supervisor. The grievance was really directed against him by seeking to move him to near the bottom of the seniority list. I asked if he were present; he was not. I asked if he had been notified of the hearing; no one knew. After only a few words concerning the duty of fair representation, the parties decided to call him and ask him if he wanted to be present and testify. He did, and we waited an hour until he could get there. Though not helpful to him, his testimony was helpful to the proceedings by providing a complete picture of his original promotion, past practices, and general understandings. He did not retain the seniority, but he had his opportunity to present his case. I had a more complete understanding of the case; the union recognized that he had a right to participate; and the award was protected from legal challenge.

Other seniority cases may present less sharply focused issues, for those who will lose if the union wins may include a large group of employees. A claim by one employee that he or she is entitled to a certain place on the seniority list will move all those below down one notch. When seniority units are merged, the contest is between two groups, and the seniority rights the union seeks on behalf of one group are at the expense of the other. In these cases, if some of the disadvantaged employees disagree with the union's position in the arbitration, they should be allowed to have a representative at the hearing to present their view. For this purpose, they should be given notice, by posting or otherwise, of the hearing and their right to participate. The arbitrator should, before proceeding, make sure that an adequate notice has been given. Otherwise, the arbitrator can have no assurance of being fully informed as to all the facts and considerations, or that the award will not be vacated because some of the employees have not been fairly represented.

In theory, giving the disadvantaged employees the right to appear and participate could raise difficult questions of how many should be allowed to be present and who should act as their spokesperson. In practice, these problems seldom arise. If there are no clearly identified disadvantaged groups, there are seldom objectors who seek to participate. Clearly identified groups have sufficient common interests to select a spokesperson.

Once we say that an individual has a right to be present at the arbitration, whether in discipline, promotion, or seniority cases, we must confront the question of what form his or her participation should take. My view is that the individual should be treated essentially as a full party to the proceedings, with the rights to submit evidence, cross-examine witnesses, and present argument.

In most discipline cases, the individual will not want to act as an independent party, but will be content to allow the union to represent him or her. The individual's presence serves to aid the union in presenting the case, to add to the union's evidence or argument where he or she thinks the union's presentation is not adequate, and to be available to the arbitrator for answering questions to allow the arbitrator a more full understanding of the case. This means that the individual should be made to feel free to add whatever relevant evidence or argument he or she wishes, and the arbitrator should not feel restricted by the questions asked by the union and employer representatives.

In rare cases, the grievant appears with his or her own lawyer or other spokesman. The union, of course, takes umbrage at the grievant's lack of confidence and will commonly object to any participation by an "outsider." In most cases, the grievant's distrust is not justified, and the union is willing and able to defend him. There is danger, however, that the union's advocacy will be indifferent or incompetent; and there is need for a guarantee of fairness and a substantial value in giving the grievant a feeling of being fairly represented. These considerations weigh persuasively in favor of allowing the employee to participate with his or her own lawyer. In addition, the potential for legal liability under *Vaca* v. *Sipes,* and *Hines* v. *Anchor Motor Freight* is so great for the parties that the parties ought to accept the participation by the individual's lawyer. If the grievant is so distrustful of the union as to hire his or her own lawyer, then the situation is a breeding ground for litigation. The best protection is to give the individual the fullest measure of fairness.

Managing the proceedings with three parties rather than two is no major problem. Courts and administrative agencies hold hearings with double the number. The employer and union can be treated as the leading parties to present evidence and cross-examine witnesses, with the individual's lawyer also cross-examining each witness in turn. When both of the leading parties have presented all their evidence, the individual's lawyer can be allowed to present any additional relevant evidence, and his or her witnesses will be subject to cross-examination by the union and employer. The case may take somewhat longer, but the arbitrator can insist that the parties not duplicate evidence or repeat questions on cross-examination.

Whenever procedural problems that may be related to fair representation arise, it is crucial that they be spelled out in the arbitration opinion. If the grievant is not present, that should be stated in the opinion with any explanation as to this absence. In a discipline case, for example, the grievant who was not present was telephoned and told that he had a right to appear. He said that he did not want to come as he had another job. In a promotion case, the promoted employee was not present and was called. He was told that he was entitled to appear and add anything he wanted, but he said he was willing to go along with the union. These facts were set out in the opinion to avoid any question being raised at a later time. If the individual actively participates or has a personal lawyer, this should be indicated. The record should be clear as to what extent the individual has had his or her day in court, so that if there is litigation, the judge and jury will know what happened.

Statutory versus Contract Right

What is the function of the arbitrator when the individual has a potential statutory right that overlaps a contract right? For example, if a union steward is discharged because he files too many grievances, his discharge may violate the just cause clause of the contract and also the prohibition against discrimination for union activity in section 8(a) (3) of the National Labor Relations Act. Or a pregnant woman denied paid leave for childbirth may claim denial of the right to sick leave under the contract, and also sex discrimination under Title VII of the Civil Rights Act of 1964. In such a case, should the arbitrator adjudicate both the contract right and the statutory right, or decide only the contract right, regardless of whether that is consistent with the statutory right?

Two lines of Supreme Court cases are directly relevant. First, in the Steelworkers Trilogy, the Supreme Court gave strong endorsement to grievance arbitration and the competence of arbitrators to interpret and apply the collective agreement. In *Steelworkers* v. *Enterprise Wheel*, 363 U.S. 593 (1960), the Court declared, "The refusal of courts to review the merits of an arbitration award is the proper approach to arbitration under collective agreements . . ." Nevertheless, the arbitrator is confined to interpretation and application of the collective agreement: he does not sit to dispense his own brand of industrial justice . . . his award is legitimate only so long as it draws its essence from the collective agreement" (p. 596–97).

In short, the arbitrator's function is to interpret and apply the collective agreement. That is the arbitrator's area of special competence; that is the function which is given to him or her by the contract; that is where the courts will defer to his or her judgment.

The second line is exemplified by *Alexander* v. *Gardner-Denver Co.*, 415 U.S. 36 (1974). In that case, a black employee was discharged, allegedly for creating excessive scrap. The discharge was submitted to arbitration, and in the arbitration proceedings he claimed that the discharge resulted from racial discrimination. The arbitrator ruled that the discharge was for just cause. In the meantime, he had filed a charge of racial discrimination under Title VII. When this case came to court, the federal district court dismissed the claim on the grounds that it had already been submitted to the arbitrator and resolved against him.

The Supreme Court reversed, holding that the arbitration decision did not foreclose judicial enforcement of the individual's statutory rights. The employee has two independent sets of rights, the rights under the contract and the rights under Title VII: "Arbitral procedures, while well suited to the resolution of contractual disputes, make arbitration a comparatively inappropriate forum for the final resolution of rights created by Title VII. This conclusion rests first on the special role of the arbitrator, whose task is to effectuate the intent of the parties rather than the requirements of enacted legislation. Where the collective bargaining agreement conflicts with Title VII, the arbitrator must follow the agreement" (pp. 56–57).

More recently, the Supreme Court has held in *Barrentine* v. *Arkansas–Best Freight System, Inc.*, 450 U.S. 728 (1981), that an unfavorable arbitration award could not prejudice an individual's claim for overtime under the Fair Labor Standards Act. The statutory rights were "independent of the collective bargaining process," and the arbitrator's task is limited to construing the collective agreement.

The direction these two lines of cases take seems unmistakable. The arbitrator's function is to interpret the contract; he or she has no authority or special competence to interpret and apply the statute. Whether the contract conflicts with the statute is for the courts to decide.

In operational terms, if a case that potentially raises a statutory issue as well as a contractual issue comes to arbitration, the arbitrator should look to the intent of the parties to interpret and apply the contract. The award should be based on the contract, not the statute. If that result conflicts with the statute, it can be set aside by the procedure and tribunal designed to enforce the statutory right, the court. To be sure, it is troubling for an arbitrator to issue an award that he or she may believe is contrary to law. But the arbitrator's charter is the contract. The arbitrator has no general charter to enforce the law or remedy all injustices.

There are strong practical and policy reasons for this. One reason is that many arbitrators, even the most experienced and competent in collective bargaining practices and industrial relations, have no special competence in discerning legislative intent or interpreting statute. It behooves arbitrators to salt their pride of profession with a grain of modesty. Even though a particular arbitrator believes himself specially learned in the law, he should not undertake functions that are not appropriate to the process generally.

More important, adjudicating statutory rights can place an arbitrator in an exceedingly difficult position. When statutory rights are involved, the union may be less than an enthusiastic supporter of the individual's rights. Unions have at times tolerated, if not welcomed, discrimination against blacks or women, and an overaggressive union steward may be as much a thorn of the side of union officers as of management.

The union may process the case to arbitration for the purpose of obtaining an arbitrator's ratification of the discharge, and then present the evidence and argument so as to achieve that result. The arbitrator may be unaware of being used, and even if he or she becomes suspicious, may be understandably reluctant to voice suspicions of those who have selected him and who will pay the fee. The arbitrator ought not bear the responsibility for adjudicating such statutory rights.

The arbitrator, in my judgment, ought not purport or even attempt to determine statutory rights. In refusing to do so, the arbitrator should make clear in the opinion that he or she has determined only the individual's contractual rights and has not weighed or considered the individual's statutory rights. Courts, and the NLRB, at times tend to give undue deference to arbitrators' awards, perhaps out of a desire to shift responsibility. The arbitrator should not only keep to his or her proper function, but should do all possible to ensure that the courts or the board not mistake this limited role and perform their proper function.

One final question remains: What if all the parties—the union, the employer, and the individual—agree that the arbitrator should decide both the contractual and the statutory issue? The arbitrator can, of course, be empowered by the parties to decide their statutory rights. Were I involved, my first step would be to make certain that the individual had made a willing and knowing decision to submit the statutory rights to arbitration. The second step would be to insist that the parties be represented by lawyers so the statutory issues would be fully developed. The third step would be to make explicit in the arbitration opinion that the statutory issue was expressly submitted by the individual. And the fourth step would be to spell out fully the rationale and legal authority on which the statutory issue was decided so the court could, as it should, meaningfully review the decision.

Though the parties are willing to call me a judge, and I would like to be a judge, I am only an arbitrator whose primary competence is to decide contractual disputes. But as an arbitrator, appointed by the union and the employer, I consider that my responsibility includes protecting the individual employees rights under the collective agreement. Both the law and fundamental fairness require this. The parties cannot ask or expect me to do otherwise, nor would I serve their long-run interests to do otherwise.

Deciding the Case

11

Weighing the Decision

Arnold M. Zack

THE DECISION-MAKING process is a very personal one, and this is an analysis of how *I* decide cases. But I suspect that arbitrators all go through a similar process in reaching the bottom line in a case. Decision making is much like a continuum, paralleling your participation in the case from the time you are first appointed as arbitrator until you complete the writing of the decision.

The first knowledge most of us have of a case comes at the start of the hearing. We may get a demand for arbitration, which briefly states the issue, or a letter from either or both of the parties listing a grievance number or the title of the case, or a telephone call from one of the parties informing us that they want us to hear a case. One of the reassuring traditions in this business is that clients purposely avoid giving arbitrators more than the minimum amount of information. They respect the practice of avoiding ex parte exchanges and recognize that the arbitrator might become uncomfortable or seek to be excused from the case for allowing too much input from one side.

As a result, you have very little information about a case before the hearing. But at that time, information comes at you fast and furious: each little bit of information becomes a prejudice that may be quickly supplanted by a new piece of information as the case proceeds. Let me give you a few examples.

You walk into the hearing room and observe counsel for one side sitting with a stack of law books in front of him and two people at his side, while the other party has a large group of workers present and little or no paraphernalia. This may send a message that the company is weak on the facts and strong on the law; or that its case, based on the contract, is weak and it is going to try and rely on external law; or that the workers are solidly behind the grievant and will testify to back up his or her version of what has occurred.

Suppose you find the grievant alone with his or her own attorney, without the usual coterie of union officers who traditionally attend arbitration hearings. Does that convey a subtle message that the union is permitting the case to proceed only because the grievant insists on it or threatens to sue if the case is not processed? Does it mean that the union would rather have no part of this case or that it may in fact be a weak case?

What does it mean if you find the two presenters out in the hall, walking back and forth between the two camps? Does that mean a settlement is imminent? Or that the employer is willing to resolve the case because its position is weaker? Or that the union is trying to salvage what it can of its demand to avoid having the grievant lose the case and get nothing?

First impressions may well be misleading, but they tend to create a mind-set on the part of the arbitrator, which, while it may be overcome by subsequent events, creates a threshold of expectation.

Evaluating Testimony

Unless the parties have agreed in advance on the issue to be arbitrated, the first real exchange with the parties is probably in the discussion surrounding framing of the issue. While arbitrators are supposed to decide cases based on testimony presented at the hearing, on the evidence, and on the arguments of the presenters, I suspect we are all influenced by a visceral reaction to the parties' first presentation of the issue in dispute. If the issue is proposed as, Was Jones properly terminated for coming to work five minutes late?, then the company had better show why it took such drastic action for tardiness. But if the issue is proposed as, Was Jones properly terminated for stealing three hundred pounds of copper tubing?, the prejudice might lie the other way. I will be waiting to see how the grievant is going to get out of this one.

Even in a contractual interpretation case, the framing of the issue may instill some initial prejudice in the arbitrator. The question, Did the company violate the parties' agreement by subcontracting the building of its new warehouse? leads me in a different direction if the company is small than if it is a large construction firm. I suspect we are all vulnerable to a ripple of prejudice in reaction to the framing of the issue.

The response to the proposed issue also raises some problems. Rapid agreement to a routinely or fairly phrased issue creates no problems. But, if the question is loaded—Was the three-week suspension, for just cause in light of the grievant's insubordinate behavior?—and both sides rapidly agree to it, then I must ask myself whether this is some kind of a setup. The answer to that may lie in the experience of the spokespersons. Are they knowledgeable and sophisticated, or is one side particularly naïve? If so, should I intervene or stay out of the matter? These responses may reveal some paranoia on my part. But the mind does have reactions to such stimuli, and our thinking may be affected until later in the presentation.

Indeed, all these concerns may be wiped out by the next step in the proceedings, the opening statements of the spokespersons. Obviously, the spokespersons want to make the best possible impression on the arbitrator by presenting the most favorable facts and perhaps omitting others that are less favorable. This tilt can also be accomplished by the use of carefully selected language. One party might tell you, "The grievant then entered the room and threatened his supervisor by starting to jab at his face," while the other side reports, "The grievant then answered the foreman's demand that he come into the room and raised his finger to emphasize that he thought the foreman should not harass him." Which one is lying? Which one is telling the truth? Or does the real truth lie somewhere in between? With these initial recitations, however, you do recognize that the parties know that examination and cross-examination of the witnesses will provide a more exact description of what happened. In some cases, however, where the dispute occurred without outside witnesses, you also recognize that the case must be resolved on the basis of credibility of the two participants.

Likewise, in the recitation of relevant contract provisions in the opening statements, the employer points out that its contracting out of the disputed work is authorized by the management rights clause. You read that section and find that it supports the employer's position. So, you say to yourself, "What will the union come up with to overcome that?" Then the union calls your attention to language from another contract provision that specifically prohibits subcontracting certain work, which sounds like the work in dispute. Then you think, "Aha! the company obviously knew about that clause, so this work must be of a differnet type—or there is a contrary past practice."

So it goes, throughout the framing of the issue and the presentation of opening statements. Indeed, this skepticism continues through the actual presentation of witnesses and evidence and on into the final arguments. You have to keep up a subliminal guard to defend against accepting any position too quickly. Eventually, this may blossom into cynicism about what the parties are trying to present to you. Remember, though, that the biased presentations are part of the spokespersons' obligation as partisans and advocates. You have the superior responsibility to be critical enough about such presentations that you are ultimately convinced that one side should prevail and that the argument of the other side, although its view was presented equally well or perhaps even better, is not of equal merit or not as persuasive or not in conformity with the requirements of the parties' contract.

Questioning by the Arbitrator

In trying to fulfill this responsibility, you may be tempted to plunge into the parties' exchange to raise certain questions that have not been asked, to extract information that has been omitted or avoided, and to place the need for knowing the truth above and beyond the parties' responsibilities in presenting their cases. Such intervention not only disrupts the parties' priorities in presenting their cases, it may reveal skeletons that both wished to keep closeted. Or, one side might view your participation as being too active, believing that the other party and not the arbitrator should cross-examine witnesses.

The arbitrator should not, however, play dead. He or she

will naturally have questions, perhaps even vital questions that might turn the case around. But you should sit on these questions, making notes, until the parties have finished their examination and cross-examination of a witness. Many of the questions you have noted will be answered by the time the parties have finished. At the end of the questioning, review any remaining questions and ask yourself, "Why wasn't that question asked? What would happen if I asked it now?" If you believe you really need the answer, you should ask the question, for the arbitrator must be satisfied that he or she has all the information necessary to make the determination of the case.

Other questions that do not deal with the testimony of the present witness arise. The arbitrator should also sit on these, even until the end of the hearing. By then, some of your questions about contract language, about the testimony of witnesses, may be irrelevant. They may look very naïve, in which case you will be glad you did not ask them earlier.

Arbitrators are always concerned about whether they should ask questions. Maybe the questions should have been asked by opposing counsel. Maybe asking them at the end of the hearing will appear to be helping the weaker side or embarrass one advocate in front of his or her clients. There will certainly be fewer loose strands if the parties are represented by accomplished spokespersons. But there may still be issues that the arbitrator believes need to be clarified in order to fulfill his or her obligation to the parties. It does get tricky trying to decide what questions should be asked and what issues the parties are trying to avoid, such as, What happened to the other employee who was caught falsifying his time card along with the grievant?

The most dramatic of situations in which the neutral must decide whether to intervene is in the case of the nonlawyer who is up against a sophisticated attorney and who is being effectively railroaded. The parties are obviously obligated to defend their own cases, and their choices of spokespersons are part of their strategies. So here too, the arbitrator should ask only those questions necessary for the opinion and be careful not to rattle skeletons in either party's closet.

Throughout the questioning of witnesses, the most useful question to ask yourself is whether a response was reasonable.

What would you have done in that situation? Does what transpired make sense? Could it, in fact, have occurred? Certainly, some implausible situations come to light in arbitrations, but the standard of reasonableness usually prevails and helps resolve conflicts of testimony and fact.

Caveats for Discipline Cases

In discipline cases, you may be presented with the grievant's prior record. Although guilt in prior instances does not constitute guilt in the offense before you, arbitrators may tend to view a grievant with a prior history of insubordination as less credible in the instant case. But there is also the possibility that the supervisor is contriving an incident that, because of the past record, will be more readily believed than it would with the grievant who had a clear past record. It is also possible that higher level management is trying hard to rid itself of the person, even if the facts of a particular case do not clearly indicate that there was insubordination. You must be on your guard in such cases, even against the union who wants to get rid of a bad apple because of problems caused them in the past.

Even though both parties and the arbitrator adhere to the precepts of progressive discipline, the problem of deciding the case may also be exacerbated when the final offense follows a long period of good behavior or when the grievant is a long service employee. There is little difficulty in reaching a decision when the grievant is a two-year employee and has four or five instances of insubordination within that time. But what if the grievant is a twenty-year employee who had a clear record until his wife died and then amassed four instances of insubordination within eight months? Or, what if the employee is a ten-year employee who had four instances of insubordination in the first two years and who was warned that he would be fired if it happened again, and the next insubordination occurred ten years later?

The problem in deciding such cases goes beyond the question of guilt or innocence in the incident leading to the arbitration. The question is the appropriate penalty for such infractions in light of the grievant's record. You react differently to the size of the penalty. Even aside from such capital offenses as theft, punching a foreman while at work, and smoking in a dynamite factory, you will still question the appropriateness of the penalty for the offense. Does it conform to progressive discipline? Will it impress upon the employee his or her need to reform behavior? Is the grievant indeed incorrigible? What effect will it have on other employees in a similar situation? What will it do to the company's system of discipline in the plant?

Arbitrators are influenced by the grievant's appearance. I remember a case in which the witness, accused of theft in a factory, was wearing a gold Rolex watch at the hearing. This glaring inconsistency with his position as a factory worker was so subject to an incorrect interpretation that I found myself fantasizing scenarios by which he might have obtained such a watch legitimately. I even asked him what time it was, so I could get a better look and make sure it was a Rolex.

Similarly, we tend to judge on the basis of facial expressions or manner. In one case, a second grade teacher was described by her spokesperson as having been intimidated by her supervisor and as having broken down in tears at a conference about an adverse evaluation. I developed a mental image of this person as a shy wallflower. Yet she was one of the most belligerent witnesses I have ever heard, arguing with her spokesperson, the other side's spokesperson, and even with the arbitrator. She really changed my perception.

The same problem may arise when a grievant does not testify, such as in a theft case. The arbitrator wonders why he was not called, what he would say if he did testify, whether he was not called because he was such a bungler, or whether he would be so strident that he would belie all the wonderful things his union had said about him. Arbitrators are probably prejudiced against grievants who fail to take the stand in their own defense, since it would be reasonable to have such persons testify and there is bound to be some question as to why they did not.

Final Presentations

After the parties have completed their presentations of evidence and witnesses and the hearing has been closed, the arbitrator is left to wrestle with the decision. If he or she is anything like me, the arbitrator had started to lean one way, then the production of a particular document changed that view, then the production of a rebuttal document changed it back, and so on. This pendulum swings throughout the hearing until the parties conclude the presentation of their cases. By that time, the arbitrator often has a pretty good idea of the outcome of the case and the reasoning process that will lead to it. I would suggest that in 60 or 70 percent of cases, the arbitrator has made up his or her mind by the time the last witness testifies. As a result, the arbitrator may feel little need for the oral arguments or written briefs the parties often provide. Nonetheless, he or she should not bypass the arguments, but take advantage of this additional opportunity to reinforce the parties' positions and his or her reasoning. It is also important to review the arguments raised by the party who seems to be losing the case.

In the remaining 30 or 40 percent of cases, the arbitrator's mind may not be made up. In such cases, the closing arguments or briefs are essential. There is a tendency for the spokespersons who have presented the case to welcome the respite (or perhaps the fee building) that comes with the opportunity to file a posthearing brief a few weeks later, after they have reviewed their notes or the transcript of the hearing and have developed a logical recitation of why their side should win the case.

I prefer oral final argument for several reasons. First, I want to review the argument of counsel while it is fresh in my mind and I can readily recall the testimony. Second, it is possible that such a review may reveal that I missed some crucial evidence during the hearing itself, or that there are additional questions I would like to ask. Perhaps some element of the case that I thought insignificant is now being relied on as crucial to the case. Third, I want to be sure that the parties have been exposed to and had an opportunity to respond to the arguments raised by the other side. Frequently, when the briefs are filed simultaneously with no provision for reply briefs, there is inadequate rejoinder to the argument anticipated from the other side. I seek to avoid the situation of the company relying on article 2 of the contract and the union relying on article 3 in their briefs and neither anticipating the argument of the other. If this confrontation occurred during oral argument, it could be dealt with easily. Finally, I believe the process of oral argument facilitates the arbitrator's earlier writing and issuing of a decision without the additional delays and costs caused by the filing of briefs and the arbitrator's need to refresh the memory of a case heard long ago.

I do not preclude briefs if either party really wants to file them, nor do I preclude the raising of additional arguments in their briefs; nor do I insist on oral argument if neither party wants to provide it. In a recent case, after the company made its closing argument, the union spokesperson leaned forward and said, "That is very persuasive. I believe your interpretation is correct. We drop that portion of our claim." There are also cases where the parties agree, after closing argument, to settle the matter, which, after all is the goal of the process. Oral arguments often lead to a joint conclusion not to file briefs, since both sides believe that they have summarized their cases effectively and that the arbitrator understands the issue.

What happens next?

The natural response after the hearing is, "Thank goodness this day is over! I have all the information I need and I will write the opinion." But then, due to the press of personal matters or other business or to laziness, the case is put at the bottom of the pile. Naturally, if briefs are to be filed or you are waiting for a transcript, there is added incentive to tell yourself, "Well, there is nothing I can do now." But even when the awaited materials come in, it is still tempting to put off writing the decision. Perhaps the intervening time has dulled your recollection of the case. That can make the task of writing the decision even more onerous than it seemed at the end of the hearing. But the most insidious effect of delays in cases in which briefs are filed is that the arbitrator tends to rely upon the biased statements of the facts related in the parties' briefs.

The preferable route, and the one which requires the most discipline, is the immediate writing of the opinion on the evening of the hearing or the next day, before the curve of memory loss has taken its toll. The facts, the testimony, the nonverbal responses of the witnesses are fresh in mind, and you are still wrestling with the arguments raised by the parties. The greatest benefit from immediate writing of the opinion is the economy of time; it is more efficient to write up something while it is fresh in your mind, before your notes become stale and without meaning and you forget some unnoted matter that occurred at the hearing.

I do not recommend sending out the decision immediately after writing it. A subsequent objective review of the decision may disclose another opinion, or part of the opinion may not be phrased exactly the way you would like it to be. If there are no briefs coming, write up the whole case subject to further editing. If briefs are to be filed, write up the facts and an outline of the parties' arguments. Once that is done, you can write an outline of your opinion in a very short time. When the briefs come in, the overwhelming arguments of counsel may change your opinion, but the likelihood is that your initial judgment will not be changed. It is thus advisable to write up your own view of the case before you have forgotten it. You can always change what you have written, but you cannot re-capture the alertness of response and thought that you have immediately after the hearing.

If you have to rely on a transcript, it is not much different from writing up someone else's arbitration hearing. As for those few cases where your mind is not made up by the conclusion of the hearing, the writing itself may be a stimulus toward reaching your decision in the case.

Weighing the Choices

What I have described is largely what I do. But two articles on the decision process seem particularly apt, probably because they support my prejudices. The first is the fourth lecture by Benjamin Cardozo on the nature of the legal process, delivered at Yale Law School in 1921, in which he observes, "Deep below consciousness are other forces, the likes and dislikes, the predilections and the prejudices, the complex of instincts and emotion and habits and convictions which make the man, whether he be litigant or judge" (1921, p. 67). I strongly recommend the volume because it underscores the fact that the judge is really very little different from any reasonable man in reaching conclusions on the evidence presented to him.

A similar view is presented by a former teacher at Yale Law School, Jerome Frank, in his book *Law and the Modern Mind.*

The process of judging, so the psychologists tell us, seldom begins with a premise from which a solution is subsequently worked out. Judging rather begins the other way around—with a conclusion more or less vaguely formed; a man ordinarily starts with such a conclusion and afterwards tries to find premises which will substantiate it. If he cannot to his satisfaction find proper arguments to link up his conclusion with premises which he finds acceptable, he will, unless he is arbitrary, or mad, reject the conclusion and seek another.... Judicial judgments, like other judgments, doubtless in most cases are worked out backwards from conclusions tentatively formed.... The vital motivating impulse for the decision is an intuitive sense of what is right and what is wrong in a particular case (1949, pp. 100–101).

Thus, when you are deciding a case, intuition comes first and will prevail if borne out by the evidence and the testimony. But there are times when this visceral reaction is outweighed by reality, for instance, by a specific contract provision. Perhaps the parties have negotiated something that you know without thinking is wrong, unfair, nonsensical, not what you would have ordained in the absence of a contract. But arbitrators are creatures of the contract and are bound by it. If the parties have negotiated a clause covering the situation, then the arbitrator must support it.

There are cases where the arbitrator is faced with a choice between adhering to that strict construction or doing what he or she thinks is better for the parties. Obviously, there are cases that fall on the razor's edge, where the contract language is clear but there is a contrary past practice. There, the arbitrator may feel compelled to bring the parties back into compliance with the agreement or may believe that equity dictates a different result and rely on the past practice.

Arbitrators have an obligation to adhere to the terms of the parties' agreement. They negotiated it expecting to comply with it, and it is only right that if they are expected to live up to its terms for the length of the contract, any disputes resolved by an outside arbitrator should be decided in the manner that does the least violence to their agreement and their expectancies. To do otherwise places a premium on grieving and resort to arbitration to secure a result other than that which was negotiated.

Having said that, let us turn to the situation where there is no clear contract language, such as in discipline and discharge cases, to guide the arbitrator. The universal standard is just cause, but there is little guidance in interpreting precisely what just cause is. Other cases within the enterprise, other arbitrators' awards, and the standard of progressive discipline may aid you in reaching your final determination of whether the offense in a particular case was deserving of penalty, and, if so, how much. Your subjective lending of credibility to the employer's disciplinary standards must be weighed against justice for the individual and the chance to rehabilitate. These are troublesome cases, the just resolutions to which continue to be evasive.

Elements of the Opinion

Several problems arise in thinking out the opinion and decision: arbitrability, contract interpretation, precedents, and legal constraints and remedy.

On the issue of arbitrability, I should emphasize that arbitrators prefer to decide cases on their merits because a problem exists, and it should be resolved and the substantive issue put to rest. Arbitrability issues are impediments to such issues being resolved on their merits. Yet, we are limited to the contract terms the parties have negotiated. We are bound by the procedural limitations as well as by the substantive limitations they have imposed on each other. We cannot and should not ignore the rights of the party that invokes arbitrability. To do so erodes the parties' regard, not only for the negotiating process, but for the arbitration process as well. The preference for hearing cases on their merits is what has placed the burden of proving that a case is *not* arbitrable on the challenging party, usually the employer.

Arbitrators are faced with two types of arbitrability challenges, those involving substantive authority (the jurisdiction to continue arbitrating) and those involving procedural arbitrability (conformity to the negotiated procedures in the contract for taking cases to arbitration).

On substantive issues of arbitrability, the arbitrator has no right to decide a case if the contract does not give him or her jurisdiction to do so. If the contract says that the arbitrator shall not decide the issue that is the subject of the grievance, that should bar the arbitration. The party challenging substantive arbitrability may do so at any time. In disputes over whether the contract permits arbitration of an issue the parties may agree to give the arbitrator jurisdiction to decide that subject, but unless they have ceded to an arbitrator jurisdiction in substantive arbitrability, they may go to court to overturn the arbitrator who asserts jurisdiction where the contract denies it. As arbitrator Harry Shulman stated in his famous Holmes Lectures at Harvard Law School, "An arbitrator worthy of appointment in the first place, must conscientiously respect the limits imposed on his jurisdiction, for otherwise, he will not only betray his trust, but also undermine his own future usefulness, and therefore endanger the very system of self-government in which he works" (1956, p. 180).

Procedural arbitrability does not challenge the arbitrator's right to hear a particular case. Rather, it challenges whether the contract provisions have been adhered to in the steps leading to arbitration. The arbitrator is the final authority in deciding matters of procedural arbitrability. Although the arbitrator will be careful not to assume jurisdiction where the contract bars the hearing of a particular kind of case, as in substantive arbitrability cases, he or she will probably try to find a case arbitrable on procedural grounds unless the parties have been strict in their adherence to procedural restrictions in processing cases. Thus, the arbitrator may rely on the parties' casual adherence to time limits to find that a one- or two-day delay in processing a particular case does not make it nonarbitrable. Or if certain requirements, such as signatures or contract citations, have not been strictly relied on in the past, the arbitrator may excuse such an omission in the instant case. Strict adherence to time limits and signatures and citing contract clauses in the past, however, may mandate adherence in the instant case, and the arbitrator may conclude that the case is not arbitrable. The arbitrator must require adherence to *all* contract provisions, not merely those he or she finds convenient or appealing.

The issue of compliance with the parties' contract constitutes the thrust of most contract interpretation issues. There are frequently conflicting or fuzzy contract terms on which the parties disagree as to the interpretation or application. The arbitrator may have to weigh the arguments about which language applies or resolve ambiguities in the language. What was the intent of the parties? Was there a mutual desire to achieve a particular end? Does their negotiating history show any meeting of the minds? Sometimes there is no credible negotiating history, and you may have to resolve ambiguity by reference only to the agreement. Even here, there are standards to assist you, such as controlling language adopted in a later contract, or specific terms controlling over general terms, or the list of a number of items that presumes deliberate exclusion of any others (inclusio unis, exclusio alterius).

The arbitrator faced with these choices will make the determination he or she believes most appropriate to the situation, an equitable result, and the one that conforms most closely to what the parties would have negotiated had they anticipated this problem. As Justice Douglas in the U.S. Supreme Court decision in *Warrior & Gulf,* said of arbitrators, "The parties expect that his judgment of a particular grievance will reflect not only what the contract says, but insofar as the agreement permits, such factors as the effect on productivity of a particular result, its consequences to the morale of the shop, his judgment whether tensions will be heightened or diminished," 363 U.S. 574 (1960).

I suspect that one of the reasons the parties opt for the more senior arbitrators, those who have more experience in the field of labor relations, is that such arbitrators understand what happens in the late hours of negotiating sessions. They are familiar with how words get put into a contract, and they know what weight is to be given to what is agreed upon and how the parties expect reliance on those standards in later cases. As Shulman noted, "No matter how much time is allowed for the negotiation there is never time enough to think every issue through in all its possible applications, and never ingenuity enough to anticipate all that does later show up. Since the parties earnestly strive to complete an agreement, there is almost irresistible pressure to find a verbal formula which is acceptable, even though its meaning to the two sides may in fact differ" (1956, p. 175). Shulman believed that all parts of the agreement do not necessarily make a consistent pattern, but the interpretation that is most compatible with the agreement as a whole is to be preferred over one that creates an anomaly.

When there is little guidance from the negotiating history or from the agreement, the guidance may come from the opinions of other arbitrators. While the decisions of other arbitrators dealing with other parties are not binding on your case, they may provide some guidance as to how other arbitrators have decided similar cases. Because no arbitration case is identical to one coming before it in another installation and under another collective bargaining agreement, you have to be careful not to buy the argument of counsel that another case involving two other parties is determinative of the case before you—it is not. It is *your* decision that will be determinative. Although it is worthwhile to read such cited decisions to learn how other arbitrators have approached such a problem, remember that only a fraction of all awards issued are published, and an unusual one is more likely to be published than a routine decision that lacks pizazz. If you seek guidance, I suggest looking into the earlier volumes of the publishing services (before 1960), which will reveal the reasoning of the giants of the field, rather than reading decisions by less experienced arbitrators. One of the ways to achieve standing is to decide cases by your own reasoning, rather than to borrow from someone else who may have done a less-than-accurate survey of published precedents in the field.

A different rule of thumb applies to prior arbitration decisions issued under the same agreement under which you are working. Such precedents are not necessarily binding on you, but if the parties have submitted the issue to another arbitrator, it makes sense to concur with that decision if it is one you can live with. The consequence of issuing a different award is that the parties will seek a third case to test before a third arbitrator, which will reinforce either your decision or the earlier one, and so on. I recommend endorsement of the previous decision, which leaves it to the parties to negotiate any changes in their next collective bargaining negotiations. Try to deter them from arbitrator shopping and make a small contribution to the stability of the parties' relationship.

The awards must necessarily set precedents for recurring cases and the opinions must necessarily provide guidance for the future in relating decision to reason and to more or less mutually accepted principle. Consistency is not a lawyer's creation. It is a normal urge and a normal expectation. It is part of the ideal of equality of treatment. The lawyer's contribution, indeed, is his differentiation of rational, civilized consistency from apparent consistency. Let me give you an example. In many appeals from disciplinary penalties imposed by the employer, I heard the union argue earnestly that the penalty should be reduced because of the employee's long service record. I was persuaded and held that the employee's seniority should be considered in fixing the size of the penalty. Then came a case in which two employees committed the same offense at the same time and one was given a larger penalty than the other. The union protested the larger penalty as being an obvious impairment of the principles of equality. This was not necessarily conscious opportunism, although there is always a good deal of that. A period of education was required to effect the realization, not only by the advocates, but by the rank and file that the equality for which they themselves contended in the area of discipline necessitated different penalties for the same offense whenever factors other than the offense itself were considered" (Shulman 1956, p. 195).

A word should be said here about the issue of legal restraints on the arbitrator. For many years arbitrators basked in the light of the Steelworkers Trilogy, with little concern about what the courts might do to their awards. Certainly there were some reversals, in cases where the arbitrator exceeded jurisdiction or did not draw the essence of a decision from the terms of the parties' contract. It was a golden era. That lasted until the courts, in fulfilling their obligation to protect individual statutory rights, such as those under the Civil Rights Act of 1964 or ERISA or OSHA or FLSA, held that arbitration awards rendered as part of a collective scheme of negotiations cannot deprive individuals of any statutory rights they might have, *Alexander* v. *Gardner-Denver Co.*, 415 U.S. 36 (1974). Since that time, there has continued to be little interference with arbitrators' awards, but there is growing concern that the arbitration award is less likely to be final and binding than contemplated by unions and management.

Some arbitrators, more concerned about this prospect than others, seek to forestall reversal by incorporating into their opinions consideration of the statutory issues that may arise. My personal view is that watching over your shoulder is a futility; that the arbitrator seldom, if ever, gets full information from counsel as to what the law requires; that the courts still retain the right of review of an arbitrator's opinion; and that in so doing, the arbitrator may be unnecessarily sacrificing what he or she believes to be the correct decision under the parties' contract. My practice has been to confine myself to the interpretation and application of the contract, noting that if my decision is not in conformity with the existing law, that is a concern for a different forum. The alternative is that the arbitrator may deny a grievance based on an improper interpretation of the law, only to have the court say subsequently that while the arbitrator may have been wrong, the parties had agreed that the decision would be final and binding, and thus dismiss the appeal.

The final consideration is remedy. What if the grievance is sustained in whole or in part? What should the remedy be? The arbitrator is usually deprived of any influence on this subject by the employer, who fears that discussion of any possibility of remedy will be viewed as an acknowledgment that it does not believe its case to be very strong on the merits. Thus, the arbitrator is in the dark as to how to fashion the remedy. Some arbitrators retain jurisdiction on the issue of remedy, postponing any decision and leaving it up to the parties to decide. I feel uncomfortable doing that, forcing the losing party back before the same arbitrator. My practice is to formulate the general standards of a remedy I believe is appropriate and then to sign the decision without retaining jurisdiction. That way the parties are free to come back to me if they wish, which happens on occasion, or they may go to another arbitrator with what is, in effect, a new dispute.

Arbitrators do not have the authority to create remedies not called for in the agreement or the right to impose punitive damages. In this area, too, the arbitrator may temper his decision according to what he heard at the hearing, what he has determined concerning culpability and the potential for rehabilitation, and what he believes to be an equitable result. The standard I follow in fabricating a remedy is to try to place the individual in the position he or she would have been in had the employer not violated the parties' agreement.

Many of these issues involved in thinking out the opinion do not surface until the actual writing is in progress. Because it is the act of writing that helps many arbitrators to assemble their facts and work out the logic of their opinions, the writing itself is not always easy or quick. It may make painfully obvious one's errors in thinking and may even cause a complete revision of the opinion with an opposite conclusion. But write we must, and as Shulman warns, ". . . the greater danger to be guarded against is that too much will be said rather than too little" (1956, p. 195).

12

Past Practice and the Administration of Collective Bargaining Agreements

Richard Mittenthal

ARCHIBALD COX has suggested that before "a rationale of grievance arbitration can be developed, more work must be done in identifying and analyzing the standards that shape arbitral opinions" (1959, p. 46). This chapter is a product of Cox's suggestion. It examines in depth one of the more important standards upon which so many of our decisions are based—past practice.

Custom and practice profoundly influence every area of human activity. Protocol guides the relations among states; etiquette affects an individual's social behavior; habit governs most of our daily actions; and mores help to determine our laws. It is hardly surprising, therefore, to find that past practice in an industrial plant plays a significant role in the administration of the collective agreement. Justice Douglas of the United States Supreme Court stated that "the labor arbitrator's source

Published by permission from *Arbitration and Public Policy*, Proceedings of the Fourteenth Annual Meeting, National Academy of Arbitrators, pages 30–58, copyright © 1961 by The Bureau of National Affairs, Inc., Washington, D.C.

of law is not confined to the express provisions of the contract, as the industrial common law—the past practices of the industry and the shop—is equally a part of the collective bargaining agreement although not expressed in it," *United Steelworkers of America* v. *Warrior & Gulf Navigation Co.,* 363 U.S. 574 (1960). Past practice is one of the most useful and hence commonly used aids in resolving grievance disputes. It can help the arbitrator in a variety of ways in interpreting the agreement. It may be used to clarify what is ambiguous, to give substance to what is general, and perhaps even to modify or amend what is seemingly unambiguous. It may also, apart from any basis in the agreement, be used to establish a separate, enforceable condition of employment.

The Nature of a Practice

The facts in a case may be readily ascertainable, but the arbitrator must then determine what their significance is, whether they add up to a practice, and if so, what that practice is. These questions confront us whenever the parties base their argument on a claimed practice. They cannot be answered by generalization. For a practice is ordinarily the unique product of a particular plant's history and tradition, of a particular group of employees and supervisors, and of a particular set of circumstances that made it viable in the first place. Thus, in deciding the threshold question of whether a practice exists, we must look to the plant setting rather than to theories of contract administration.

Although the conception of what constitutes a practice differs from one employer to another and from one union to another, there are certain characteristics that typify most practices. These characteristics have been noted in many arbitration decisions (see, e.g., *Curtis Companies, Inc.,* 29 *Lab. Arb.* 434 (1957); *Celanese Corp. of America,* 24 *Lab. Arb.* 168 (1954); *Sheller Mfg. Corp.,* 10 *Lab. Arb.* 617 (1948)). For example, in the steel industry, Sylvester Garrett has lucidly defined a practice:

> A custom or practice is not something which arises simply because a given course of conduct has been pursued by Management or the employees on one or more occasions. A custom or a practice is a usage evolved by men as a normal reaction to a recurring type situation. It must be shown to be the *accepted* course of conduct

characteristically repeated in response to the given set of underlying circumstances. This is not to say that the course of conduct must be *accepted* in the sense of both parties having agreed to it, but rather that it must be *accepted* in the sense of being regarded by the men involved as the *normal* and *proper* response to the underlying circumstances presented (2 *Steelworkers Arbitration Bulletin* 1187).[1]

In short, something qualifies as a practice if it is shown to be the understood and accepted way of doing things over an extended period of time.

What qualities must a course of conduct have before it can legitimately be regarded as a practice?

First, there should be clarity and consistency. A course of conduct that is vague and ambiguous or has been contradicted as often as it has been followed can hardly qualify as a practice. But where those in the plant invariably respond in the same way to a particular set of conditions, their conduct may very well ripen into a practice.

Second, there should be longevity and repetition. A period of time has to elapse during which a consistent pattern of behavior emerges. Hence, one or two isolated instances of a certain conduct do not establish a practice. Just how frequently and over how long a period something must be done before it can be characterized as a practice is a matter of judgment for which no formula can be devised.

Third, there should be acceptability. The employees and the supervisors alike must have knowledge of the particular conduct and must regard it as the correct and customary means of handling a situation. Such acceptability may frequently be implied from long acquiescence in a known course of conduct. Where this acquiescence does not exist, that it is, where em-

---

1. A similar definition can be found in some judicial opinions. In *Jarecki Mfg. Co. v. Merriam*, 104 Kan. 646, 180 P. 224 (1919), the court stated: "Persons are presumed to contract with reference to a custom or usage which pertains to the subject of the contract. To constitute a custom which tacitly attends the obligation of a contract, the habit, mode, or course of dealing in the particular trade, business, or locality must be definite and certain; must be well settled and established; must be uniformly and universally prevalent and observed; must be of general notoriety; and must have been acquiesced in without contention or dispute so long and so continuously that contracting parties either had it in mind or ought to have had in mind, and consequently contracted, or presumptively contracted, with reference to it. . . ." See also *McComb v. C. A. Swanson & Sons*, 77 F. Supp. 716, 734 (1948).

ployees have constantly protested a particular course of action through complaints and grievances, it is doubtful that any practice has been created.

One must consider, too, the underlying circumstances that give a practice its true dimensions. A practice is no broader than the circumstances out of which it has arisen, although its scope can always be enlarged in the day-to-day administration of the agreement. No meaningful description of a practice can be made without mention of these circumstances. For instance, a work assignment practice that develops on the afternoon and midnight shifts and is responsive to the peculiar needs of night work cannot be automatically extended to the day shift. Every practice must be carefully related to its origin and purpose.

Finally, the significance to be attributed to a practice may possibly be affected by whether or not it is supported by mutuality. Some practices are the product, either in their inception or in their application, of a joint understanding; others develop from choices made by the employer in the exercise of its managerial discretion, without any intention of a future commitment.

Subject Matter
Practices usually relate to some phase of the contractual relationship between the employer and employees. They may concern such subjects as scheduling, overtime, promotions, and the uses of seniority, all of which are covered to some extent in the typical collective agreement. But practices may also involve extracontractual considerations from the giving of Thanksgiving turkeys and Christmas bonuses to the availability of free parking.

Still other practices, although this characterization may be arguable, have more to do with managerial discretion in operating a plant than with the employment relationship. For example, the long-time use of interdepartmental hand trucks for moving material might be regarded as a practice, and the truckers who do this work certainly have an interest in preserving this method of operation. But could it be seriously argued that this practice would prohibit the employer from introducing a conveyor belt to replace the hand trucks? Most agreements provide, usually in a management rights clause, that methods of manufacture are solely within the employer's discretion.

There may even be practices that have nothing whatever to do with the employment relationship. The long-time assignment of a certain number of foremen to a given department might be viewed by some as a practice, but it could hardly preclude the employer from using fewer foremen. The mere existence of a practice, without more, has no real significance. Only if the practice clarifies an imperfectly expressed contractual obligation or lends substance to an indefinitely expressed obligation or creates a completely independent obligation will it have some effect on the parties' relationship.

Because practices may relate to any phase of an employer's business, some parties have seen fit to spell out limitations on the kind of subject matter a practice may cover. In the steel industry, for instance, a practice is referred to as a "local working condition" and it is binding only if it provides "*benefits* . . . in excess of or in addition too" those provided in the agreement (U.S. Steel and United Steelworkers Agreement, §2 B-3). In determining what constitutes a benefit, steel arbitrators have applied an objective rather than a subjective test. Hence, whether the aggrieved employees like or dislike the practice in dispute is irrelevant. The decisive question, instead, is whether an ordinary employee in the same situation would reasonably regard the practice as a substantial benefit in relation to his job. If so, the practice may be an enforceable "local working condition."

The wide variety of possible subjects may make it difficult to decide the exact nature of a practice. Suppose that certain extra work that periodically arises in department X has, as a matter of practice, been performed by X's employees at overtime rates, but that this has always occurred when the entire plant was on a forty-hour week. Suppose too that this kind of practice is enforceable under the agreement. One day this extra work is made available when the plant is on a thirty-two-hour week, and the employer gives the work to employees from other departments as well as from X so as to provide the maximum number of men with thirty-six hours' work. How is the practice to be described? The union says it is a work assignment practice, giving X's employees an exclusive claim to the disputed work whenever it is performed. The employer says it is an overtime practice, giving X's employees the disputed work only when it is to be performed at overtime rates.

The problem—the proper scope of the practice—is manifest. Was it intended that the practice apply without limitation to all levels of operation or was it intended that the practice be restricted to the precise situation in which it had previously been applied? Some help in formulating an answer may be found in the purpose behind the practice. Hence, if it could be shown that the purpose was to have the work done in department X alone and that it was mere coincidence that the practice had always been applied when the employees were on a 40-hour schedule, the broad interpretation urged by the union would seem to be correct. Absent such a showing, I would think the narrow interpretation would have to be adopted.

We must also be careful to distinguish between a practice and the results of a practice. Assume that a plant has two separate electrical crews, one for existing equipment and the other for new installations, and that overtime on a particular job has always been given to the crew that was actually working that job. Assume too that in implementing this practice over the years there has been a relatively equal distribution of overtime between the crews. From these facts, it cannot be said that equalization of overtime thereby became a practice. The equalization was simply one of the consequences, probably unintended, of applying the overtime assignment practice. If a practice were defined in terms not only of its subject matter but of its consequences as well, it would surely develop a breadth far beyond what was originally intended.

Proof

To allege the existence of a practice is one thing; to prove it is quite another. The allegation is a common one. But my experience indicates that where past practice is disputed, the party relying upon the practice is often unable to establish it. This is not surprising. For the arbitrator in such a dispute is likely to be confronted by irreconcilable claims, sharply conflicting testimony, and incomplete information. Harry Shulman expressed our dilemma in these words:

> The Union's witnesses remember only the occasions on which the work was done in the manner they urge. Supervision remembers the occasions on which the work was done otherwise. Each remembers details the other does not; each is surprised at the other's perversity; and both forget or omit important circumstances. Rarely

is alleged practice clear, detailed, and undisputed: commonly, inquiry into past practice . . . produces immersion in a bog of contradictions, fragments, doubts, and one-sided views . . . (*Ford Motor Co.-United Automobile Workers,* 19 *Lab. Arb.* 237 (1952)).

The arbitrator, abandoned in this kind of maze, is almost certain to decide the grievance on some basis other than past practice. The only means of resolving the confusion, short of credibility findings, is through written records of the disputed events. Such records may be the best possible evidence of what took place in the past. Unfortunately, records such as scheduling and work assignments are seldom maintained for any length of time. Even when available, they may be incomplete, or it may be difficult and costly to reduce them to some meaningful form. Considering these problems, it is understandable that practices are most often held to exist where the parties are in substantial agreement as to what the established course of conduct has been.

Functions of Past Practice

Clarifying Ambiguous Language
The danger of ambiguity arises not only from the English language with its immense vocabulary, flexible grammar, and loose syntax but also from the nature of the collective bargaining agreement. The agreement is a means of governing "complex, many-sided relations between large numbers of people in a going concern for very substantial periods of time" (Cox 1958, p. 22). It is seldom written with the kind of precision and detail that characterize other legal instruments. Although it covers a great variety of subjects, many of which are quite complicated, it must be simply written so that its terms can be understood by the employees and their supervisors. It is sometimes composed by persons inexperienced in the art of written expression. Issues are often settled by a general formula because the negotiators recognize they could not possibly foresee or provide for the many contingencies which are bound to occur during the life of the agreement.

Indeed, any attempt to anticipate and dispose of problems before they arise would, I suspect, create new areas of disagreement and thus obstruct negotiations. Sooner or later the employer and the union must reach agreement if they wish to avoid the economic waste of a strike or lockout. Because of this pressure, the parties often defer the resolution of their differences—either by ignoring them or by writing a provision that is so vague and uncertain as to leave the underlying issue open.

These characteristics inevitably cause portions of the agreement to be expressed in ambiguous and general terms. With the passage of time, however, this language may be given a clear and practical construction, either through managerial action that is acquiesced in by the employees (or, conceivably, employee action which is acquiesced in by management) or through the resolution of disputes on a case-by-case basis. This accumulation of plant experience results in the development of practices and procedures of varying degrees of consistency and force.

Those responsible for the administration of the agreement can no more overlook these practices than they can the express provisions of the agreement. For the established way of doing things is usually the contractually correct way of doing things, and what has become a mutually acceptable interpretation of the agreement is likely to remain so. Hence, the full meaning of the agreement may frequently depend upon how it has been applied in the past.

Consider, for example, an agreement that provides for premium pay for "any work over eight hours in a day." An employee works his regular 8 a.m. to 4 p.m. shift on Monday but works from 6 a.m. to 2 p.m. on Tuesday pursuant to a request by supervision. He asks for overtime for his first two hours (6 a.m. to 8 a.m.) on Tuesday. Whether his claim has merit depends upon how you construe the term "day." Did the parties mean a "calendar day" as the employer argues, or did they mean a "work day," that is, a 24-hour period beginning with the time an employee regularly starts work, as the union argues?

It may be possible to resolve this ambiguity through resort to practice. How the parties act under an agreement may be just as important as what they say in it. To borrow a well-known adage, "actions speak louder than words." From the conflict and accommodation that are daily occurrences in plant life, there arises "a context of practices, usages, and rule-of-the-thumb interpretations," which gradually gives substance to the ambiguous language of the agreement (*Eastern Stainless Steel Corp., 12 Lab. Arb.* 713 (1949)). A practice, once developed, is the best evidence of what the language meant to those who wrote it.

By relying upon practice, the burden of the decision may be shifted from the arbitrator back to the parties. For to the extent to which the arbitrator adopts the interpretation given by the parties themselves as shown by their acts, he minimizes his own role in the construction process. The real significance of practice as an interpretive aid lies in the fact that the arbitrator is responsive to the values and standards of the parties. A decision based on past practice emphasizes not the personal viewpoint of the arbitrator but rather the parties' own history, what they have found to be proper and agreeable over the years. Because such a decision is bound to reflect the parties' concept of rightness, it is more likely to resolve the underlying dispute and more likely to be acceptable. A solution created from within is always preferable to one which is imposed from without (see Seward 1957, pp. 72–73).

Implementing General Contract Language
Practice is also a means of implementing general contract language. In areas that cannot be made specific, the parties are often satisfied to state a general rule and to allow the precise meaning of the rule to develop through the day-to-day administration of the agreement.

For instance, the right to discipline and discharge is usually conditioned upon the existence of "just cause." Similarly, the right to deviate from a contract requirement may be conditioned upon the existence of "circumstances beyond the employer's control." General expressions of this kind are rarely defined. For no definition, however detailed, could anticipate all the possibilities that might take place during the term of the agreement.

But, in time, this kind of general language does tend to become more concrete. As the parties respond to the many different situations confronting them—approving certain principles and procedures, disputing others, and resolving their disputes in the grievance procedure—they find mutually acceptable ways of doing things which serve to guide them in future cases. Instead of rearguing every matter without regard to their earlier experiences, acceptable principles and procedures are applied again and again.

Thus, practices arise that represent the reasonable expectations of the parties. These practices provide a sound basis for interpreting and applying general contract language. They can be used to help determine whether a particular condition was actually "beyond the employer's control" or whether a particular employee's behavior was "just cause" for discipline.

Suppose, for example, that tardiness of less than five minutes has always been overlooked but that after it becomes extremely widespread, management disciplines a few employees without any advance notice of its change in policy. In view of this long toleration of tardiness, it is doubtful that there would be "just cause" for discipline. Plant practice thus injects something tangible into the "just cause" provision, giving employees a clear notion of what is acceptable and unacceptable in plant behavior. Of course, once they are notified that tardiness will no longer be ignored, the employer would be free to take reasonable disciplinary action.

Although discipline that is completely inconsistent with past practice is likely to lack "just cause," it does not follow that discipline must be perfectly consistent with past practice in order to establish "just cause."

Suppose that fighting in the plant has in the past resulted in disciplinary suspensions of two to five weeks and that those who have been so disciplined were all men with considerable seniority. Then, a recently hired employee starts a fight with no justification whatever and is discharged. The union may argue that because others had received suspensions, the discharge was too severe a penalty. But one must remember that there are degrees of culpability and that discharge is hardly the same penalty when applied to an employee with one year's seniority and to another with twenty years' seniority. The employer should not be precluded from discharging this man merely because on earlier occasions it had good reason to be lenient.

The point is that "it is not the fact of seeming inconsistency in past practice, but the cause of it, that ought to engage the arbitrator's attention." Hence, what seems on the surface to be capricious administration of a disciplinary rule "may prove on closer inspection to be a flexible and humane application of a sound principle to essentially different situations" (Aaron 1955).

Modifying or Amending Apparently Unambiguous Language
What an agreement says is one thing; how it is carried out may be quite another. A study at the University of Illinois revealed that differences between contract provisions and actual practice are not at all unusual (Derber, Chalmers, and Stagner 1958). Thus, an arbitrator occasionally is confronted with a situation where an established practice conflicts with a seemingly clear and unambiguous contract provision. Which is to prevail? The answer in many cases has been to disregard the practice and affirm the plain meaning of the contract language (see, e.g., *Sun Rubber Co.*, 28 *Lab. Arb.* 362, 368 (1957); *Price-Pfister Brass Mfg. Co.*, 25 *Lab. Arb.* 398, 404 (1955); *Bethlehem Steel Co.*, 21 *Lab. Arb.* 579, 582 (1953); *Tide Water Oil Co.*, 17 *Lab. Arb.* 829, 833 (1952). See also the celebrated case of *Western Union Telegraph Co.* v. *American Communications Assn.*, 12 *Lab. Arb.* 516 (1949)).

At the National Academy meeting in 1955, Ben Aaron forcefully argued that sometimes practice should prevail. He posed a hypothetical situation based upon this contract provision:

> Where skill and physical capacity are substantially equal, seniority shall govern in the following situations only: promotions, downgrading, layoffs, and transfers.

He assumed that the consistent practice for five years immediately preceding the dispute has been to treat seniority as the controlling consideration in the assignment of overtime work and that a grievance has arisen out of the employer's sudden abandonment of that practice. He assumed further that the agreement vests in management the right to direct the working forces, subject only to qualifications or restrictions set forth elsewhere in the agreement, and that the parties have expressly forbidden the arbitrator to add to, subtract from, or modify any provision of the agreement (Aaron 1955).

The conventional analysis of the problem begins with the proposition that the contract should be construed according to the parties' original intention. The best evidence of their intention is generally found in the contract itself, that is, in the words the parties themselves employed to express their intent. If these words are free from ambiguity and if their meaning is plain, there is no need to resort to interpretive aids such as past practice. This reasoning is well established in the law of contracts.[2]

In the hypothetical case, the contract asserts that seniority is controlling "in the following situations only: promotions, down-grading, layoffs, and transfers." On its face, this language contains no ambiguity whatever. By using the word "only," a more exclusive term would be hard to imagine, the parties evidently intended seniority to apply in the four situations mentioned but in no others. Hence, pursuant to the plain meaning of this clause, seniority would not govern overtime assignments and any practice to the contrary would have to be ignored.

Aaron, however, says this may be too rigid an approach to the problem because it borrows principles from the law of contracts without giving adequate consideration to the unique characteristics of the collective bargaining contract and the relative flexibility with which even commercial contracts are construed today. He argues persuasively that no matter how clear the language of the collective bargaining contract seems to be, it does not always tell the full story of the parties' intentions.

Suppose, in our hypothetical case, the testimony reveals that the matter of overtime assignments was never considered during the negotiation of the seniority clause—either because the parties overlooked it under the mistaken impression that they had covered all possible contingencies or because the parties concerned themselves only with those situations they had previously experienced. Or suppose the parties simply found this seniority clause in some other agreement and

---

2. See the following excerpt from 55 *Am. Jur.* § 31:
Perhaps the most fundamental of the rules which limit the introduction of a custom or usage . . . is that which denies the admissibility of such evidence where its purpose or effect is to contradict the plain, unambiguous terms . . . expressed in the contract itself or to vary or qualify terms which are free from ambiguity. . . . It [custom or usage] may explain what is ambiguous but it cannot vary or contradict what is manifest or plain. . . . An express written contract embodying in clear and positive terms the intention of the parties cannot be varied by evidence of usage or custom which either expressly or by necessary implication contradicts the terms of such contract.

adopted it without discussion. Anyone familiar with collective bargaining knows this sort of thing does happen. The contract itself is not usually written by people trained in semantics. It is hardly surprising therefore to find in the typical contract an "inartistic and inaccurate use of words that have a precise and commonly accepted meaning in law" (Aaron 1955, p. 5). The word only in the hypothetical case may merely be attributable to an inexperienced or over-eager draftsman.

Under these assumed circumstances, it cannot confidently be said that the parties intended to exclude overtime assignments from the scope of the seniority clause. Absent any original intention with respect to this problem, Aaron concludes that the long-standing practice of making overtime assignments by seniority should be controlling.

This conclusion appears to be supported by two different rationales. First, the argument seems to be that contract language is no clearer than the underlying intention of the parties. As Judge Cardozo put it, "few words are so plain that the context or the occasion is without capacity to enlarge or narrow their extension." Hence, where it is shown that their intention was uncertain or incomplete, the language cannot be considered truly ambiguous. It follows that past practice is being used not to contradict what is plain but rather to add to what is already a part of the agreement.

Second, the argument is that to adopt the overtime assignment practice "does not alter the agreement but merely takes note of a modification that has already been made either by the parties jointly or by the unilateral action of the employer tacitly approved by the union (Aaron 1955, p. 6). The practice, in short, amounts to an amendment of the agreement.

I find much merit in what Aaron says, and there are several reported decisions that indicate his views are shared by others as well (see, e.g., *Metropolitan Coach Lines*, 27 *Lab. Arb.* 376, 383 (1956); *Smith Display Service*, 17 *Lab. Arb.* 524, 526 (1951)). The real question, however, is whether as serious a matter as the modification of clear contract language can be based on practice alone. Some arbitrators have held, I think with good reason, that practice should prevail only if the proofs are sufficiently strong to warrant saying there was in effect mutual agreement to the modification (see, e.g., *National Lead*

Co., 28 *Lab. Arb.* 470 (1957); *Gibson Refrigerator Co.*, 17 *Lab. Arb.* 313, 318 (1951); *Texas-New Mexico Pipe Line Co.*, 17 *Lab. Arb.* 90, 91 (1951); *Merrill-Stevens Dry Dock & Repair Co.*, 10 *Lab. Arb.* 562, 563 (1948); *Pittsburgh Plate Glass Co.*, 8 *Lab. Arb.* 317, 332 (1947)).[3] The parties must, to use the words in one decision, "have evinced a positive acceptance or endorsement" of the practice, *Bethlehem Steel Co.*, 13 *Lab. Arb.* 556, 560 (1949). Thus, I believe that the modification is justified not by practice but rather by the parties' agreement, the existence of which may possibly be inferred from a clear and consistent practice.

None of this reasoning is radical. The notion that the collective bargaining contract is a "living document" has already won wide acceptance. Those responsible for a contract are free to change it at any time by adding an entirely new provision, by rewriting an existing clause, or by reinterpreting some section to give it a meaning other than that which was originally intended. Grievance settlements often result in "understandings that are as durable, or more so, than the actual terms of the labor contract. . . ." (Taylor 1957, pp. 20–21).

If a contract is susceptible to change in these ways, why should it not be equally susceptible to change by reason of practice, at least where the practice represents the joint understanding of the parties? After all, the only ground for recognizing the modification or amendment of a contract is some mutual agreement. And it can be strongly argued that the *form* the agreement takes is not important. Whether it be a formal writing, an oral understanding, or a long-standing practice, so long as each is supported by mutuality, the parties have indeed chosen to change their contract.

It is also worth emphasizing that Aaron's hypothetical case just illustrates a situation where practice conflicts with the apparent meaning of a seemingly unambiguous provision. But what of a situation where practice conflicts with the real meaning of a truly unambiguous provision?

Suppose, for instance, that a contract says "seniority shall

---

3. For still another viewpoint, see Pearce Davis's comments on Aaron's hypothetical case. He stated he too would consider the overtime assignment practice to be enforceable but only if it were established "that the practice had been initiated by actual discussion and agreement of both parties" (Aaron 1955, p. 15).

not govern the assignment of overtime work," that the parties meant to restrict the application of seniority, that a practice of distributing overtime according to seniority later developed, and that this practice was not initiated until the union had stated in discussions with the employer that it approved of this means of distributing overtime. On these facts, would the employer's unilateral discontinuance of the practice constitute a contract violation?

Applying the rationale stated in Aaron's paper, I would find no violation on the ground that practice can be decisive only if there is some uncertainty, however slight, with respect to the parties' original intention. My hypothetical case contains no such uncertainty, the parties' intention being perfectly obvious. Yet, if the "living document" notion is carried to its logical conclusion, a violation may exist on the ground that the practice, being a product of joint determination, amounts to an amendment of the contract and that thereafter the practice could only be changed by mutual agreement.

Some may complain that the contract is so clear and compelling here that no room is left for consideration of past practice. However, as Williston has explained in his famous treatise on contracts, "if the meaning of the contract is plain, the acts of the parties cannot prove an interpretation contrary to the plain meaning" but nevertheless "such conduct of the parties . . . may be evidence of a subsequent modification of their contract" (1936, § 623).

As a Separate, Enforceable Condition of Employment
Sometimes an established practice is regarded as a distinct and binding condition of employment, which cannot be changed without the mutual consent of the parties. Its binding quality may arise either from a contract provision that specifically requires the continuance of existing practices or, absent such a provision, from the theory that long-standing practices that have been accepted by the parties become an integral part of the agreement with just as much force as any of its written provisions.

There are different kinds of contract provisions regarding past practice. Some merely state that practices shall govern one small phase of the employment relationship. For instance, "bidding on job vacancies shall be in accordance with past practice." Others broadly embrace practices with little or no qualification. For instance, "all practices and conditions not specified in this contract shall remain the same for the duration of the contract" (see Reilly 1957 for the attitude of many management attorneys on such clauses). Still others require that practices be continued during the term of the agreement but allow management to change or eliminate a practice upon the occurrence of certain stated conditions.

No discussion of this subject would be complete without some mention of the experiences of the basic steel industry. The typical steel agreement provides that "any local working conditions in effect which have existed regularly over a period of time under the applicable circumstances . . . shall remain in effect for the term of this Agreement. . . ." (*U.S. Steel and United Steelworkers Agreement* § 2B; *Republic Steel and United Steelworkers Agreement* art. 1, § 3). In this way, there has been incorporated into the steel agreements a wide variety of practices affecting wages, crew sizes, relief time, work assignments, and many other matters.

The "local working conditions" clause is thus the source of important rights and obligations, many of which are somewhat obscured by the bustle of daily plant operations. Local working conditions are defined in the steel agreements as "specific practices or customs which reflect detailed application of the subject matter within the scope of wages, hours of work, or other conditions of employment and includes local agreements, written or oral, on such matters." It is this uncertainty as to the nature and extent of the commitment that seems most disturbing to steel management. But a local working condition is not by nature unalterable. It may be changed or eliminated either by mutual agreement *or* by the employer if it can establish (1) that it has through the exercise of managerial discretion changed or eliminated "the basis for the existence of the local working condition" and (2) that a reasonable causal relationship exists between the change in the basis for the working condition and the change in the working condition itself.

The steel agreements thus seek to balance the employee's interest in preserving benefits from established practices and the manager's interest in being able to alter practices to suit changing industrial circumstances and thereby enhance efficiency. The "local working conditions" clause is, in short, a compromise between stability on the one hand and flexibility on the other.

I would like to illustrate the application of this clause with a hypothetical case. Suppose that certain mill equipment has been run by five men for many years, that this arrangement was originally based upon supervision's evaluation of the amount of work involved, and that the five-man crew has come to be recognized as a "local working condition." If technological improvements are made in the equipment and if these improvements substantially decrease the crew's workload, it has been held that the employer will have changed "the basis for the existence of the local working condition." Hence, it will be free to change the "local working condition" itself, that is, to reduce the crew size. The only proviso is that a reasonable "cause-effect" relationship exist between the change in the basis for the practice and the change in the practice itself.

Even without technological improvements, however, the employer may be confident that the operation can be adequately performed with four men instead of five by reassigning duties among the crew members or by eliminating some of their idle time. Or the employer may belatedly discover that the original supervisory estimates of the work involved were completely wrong and that the crew should never have been larger than four men. But these circumstances, it has been held, do not change "the basis for the existence of the local working condition" and hence do not justify a reduction in crew sizes. Such a reduction must almost always be based upon some technological advance, either in equipment or in manufacturing processes.

A "local working condition," in other words, need not yield to greater efficiency alone. Furthermore, the "local working conditions" clause places a premium on prompt and careful judgment in any area affecting conditions of employment. Where, for instance, an improved manufacturing process warrants a crew reduction but management fails to take any action, its failure may ultimately result in a new "local working condition," which will saddle the operation with the old crew. Thus, an employer is forced to live with an error or a mistake in judgment once it becomes embedded in a "local working condition." To this extent, the clause may prevent management from realizing optimum efficiency, but management must bear some of the responsibility for this result.

Most agreements, however, say nothing about management having to maintain existing conditions. They ordinarily do not even mention the subject of past practice. The question then is whether, apart from any basis in the agreement, an established practice can nevertheless be considered a binding condition of employment. The answer, I think, depends upon one's conception of the collective bargaining agreement. To use Harry Shulman's words, "is the agreement an exclusive statement of rights and privileges or does it subsume continuation of existing conditions?" (1955, p. 1011).

Employers tend to argue that the only restrictions placed upon management are those contained in the agreement and that in all other respects management is free to act in whatever way it sees fit. Or to put the argument in the more familiar "reserved rights" terminology, management continues to have the rights it customarily possessed and which it has not surrendered through collective bargaining. If an agreement does not require the continuance of existing conditions, a practice, being merely an extracontractual consideration, would have no binding force regardless of how well established it may be. It follows that management may change or eliminate the practice without the union's consent.

Unions take an entirely different view of the problem. They emphasize the unique qualities of the collective bargaining agreement and the background against which the agreement was negotiated, particularly those practices that have come to be accepted by employees and supervisors alike and have thus become an important part of the working environment. The agreement is executed in the light of this working environment and on the assumption that existing practices will remain in effect. Therefore, to the extent that these practices are unchallenged during negotiations, the parties must be held to have adopted them and made them a part of their agreement (see Goldberg 1956).

Many arbitrators have, at some time in their careers, been

confronted by these arguments. Some have held that the agreement is the exclusive source of rights and privileges (see, e.g., *National Distillers Products Corp.*, 24 *Lab. Arb.* 500 (1953); *Donaldson Co., Inc.*, 20 *Lab. Arb.* 826 (1953); *New York Trap Rock Corp.*, 19 *Lab. Arb.* 421 (1952); *Byerlite Corp.*, 12 *Lab. Arb.* 641 (1949); *M. T. Stevens & Sons Co.*, 7 *Lab. Arb.* 585 (1947)). Others have held that the agreement may subsume continuation of existing conditions (see, e.g., *Fruehauf Trailer Co.*, 29 *Lab. Arb.* 372 (1957); *Morris P. Kirk & Son, Inc.*, 27 *Lab. Arb.* 6 (1956); *E. W. Bliss Co.*, 24 *Lab. Arb.* 614 (1955); *Phillips Petroleum Co.*, 24 *Lab. Arb.* 191 (1955); *Northland Greyhound Lines, Inc.*, 23 *Lab. Arb.* 277 (1954); *International Harvester Co.*, 20 *Lab. Arb.* 276 (1953); *American Seating Co.*, 16 *Lab. Arb.* 115 (1951); *California Cotton Mills Co.* 14 *Lab. Arb.* 377 (1950); *Franklin Assn. of Chicago*, 7 *Lab. Arb.* 614 (1947)). The latter is the more prevalent view. Those who follow it have prohibited employers from unilaterally changing or eliminating practices with regard to efficiency bonus plans, *Libby, McNeill & Libby*, 5 *Lab. Arb.* 546 (1955), *Pullman-Standard Car Mfg. Co.*, 2 *Lab. Arb.* 509 (1945); paid lunch periods, *E. W. Bliss Co.*; wash-up periods on company time, *International Harvester Co.*; maternity leaves of absence, *Northland Greyhound Lines, Inc.*; free milk, *Ryan Aeronautical Co.*, 17 *Lab. Arb.* 395 (1951); and home electricity at nominal rates *Phillips Petroleum Co.*

The reasoning behind these decisions begins with the proposition that the parties have not set down on paper the whole of their agreement. "One cannot reduce all the rules governing a community like an industrial plant to fifteen or even fifty pages" (Cox 1959).

Thus, the union-management contract includes not just the written provisions stated therein but also the understandings and mutually acceptable practices that have developed over the years. Because the contract is executed in the context of these understandings and practices, the negotiators must be presumed to be fully aware of them and to have relied upon them in striking their bargain. Hence, if a particular practice is not repudiated during negotiations, it may fairly be said that the contract was entered into upon the assumption that this practice would continue in force. By their silence, the parties have given assent to existing modes of procedure.[4] In this way, practices may by implication become an integral part of the contract.[5]

Cox (1959) not only agrees with this view but states the argument more strongly. In asserting that words of the contract cannot be the exclusive source of rights and duties, he emphasizes the following point: "Within the sphere of collective bargaining, the institutional characteristics and the governmental nature of the collective-bargaining process demand a common law of the shop which implements and furnishes the context of the agreement. We must assume that intelligent negotiators acknowledged so plain a need unless they stated a contrary rule in plain words." The common law of the shop would include, at the very least, long-standing practices in the plant.

None of this is incompatible with ordinary contract law. Williston says that a usage, in our jargon a practice, is admissible "for the purpose of adding a new element or term or incident, whichever one is pleased to call it, to the expressed terms of the contract" and that "it may be shown that a matter con-

---

4. Note the analysis made by Douglass V. Brown (1949):

But when all of the provisions are written, it will be found that many matters which affect conditions of employment are not specifically referred to. Does this mean that these matters are of no concern to the parties, or that the agreement has no meaning with respect to them? I think not. On some of these matters, the parties are satisfied with existing modes of procedure, consciously or unconsciously. On others, one party or the other may be dissatisfied but may be unable to devise better modes. On still others, one party may have preferred an alternative but may have been unable to secure agreement from the other party, or may have been unwilling to pay the price necessary for acceptance. In any event, the omission of specific reference is significant.

. . . The agreement, no matter how short, does provide a guide to modes of procedure and to the rights of the parties on *all* matters affecting the conditions of employment. Where explicit provisions are made, the question is relatively simple. But even where the agreement is silent, the parties have, by their silence, given assent to a continuation of the existing modes of procedure.

5. This implication, of course, would not be possible if it conflicted with the express language of the contract. For example, if a contract said "the written provisions constitute the entire agreement of the parties," it would be difficult to imply that the parties meant to make practices a part of their contract.

cerning which the written contract is silent, is affected by a usage with which both parties are chargeable" (1936, § 652).

Indeed, some courts have decided that when an employee is hired or an agent appointed, the nature of his duties and compensation as well may not be stated but may nevertheless be fixed by what is customary and reasonable (see *Venembury* v. *Duffey,* 177 Ark. 663, 7 S.W. 2d 336 (1928) (broker's commission fixed by practice); *Voell* v. *Klein,* 184 Wis. 620, 200 N.W. 364 (1924) (authority of sales agent to accept used car as part payment for new one held established by practice of automobile dealers)). In one case, a practice between railroads and their employees was held admissible to establish an implied agreement to pay time and one-half for overtime work, *McGurie* v. *Interurban Ry.,* 99 Ia. 203, 200 N.W. 55 (1924).

But this theory, insofar as it relates to the collective bargaining agreement, is open to criticism. To repeat, the majority view is that established practices which were in existence when the agreement was negotiated and which were not discussed during negotiations are binding upon the parties and must be continued for the life of the agreement. This is said to be an implied condition of the agreement. In the courts, implications of this kind are "based on morality, common understanding, social policy, and legal duty expressed in tort or quasi-contract" (Shulman 1955, pp. 1011–13).[6]

These considerations, however, are not much help to arbitrators. If we are the servants of the parties alone and not the public, I doubt that social policy would be a sound basis for drawing an implication. If our job is to seek out the parties' values and not to impose others' values upon them, I doubt that morality would provide the basis for an implication. If our powers arise from the parties' agreement and not from the labor laws, I doubt that a legal duty found in such legislation would be relevant.

Consider, for instance, the legal duty to bargain under the Labor-Management Relations Act. Apart from the question of whether we may enforce that duty, the real issue is "whether the practice may be changed without mutual consent when bar-

---

6. The analysis made in this paragraph is based upon Shulman's paper.

gaining has failed to achieve consent" (Shulman 1955, pp. 1011–13). Thus, the arbitrator's power to establish implied conditions derives not from the superior authority of the law but rather from the parties' will, from their common understanding. He may find implications that "may reasonably be inferred from some term of the agreement" (Shulman 1955, pp. 1101–13) or even from the agreement as a whole.

The implication here that existing practices must be continued until changed by mutual consent is drawn from the nature of the agreement itself and from the collective bargaining process. It would be justified, I am sure, wherever there is a real or tacit understanding during negotiations that existing practices would be continued. While such an understanding may exist in some relationships, I think Shulman is probably correct in concluding that

> it is more than doubtful that there is any general understanding among employers and unions as to the viability of existing practices during the term of a collective agreement. . . . I venture to guess that in many enterprises the execution of a collective agreement would be blocked if it were insisted that it contain a broad provision that 'all existing practices, except as modified by this agreement, shall be continued for the life thereof, unless changed by mutual consent.' And I suppose that execution would also be blocked if the converse provision were demanded, namely, that 'the employer shall be free to change any existing practice except as he is restricted by the terms of this agreement.' The reasons for the block would be, of course, the great uncertainty as to the nature and extent of the commitment, and the relentless search for cost-saving changes . . . (1955, pp. 1101–13).

It is one thing to say, as Shulman suggests, that the implication is warranted where the evidence indicates that the parties had a "common understanding" to continue existing practices: it is quite another to say, as the majority suggest, that the implication is warranted because it may be assumed, unless otherwise stated in negotiations, that the parties had such a "common understanding."[7] The difference in viewpoints is clear. Shulman wants some proof of what the majority ordinarily assumes.

---

7. Or to take this one step further, as Cox suggests, it may be assumed, unless otherwise stated in the agreement, that the parties had such a "common understanding" (Cox 1959).

Shulman's approach places a heavy burden on anyone who claims that a practice is a binding condition of employment. Think of the difficulty one might encounter in trying to establish that the unstated assumption of the negotiators on both sides of the table was to continue existing practices. The majority approach, on the other hand, comes close to engrafting a past practice clause onto the typical collective agreement without regard to the actual assumptions of the negotiators. Their silence at the bargaining table is presumed to constitute assent to existing conditions, whether they thought of this or not.

There are other possibilities too. We may find that the parties had no common understanding to continue practices in general but did have a common understanding to continue a particular practice. Much of this discussion has related to practices in general. Yet, an arbitration case rarely poses so broad a problem. We are usually asked to decide only whether a specific practice, say, a paid lunch period, must be continued in effect. Where possible, the answer should be as narrow as the question. To the extent to which the answer goes further and seeks to determine whether the agreement subsumes the continuation of existing conditions, the arbitrator risks deciding far more than the parties want him to decide. The dangers are magnified too by the fact that the arbitrator is not likely to elicit a clear picture of the assumptions upon which the agreement was negotiated.

Still another problem exists. Those of us who accept the principle that an agreement may require the continuance of existing practices recognize that this principle cannot be allowed to freeze *all* existing conditions. For instance, the long-time use of handcontrolled grinding machines could hardly be regarded as a practice prohibiting the introduction of automatic grinding machines. Or the long-time use of pastel colors in painting plant interiors could not preclude management from changing to a different color scheme. Plainly, not all practices can be considered binding conditions of employment.

Thus, while we are willing to imply that practices are a part of the agreement, we are apprehensive of the breadth of the implication. What seems correct from a theoretical point of view does not always make sense from a practical point of view. Arbitrators, accordingly, have accepted the implication but sought to limit it to just certain kinds of practices. The difficulty is to determine what kind of rational line, if any, can be drawn between those practices that may be incorporated into the agreement and those that may not.

Some decisions enforce only those practices concerning major conditions of employment as contrasted to minor conditions (see, e.g., *Pan Am Southern Corp.*, 25 *Lab. Arb.* 611, 613 (1955); *Phillips Petroleum Co.*, 24 *Lab. Arb.* 191, 194 (1955); *Continental Baking Co.*, 20 *Lab. Arb.* 309, 311 (1953); *General Aniline & Film Corp.*, 19 *Lab. Arb.* 628, 629 (1952)).[8] But the test seems inadequate for several reasons. To begin with, it is vague and inexact. What is major to one group of employees may be minor to all the others; what is major from the standpoint of morale may be minor from the standpoint of earnings and job security. There is no logical basis for distinguishing between major and minor conditions, unless the arbitrator is to concern himself only with serious violations of the agreement.

More important, this kind of test encourages arbitrators "to commence their thinking with what they consider a desirable decision and then work backward to appropriate premises, devising syllogisms to justify that decision . . ." (Frank 1934, p. 12413). That is, if an arbitrator decides to enforce the practice he calls it a major condition, and if he decides otherwise he calls it a minor condition. To this extent, the test provides us with a rationalization rather than a reason for our ruling.

The Elkouris have suggested a comparable test. They would enforce only those practices which involve "employee benefits"; they would not prohibit changes in practices which involve "basic management functions" (1960, pp. 274–75). This test, however, is no more convincing than the major-minor test. It suffers from the same defects. It too encourages the arbitrator to work backwards from his decision, thus providing a rationalization rather than a reason for his ruling. To enforce a practice all the arbitrator need say is that it concerns employee benefits. But the fact is that most practices that create such

---

8. Cox and John Dunlop, in an article dealing with national labor policy, urged that "a collective bargaining agreement should be deemed, unless a contrary intention is manifest, to carry forward for its term the major terms and conditions of employment, not covered by the agreement, which prevailed when the agreement was executed" (1950, pp. 1097, 1116–17).

benefits are likely to impinge upon some basic management function.

Consider a situation where the employer wishes to reduce a long-established crew size based upon a recent engineering survey of the plant. How is the crew size practice to be characterized? It involves the direction of the working force and the determination of methods of operation, which are customary management functions, but it also involves the job security of one or more members of the crew, a very real employee benefit. In the closer cases, this test provides no satisfactory guidance. Besides, it seems to me that if the parties have in effect agreed to the continuation of a particular practice, it should be binding regardless of its subject matter.

A few decisions enforce the practice if it involves a "working condition" rather than a "gift" or a "gratuity" (see *Fawick Airflex Co.*, 11 *Lab. Arb.* 666, 668–69 (1948)).[9] This distinction is meaningful only in that class of cases that concern employee bonuses or other extracontractual employee compensation. Apart from its limited applicability, however, this test does suggest that what is important here is not the subject matter of the practice but rather the extent to which the practice is founded upon the agreement of the parties.

A better test, I think, is suggested by what Shulman said in a decision he made as umpire under the Ford-UAW agreement, an agreement that did not require the continuance of existing practices. He urged that the controlling question in this kind of case is whether or not the practice was supported by "mutual agreement."

> A practice thus based on mutual agreement may be subject to change only by mutual agreement. Its binding quality is due, however, not to the fact that it is past practice but rather to the agreement in which it is based. But there are other practices which are not the result of joint determination at all. They may be mere happenstance, that is, methods that developed without design or deliberation. Or they may be choices by Management in the exercise of managerial discretion as to convenient methods at the time. In such

---

9. Bonuses were held to be an integral part of the wage structure in *Nazareth Mills, Inc.*, 22 *Lab. Arb.* 808 (1954); *Felsway Shoe Corp.*, 17 *Lab. Arb.* 505 (1951). Bonuses were held to be gratuities in the following cases: *American Lava Corp.*, 32 *Lab. Arb.* 395 (1959); *Rockwell-Standard Corp.*, 32 *Lab. Arb.* 388 (1959); *Bassick Co.*, 26 *Lab. Arb.* 627 (1956).

cases there is no thought of obligation or commitment for the future. Such practices are merely present ways, not prescribed ways, of doing things. The relevant item of significance is not the nature of the particular method but the managerial freedom with respect to it. Being the product of managerial determination in its permitted discretion, such practices are, in the absence of contractual provisions to the contrary, subject to change in the same discretion. . . . But there is no requirement of mutual agreement as a condition precedent to a change of a practice of this character. A contrary holding would place past practice on a par with written agreement and create the anomaly that, while the parties expend great energy and time in negotiating the details of the Agreement, they unknowingly and unintentionally commit themselves to unstated and perhaps more important matters which in the future may be found to have been past practice (19 *Lab. Arb.* 237 (1952); see also 20 *Lab. Arb.* 276 (1953)).

Under this test, only a practice supported by the mutual agreement of the parties would be enforceable. Such a practice would be binding, regardless of how minor it may be and regardless of the extent to which it may affect a traditional function. Absent this mutuality, however, the practice would be subject to change in management's discretion.

Although this seems a sound way of distinguishing between enforceable and nonenforceable practices, one might understandably ask what constitutes mutual agreement. Is it necessary to establish an express understanding or is it sufficient to show that the practice is of such long standing that the parties may properly be assumed to have agreed to its continuance? In other words, to what extent may the required mutuality be implied from the parties' actions or from their mere acquiescence in a given course of conduct?

Even the Shulman test does not provide a complete answer to this extremely vexing problem. I suspect that we would be far more likely to infer mutuality in a practice concerning employee benefits than in one concerning basic management functions. To this extent, Shulman and the Elkouris may well have something in common.

Duration and Termination of a Practice

Once the parties become bound by a practice, they may wonder how long it will be binding and how it can be terminated.

Consider first a practice that is, apart from any basis in the agreement, an enforceable condition of employment on the theory that the agreement subsumes the continuance of existing conditions. Such a practice cannot be unilaterally changed during the life of the agreement. For, as I explained earlier in this chapter, if a practice is not discussed during negotiations, most of us are likely to infer that the agreement was executed on the assumption that the practice would remain in effect.

The inference is based largely on the parties' acquiescence in the practice. If either side should, during the negotiation of a later agreement, object to the continuance of this practice, it could not be inferred from the signing of a new agreement that the parties intended the practice to remain in force. Without their acquiescence, the practice would no longer be a binding condition of employment. In face of a timely repudiation of a practice by one party, the other must have the practice written into the agreement if it is to continue to be binding.

Consider next a well-established practice that serves to clarify some ambiguity in the agreement. Because the practice is essential to an understanding of the ambiguous provision, it becomes in effect a part of that provision. As such, it will be binding for the life of the agreement. And the mere repudiation of the practice by one side during the negotiation of a new agreement, unless accompanied by a revision of the ambiguous language, would not be significant. For the repudiation alone would not change the meaning of the ambiguous provision and hence would not detract from the effectiveness of the practice.

It is a well-settled principle that where past practice has established a meaning for language that is subsequently used in an agreement, the language will be presumed to have the meaning given it by practice. Thus, this kind of practice can only be terminated by mutual agreement, that is, by the parties rewriting the ambiguous provision to supersede the practice, by eliminating the provision entirely.

Consider finally the effect of changing circumstances on the viability of a practice during the contract term. Where the conditions that gave rise to a practice no longer exist, the employer is not obliged to continue to apply the practice. Suppose, for instance, that crane operators who handle extremely hot materials have for years been given a certain amount of relief time during their shift and that after installing an air conditioning unit in one of the crane cabs the employer refuses to give any more relief time to the operator of that crane. Whether the employer's action is justifiable depends upon the reason behind the relief time practice.

If relief was given because of the extreme heat alone, there would be good reason for denying any relief to the operator in the air-conditioned cab. The circumstances underlying the practice would no longer be pertinent to this particular craneman. If, on the other hand, relief was given because of the high degree of concentration and care demanded in running these cranes there would be good reason to continue relief time for this craneman. The circumstances underlying the practice would still be relevant to the employee's situation, even though he now has the benefit of air conditioning.

In other words, a practice must be carefully related to the conditions from which it arose. Whenever those conditions substantially change, the practice may be subject to termination.

Conclusion

Through past practice, the arbitrator learns something of the values and standards of the parties and thus gains added insight into the nature of their contractual rights and obligations. Practices tend to disclose the reasonable expectations of the employees and managers alike. And as long as our decision is made within the bounds of these expectations, it has a better chance of being understood and accepted.

The ideas expressed here may be useful as a general guide to the uses of past practice in administering the collective agreement. They do not provide an easy formula for resolving disputes; they are no substitute for a thorough and painstaking analysis of the facts. In the problem areas of past practice, there are so many fine distinctions that the final decision in a case will rest not on any abstract theorizing but rather on the arbitrator's view of the peculiar circumstances of that case.

No matter how successful we may be in systematizing the standards which shape arbitral opinions, we must recognize that considerable room must be left for "art and intuition," for good judgment (Cox 1959, p. 1500).

13

Writing the Opinion

Charles M. Rehmus

WRITING THE arbitration opinion is the least glamorous part of an arbitrator's occupation. Most arbitrators enjoy their work, but few have ever told me that they enjoyed writing the opinion itself. Satisfaction with a well-done opinion is universal, but the process of drafting and redrafting is largely drudgery. Nevertheless, this is an important part of the job, not the sine qua non of arbitral success perhaps, but certainly an element to which careful attention should be paid.

As a legal matter, we are required only to give awards. The Supreme Court in *Enterprise Wheel*, 363 U.S. 593 (1960), said that while arbitrators do not owe the Court an explanation of their decisions, "a well reasoned opinion tends to engender confidence in the integrity of the process and aids in clarifying the underlying agreement." And the parties themselves, when asked, invariably want an opinion. Although the parties may of course waive an opinion, except in the small minority of cases involving bench decisions, there is no demand for awards without opinions. The parties almost always want something in writing, something that will explain why we awarded as we did. The reason is quite understandable. The parties do not retain counsel, then spend days in preparation and more days in hearing simply to find out whether Jones rather than Smith should have been promoted from the labor pool to machine operator. The parties are interested in principles and guidelines for the future. For their future guidance, they are entitled to the arbitrator's findings of fact, his or her view of the evidence, understanding of the respective contentions of the parties, and finally, the relevant interpretation and application of the parties' agreement. The question then arises—What kind of opinions should we write and for whom?

The Code of Professional Responsibility (see Appendix) says that awards should be definite, certain, and as concise as possible. That is the award. The Code's commentary regarding opinions states the factors the arbitrator should consider, including the desirability of brevity consistent with the nature of the case and the desires of the parties; style and form understandable to responsible representatives of the parties, the grievant, supervisors, and others; necessity for meeting the issues; forthrightness to an extent not harmful to the relationship of the parties; and the avoidance of gratuitous advice.

In my judgment, the Code raises the right questions but does not give any of the answers. There seem to be many different styles in writing of arbitral opinions, so many that I am not sure that there is any best way. But I can tell you how I do it and how some others seem to.

When I began arbitrating I sought advice on opinion writing from three distinguished arbitrators. The first told me what he believed to be the appropriate format for an arbitration award. The second gave me a copy of one of his opinions and the advice that I should be far more careful to explain to losers why they lost than to winners why they won. The third arbitrator told me that when, somehow or other, he made his decision as to who was going to win and who was going to lose, no matter how agonizing it may have been for him to reach that decision, he wrote it as if there had never been the slightest doubt in his mind. To some degree, I have found the advice of each worthwhile.

Elements of the Opinion

What are the essential ingredients that make up the format of the opinion? First, an arbitration award has to have certain preliminaries: who the parties to the grievance are, when and where the hearing was held, who appeared for each party, who were the witnesses, whether briefs were filed and if so, when.

Second, I believe one must set forth a statement of the issue the parties stipulated, or, if they left the formulation of the issue up to you, the issue that you determined had to be answered in the particular case. Third, it is common to set out the contract clauses that bear upon the matter in contention. Fourth, all of us lay out the background of the dispute, who hit whom, so to speak. How did the case come to arbitration? What were the facts that led to the grievance coming forward? Fifth, one lays out the positions of the parties. What does each side argue with regard to these background facts in light of their specific contract clauses? Sixth, the arbitrator discusses these positions of the parties as they apply to the background and the relevant contract clauses, giving his or her considered conclusion on each argument made and the reasons for it. Seventh, the award, where the arbitrator says what is going to happen to this particular grievance.

That is the way I started out writing opinions, and I doubt many would fault me if I had continued to do so. But over the years, my view of format has changed a bit. I now believe that only three of these seven elements are immutable. First, all arbitration awards that I have ever seen begin with the essential preliminary matters, however one wishes to put them forward. Second, all arbitration awards that are worth anything must state clearly the issue that the arbitrator has been asked to decide, whether as it was stipulated by the parties or as determined by the arbitrator. Third, as a legal matter and as good common sense, all arbitration awards must conclude with an award, setting forth what is to happen to the present grievance, whether sustained or denied, and, if the former, what the remedy shall be.

I have become increasingly flexible about the rest of my seven elements, however. For example, one of the complaints most frequently leveled at arbitration opinions is that they are too long, either because the parties become confused wading through so much verbiage or because they feel that longer awards result in higher bills for them to pay. One of the things that I discovered shortened my opinions was elimination of the positions of the parties, which often had to be repeated in my discussion. Instead, I began to incorporate my statement of their positions within the discussion itself. I did not ignore what the parties had said about the contract as it applied to the factual background, but rather worked those positions into the discussion itself. I found that doing so saved both time and space, making the award more efficient.

Later I took over an umpireship where my predecessors had never separated any of the elements of the opinion, and this was the way the parties preferred it. So in that role I began writing awards that went directly from the issue to the background, incorporating the relevant facts, contentions, and contract provisions into the discussion. I found this format so satisfactory that I continued it in most cases, attempting to make facts, contentions, reasoning, and conclusions flow in coherent and logical fashion.

We often are asked why arbitrators write such long awards. Perhaps it is because many arbitrators do not have or take the time to write short ones. It is obviously much simpler to go through a transcript, repeating ad nauseum from it directly into one's dictating machine all of these matters without integration, summarization, or clarification. I think some busy arbitrators write very long opinions because they do not take the time to do a tight, neat, or concise job.

As to appropriate length, I have heard it said that most arbitration awards should take no more than eight to ten typewritten pages. My own awards are commonly of that general length. I make no claim of perfection, but I have never received complaints of either lack of clarity or prolixity.

The kind of opinion I write today varies depending upon the complexity of the case and some unarticulated considerations. Some cases are complex and multifaceted, requiring a considerable amount of structure to make the different elements clear. Other cases, probably the more simple ones, can be handled more coherently and logically by an opinion that flows in a continuous manner.

Either approach is acceptable. The technique of doing a good, integrated narrative is somewhat more difficult and probably requires more experience than breaking the opinion down into logical and discrete subdivisions. Most new arbitrators when writing their first opinions commonly do it in logical, structured fashion. It is easier for them, and makes it easier for others to follow their opinions.

Audience for the Opinion

A second consideration comes into play as soon as format has been decided upon. For whom do we write arbitration opinions? The Code gives some guidance: the responsible representatives of the parties, the grievant or grievants, the grievant's supervisor, and others involved in the collective bargaining relationship. I suppose the opinion should also be directed to other employees in the unit, other supervisors, and those at other echelons in the collective bargaining relationship who are or might subsequently be involved in a similar dispute.

I have occasionally wondered if we truly write for the grievant, because one must wonder from time to time whether the grievant ever sees or reads the opinion. In many cases, I suspect the grievant wants to know only whether he or she won or lost and may never see the opinion or award. Because of this suspicion, I have a few times put in my award, as have other arbitrators, that the grievant shall be given a copy of this opinion and award. This usually occurs in a case, such as a last chance reinstatement, in which the grievant gets some relief but we have some pretty crisp things to say about the need for the individual's behavior to improve. We want to make sure the grievant sees it and reads it.

When I do write for the grievant, I make sure I use simple, straightforward language, avoiding polysyllabic words with Latin and Greek roots. I avoid the Latin phrases that are part of the lawyer's training and experience. If you are writing for the grievant or for the supervisors, I think you should avoid all Latin, subtle witticisms, and scholarly overtones. It is not fair to the reader if a blue-collar worker is the object of your writing.

Who else do we write for? In some cases, we may be writing for a judge. Suppose you have a case that involves a minority grievant who is alleging discrimination and who happens to be represented by his personal counsel rather than his union's attorney. In the light of *Alexander* v. *Gardner-Denver*, 415 U.S. 36 (1974), I would think very carefully about whether I should enumerate the footnote 21 safeguards I had provided and whether I was writing for some court in an appellate situation. In such a case, I might write a wholly different type of opinion than I might if I were writing for the grievant or first-level supervisors.

It is conceivable that any opinion an arbitrator writes may be subject to judicial scrutiny. Most arbitrators are not concerned about that. It would justifiably rankle the parties if we were to take a routine three-day disciplinary layoff and write an opinion that included legal and arbitral citations to ensure that it would be upheld on appeal.

There are increasingly circumstances when we are writing for the NLRB. Most arbitrators get at least a case a year that has been *Collyer*-ized, either by the Board or some state instrumentality, and that we are deciding under both the contract and the law, *Collyer Insulated Wire,* 192 N.L.R.B. 837 (1971). Here too, I write a different kind of opinion than I would be if I were writing solely for the parties, for I know that my decision may well be subject to a *Spielberg* review, *Spielberg Mfg. Co.,* 112 N.L.R.B. 1080 (1955).

One also occasionally writes for other employers and unions who may look at published opinions to see how their problem might be resolved. That is the educational function of the opinion. Such cases are also written for students and other arbitrators. If we have a case involving an important principle, we would like the profession to know how we have decided this particular issue. There are contemporary cases that involve new and evolving areas of shop law, such as those involving marijuana in the plant. What distinctions should be made, if any, between possession and use? between one joint and one ounce? between sharing and selling? Does the kind of work environment make a difference, and whether it is public or private sector? Opinions dealing sensibly with these differences make up a new area of plant common law and may occasionally be written with publication in mind. I caution, however, that the parties should not be expected to pay an unusual fee just because the arbitrator intends to seek the parties' permission to publish.

Decisions may be rather didactic if we are trying to tell public employers how to administer a modern, progressive disciplinary procedure or public employee union representatives the circumstances under which arbitrators may or ordinarily will not reverse management's disciplinary actions. Indeed, in the public sector where they are now learning through experience things that have been well established in the private sector for twenty-five years, there is a natural tendency to write a more expository and educational opinion than if the same case arose in the private sector.

It may be that the audience to which we send these explanations of basic theory may take offense at our inclusion of what may seem extraneous advice. If so, it is their option to reject that arbitrator for future cases. In the public sector, it has been my experience that if the arbitrator is reasonably tactful and not offensive, the parties will generally return with future disputes. It is through such advice that individual parties have been encouraged to develop procedures that now appear universal in application. Even though they may not have agreed with what the arbitrator did, they now recognize that they are living in a new environment. Accordingly, they have adapted their procedures to the mainstream.

Finally, arbitrators write for themselves. They want to explain how they reached their decision. Decisions in baseball salary disputes, where the arbitrator fills in the blanks without explanation or opinion, have been a sore trial for some. More important, the obligation to write an opinion to support an award is an essential part of the decision-making process. If all we had to do was decide, I am afraid that in some cases we might become very sloppy. The regimen of putting forward the basic issues and arguments, going through the facts, and explaining to someone else why and how we decided, forces us to think the problem through far more clearly than if we simply had to say yes or no. I am ordinarily a fairly facile writer; once I have decided a grievance I ordinarily have no trouble writing my opinion. Once in a while, however, I cannot write a decision up. Almost invariably, this signals me that I have not thought it through as carefully as I should have. If I cannot write it, I have probably done something slipshod. I may even have the wrong answer. I then start all over again, rereading the transcript, the contract, and the briefs. In a sense, by paying for the time we spend writing, the parties are paying to ensure that they get the sort of careful thought to which they are entitled, protection for them and for us.

Strategy

I should reintroduce the importance of being careful to explain to losers why they lost. Winners are seldom a problem, having believed they were right all along. But for losers, who usually also thought their case had merit, it is important to explain why each of the arguments was not satisfactory. I am careful to mention each of the arguments put forth by the loser. I do not suggest they are all equal. There are major arguments that must be dealt with in care and detail. I avoid the easy way out about the other arguments, that they are "sterile and unworthy of further consideration." I think the loser would properly resent that approach, and so I mention each of the secondary arguments and say in a sentence or two why I do not find them persuasive. A man who loses may be unhappy with you because he lost, but if he thinks it was because you did not hear or understand one of his arguments then he has every right to be angry. For no reason other than self-protection, you must list each of the arguments and, in greater or lesser detail, explain why you did not find it persuasive.

On the subject of writing your opinion as though there were no doubt in your mind, I am reminded of one arbitration opinion in which the arbitrator with unusual and unnecessary honesty said that in the course of writing the opinion he had changed his mind on the merits three times. Even if it were true, I think it inappropriate to say such things.

You have to write the opinion as if a logical person, having carefully considered these facts, these circumstances, these clauses, and these contingencies could only have come to the conclusion that you did. You have to decide the case on the issues presented to you and leave it at that. I do not care for an award saying one side or the other wins the case on the facts presented here, but if the facts had been not A, but B or C, the award might well have gone the other way. This is clearly obiter dicta. The arbitrator is trying to resolve three or four different issues or situations for the parties when he or she was asked to answer only one.

Obiter Dicta

I do not like hints to the parties, though they are often tempting. Take an example. The employer has promulgated a rule.

The union attacks it on the basis that, under the contract and the past practice of the parties, it cannot be unilaterally promulgated but can be introduced only after discussion or negotiation with the union. That is the union's sole argument. The arbitrator concludes it lacks merit, for neither the contract nor the past practice make this an area of joint decision making. Hence the employer has the unilateral right to promulgate the new rule. But upon reflection, the arbitrator also concludes that the rule is totally unreasonable, even though the union never attacked it on that ground. The arbitrator avoids saying so, for that would be obiter dicta, but wants to give them a hint. So he or she concludes the opinion, "The sole issue presented here was whether the employer had the right unilaterally to promulgate this rule. The opinion is confined to disposing of that issue." The parties now scratch their heads and ask, "I wonder what the arbitrator had in mind."

Or even worse, I have seen this conclusion: "All the opinion passes on is the company's right to take unilateral action. The opinion expresses no view of the reasonableness of the action." In both cases, all the arbitrator has done is bought them another arbitration case, probably before another arbitrator who may or may not agree with you about the reasonableness of the rule. This strikes me as unfair and unreasonable to the parties. It is wholly inappropriate to write an opinion that suggests you might have ruled differently if X had occurred or Y been cited; this simply generates another grievance.

What about the situation where you believe the union is defending the case on the wrong grounds? What should you do? If you realize this at the hearing, you should at least ensure that the parties stipulate the issue in dispute. They then eliminate your discretional uncertainty, because you must answer the issue stipulated.

Alternatively, however, they may cede to you the formulation of the issue. In that case you have greater leniency to look at the whole situation, both the employer's unilateral right to promulgate the rule as well as the reasonableness of the rule per se. But in either event, you must answer the case before you and not start hinting or suggesting to the parties that, if circumstances were different or if they had argued the case in a different way, the result might have been different. Equally important, you should ordinarily avoid sending something back to the parties for them to negotiate. That too often creates even greater problems for them.

The finality and certainty of the arbitrator's opinion and award is of course tempered when one sits as a member of a tripartite panel on which there are also partisan members of the panel appointed by the parties. On some panels, the arbitrator studies the record and then returns for an executive session with the partisan members to discuss the whole case. In other situations, the neutral first prepares a draft opinion for the partisans' examination. In my experience, partisan members only seldom have suggestions before hand as to what ought to be in the opinion. But not infrequently, they will have criticisms or comments after they have seen the draft opinion. I never think anything I write is so perfect or so lucid that, if the parties jointly agree that some particular part of my opinion ought to be changed or deleted, they should not be accommodated. If it does not harm the essential justice and reasonableness of my award, I always accept my partisan members' suggestions.

In one case I had prepared a rather lengthy opinion on a very sensitive issue that was bound to come up in the parties' forthcoming negotiations. When the partisan arbitrators saw my draft they huddled, and then asked me to write instead that the grievance had been sustained and leave it at that. They did not tamper with the result. So that is what I wrote, giving up a day and a half of hard work for a one-sentence opinion that the parties felt more comfortable with. In dealing with a tripartite panel, I think a degree of flexibility, a degree of accommodation to the parties' legitimate needs, interests, and aspirations is certainly appropriate.

Despite my reservations about obiter dicta, the case occasionally arises when one feels compelled to go beyond the issue presented. For example, I dealt with a dispute where the issue was the employer's right to make an assignment out of classification. The employer took the position that it had negotiated and achieved the right to make flexible work assignments among the various job classifications and job descriptions spelled out in the agreement. The bargaining history and the contract language were clear: the employer had negotiated to retain this right. But the employer had assigned an employee to a task specifically reserved to employees holding another classification. Although the employer had negotiated for flexibility, I concluded it had not obtained the right to go so far as to justify the assignment in dispute. The union introduced an earlier arbitration decision from another arbitrator who found as I had that the employer had exceeded the contractual authority to make flexible transfers. The issue I had before me was exactly the same issue that confronted the arbitrator in the earlier case, except for a factual difference. I could simply, as did the first arbitrator, have said, "No, this particular transfer is prohibited." That would have been appropriate within the guidelines of limited decision making, but what would have been the result? Should the parties have had to go to arbitration every time they had a disputed assignment? I concluded that it would be appropriate to give them the outer parameters for such situations, namely, "The employer is entitled to the flexibility that was negotiated, but that this did not mean unlimited flexibility." I tried to define what I meant by unlimited without trying to decide issues not before me. I gave examples of assignments that I thought the employer could not make under the contract. Clearly all of this was obiter dicta, but it seemed to me that the parties, having been to arbitration twice already over an issue that was going to confront them repeatedly, were entitled to some kind of guidance. I do not know what they thought of the award. But I did not get any nasty letters from them, and I did get some other cases.

There are cases where every arbitrator has believed it necessary to say something to the parties about the particular situation that would not absolutely be called for in making the decision in the instant case. While we all know it is beyond our strict authority and improper as a matter of general principle, on occasion we all do it. I do not recommend it. It is not something you ought to rush into. We are not so all-wise that we ought to hasten to dispense justice and wisdom generally to the labor-management community. That is the job of the parties and their advocates. Despite the temptation to solve everyone's problems, avoid obiter dicta except as an infrequent last resort.

Reliance on Precedents

This raises the question of the extent to which arbitrators rely on prior decisions of other arbitrators. There are some very acceptable and respected arbitrators whose opinions read as if they were written by the Supreme Court. They are filled with footnotes and citations—of law, of NAA papers, and most commonly, cases by other arbitrators. They analyze others' opinions. These are busy arbitrators, but ones who clearly feel comfortable with a style in which their opinions are salted and peppered with footnotes and citations.

Yet I can point out other equally acceptable arbitrators who almost never cite another arbitrator's opinion or award. I rarely cite other arbitrators' opinions and awards, even if the parties cited them to me in their briefs or gave me copies of them at the hearing. I read them. I go to the library and look them up. But my experience is that seldom are they on all squares with the issue before me. They arose from different facts under another contract with different language. There is little point in going into a detailed explanation of why this or the other case cited by one of the parties is not persuasive in my decision. Unless it is a prior award received by these parties and under the same collective bargaining agreement, I rarely bother to cite or distinguish another case. In umpireships, however, you do have to deal with the precedents. The parties are asking for continuity among and between their umpires. If you are following or varying from what has been the rule in that relationship, you are obligated to advise them of this and the reasons for it.

A somewhat trickier problem arises when one of the parties cites a prior award that I rendered myself and has been published. They think "Aha! I've got him." I am obligated to deal with that case. I have no more difficulty than do courts in distinguishing my prior awards if I think a different answer is required in a later case. But it does require an explanation of why this is a different case and why a different answer is appropriate. Otherwise the parties will think you either inconsistent or idiotic.

Generally though, when the parties do not cite prior arbitration cases and the issue is one with which I have some familiarity, I do not go near the law library. I do not look through Elkouri and Elkouri (1973) or the reporting services on the subject. The parties are asking me what should be done with the particular issue before me. Only when I have an issue with which I am wholly unfamiliar might I look at other arbitrators' opinions, even without the parties citing them to me.

One party told me he was madder than hops at an arbitrator who had relied entirely on an award cited by the other side, quoting another arbitrator's reasoning and conclusions and buying that approach entirely. My informant said, "We knew the other arbitrator was around. We could have agreed on him if we wanted him. We didn't. We jointly selected X. But we wanted X's opinion, not that of another arbitrator whom we did not select. Now we do not really know what X thought about the issue we submitted to him." I can understand their irritation. If I were presented with a situation like that, even if another decision had been influential with me, I would write the case as if I were thinking about it de novo, with only the barest reference to the other decision.

Matters of Style

Some differences in opinions and awards are simply matters of arbitral style. For example, how do you handle the issue of credibility in writing an award? A group of four of us were chatting the other day on how you write up issues of credibility. There were three different opinions among the four. One, a former president of the NAA said flatly, "I don't go into it at all. I simply assert that I find the testimony of a certain witness credible, or I find the testimony of some other witness not to be credible, and therefore the award is as follows." Another arbitrator, also a former NAA president, said he felt obligated to explain the basis for his judgment. I note that in his published awards, he goes to exhaustive length to describe the demeanor of the witnesses, such as "he was halting in the way he responded to certain questions," "he flushed as he replied," or "she answered easily." He tries to detail to the reader why he found a particular witness incredible or another believable. My own practice is not to go to that length, but I do not encapsulate my conclusion in a sentence. I try in one short paragraph to explain that based on certain considerations of credibility and motivation, to say nothing of demeanor, I find as follows on a credibility issue. Further, having abjured the mantle of omniscience many years ago, I prefer objective evidence, if I can find it, to any personal subjective conclusion. But this is a matter of style, and many excellent arbitrators differ in style.

I know an arbitrator who, if he has a transcript, invariably quotes at least once from the transcript in his opinion. I noticed this and asked why. He responded quickly, "If the parties want to pay for a transcript, I always read it. But this costs them an extra day of study time. I want them to know I read it, and therefore I always quote from it at least once in my opinion." I find this somewhat unnecessary, but this too is a very acceptable arbitrator whom I am reluctant to challenge.

There are all sorts of nuances in the way we write our opinions. While we do not want to create fodder for future arbitration cases or to give the language to one side and the decision to the other, there may be a tendency for the parties to read intended or unintended hints into the language we use. My wife once asked me, "Why, at the end of some opinions, do you just state your conclusion outright, while in other cases you write 'After careful consideration I have concluded'?" I had never realized it. After thinking it over, I concluded I used the phrase "after careful consideration" to signal the parties that I had found this one hard. But the parties do not need it and neither do I. I have tried to stop it because it is a verbal signal having no meaning to them. Even if I found the case hard to decide—and some cases *are* harder than others—why so state?

The wording of the award sometimes causes some people problems. I try to keep my awards simple: "The grievance is denied" or "The grievance is sustained," and I state what shall be the remedy. I do not attempt, as some arbitrators do, to encapsulate my whole opinion and its logic into a sentence in the award itself. I wrote the opinion to explain the award. I try to write with care, precision, and understandability to winner and loser alike. If so, I can then just specify in conclusion solely that the grievance is denied or granted. Any summarizing sentence may be misleading. It may be used by someone as a precedent, or it may exclude a pivotal fact that should be determinative in another later case.

The Code of Professional Responsibility says our awards shall be definite, certain, and as concise as possible. Finality, which used to be in the earlier revision of the Code, is now omitted. I believe that change occurred because the decision may not appropriately be final if there is a question outstanding, for example, the quantum of back pay. Rarely is the arbitrator given adequate information at the hearing on a termination case as to what the appropriate back pay amount should be if the termination was not for just cause. I do not even seek such information at hearings on discharge cases. Hence my award in a reinstatement case is that the grievant shall be reinstated and, on some occasions, be offered back pay for a certain period of time. From that back pay I may offset certain amounts of interim compensation. State laws and arbitral practices vary as to what offsets from back pay are appropriate. If the parties fall into a later disagreement as to the appropriate amount of back pay, as they occasionally do, they still have a dispute. If I had rendered a final decision, I would no longer have jurisdiction on the issue of the appropriate amount of back pay. Increasingly, I have heard parties criticize arbitrators because we have not retained jurisdiction in reinstatement cases. (In one case involving an award of reinstatement, the arbitrator rendered a final decision. The parties then went all the way to the Michigan Supreme Court to find out who should settle their remaining dispute over this remedy. The court said the original arbitrator—who then settled it in an hour!) It is now my practice and increasingly that of other arbitrators to retain jurisdiction to resolve a subsequent dispute as to the specific terms of the remedy or the appropriate amount of back pay.

The reasons I do not take evidence on the back pay issue at the hearing are that it unduly lengthens the hearing and that the parties often do not wish me to do so. The employer does not want to get into it because it somehow thinks that if the subject of back pay is even discussed it will weaken the case for just cause. Neither party may know whether the grievant mitigated damages, and if so what he or she earned. Moreover, the parties usually assume that if the issue of back pay arises they can work these problems out.

When I retain jurisdiction over an issue of back pay, I expect the parties to work it out themselves. But if they cannot, they come back to me. I do not usually hold a new hearing. Instead, I make a conference telephone call, or they each write me a letter and say what the argument is. I then write them a simple letter and straighten the problem out. I do make a deadline for parties to get back to me on any issue of remedy. I hold jurisdiction only to a specific date. I state in my original award that if I do not hear from them by that date, the matter will be considered closed. No good results from letting such matters drag out.

Appendix

Code of Professional Responsibility for Arbitrators of Labor-Management Disputes of the National Academy of Arbitrators, the American Arbitration Association, and the Federal Mediation and Conciliation Service

Preamble

Background

Voluntary arbitration rests upon the mutual desire of manage-   1
ment and labor in each collective bargaining relationship to develop
procedures for dispute settlement which meet their own particular
needs and obligations. No two voluntary systems, therefore, are likely
to be identical in practice. Words used to describe arbitrators (Arbitrator, Umpire, Impartial Chairman, Chairman of Arbitration Board,
etc.) may suggest typical approaches but actual differences within any
general type of arrangement may be as great as distinctions often
made among the several types.

Some arbitration and related procedures, however, are not the   2
product of voluntary agreement. These procedures, primarily but
not exclusively applicable in the public sector, sometimes utilize other
third party titles (Fact Finder, Impasse Panel, Board of Inquiry, etc.).
These procedures range all the way from arbitration prescribed by
statute to arrangements substantially indistinguishable from voluntary
procedures.

The standards of professional responsibility set forth in this   3
Code are designed to guide the impartial third party serving in these
diverse labor-management relationships.

Scope of Code

4   This Code is a privately developed set of standards of professional behavior. It applies to voluntary arbitration of labor-management grievance disputes and of disputes concerning new or revised
contract terms. Both "ad hoc" and "permanent" varieties of voluntary
arbitration, private and public sector, are included. To the extent
relevant in any specific case, it also applies to advisory arbitration,
impasse resolution panels, arbitration prescribed by statutes, factfinding, and other special procedures.

5   The word "arbitrator," as used hereinafter in the Code, is intended
to apply to any impartial person, irrespective of specific title, who serves
in a labor-management dispute procedure in which there is conferred
authority to decide issues or to make formal recommendations.

6   The Code is not designed to apply to mediation or conciliation,
as distinguished from arbitration, nor to other procedures in which
the third party is not authorized in advance to make decisions or
recommendations. It does not apply to partisan representatives on
tripartite boards. It does not apply to commercial arbitration or to
other uses of arbitration outside the labor-management dispute area.

Format of Code

7   **Bold Face** type, sometimes including explanatory material, is
used to set forth general principles. *Italics* are used for amplification
of general principles. Ordinary type is used primarily for illustrative
or explanatory comment.

Application of Code

8   Faithful adherence by an arbitrator to this Code is basic to professional responsibility.

9   The National Academy of Arbitrators will expect its members to
be governed in their professional conduct by this Code and stands
ready, through its Committee on Ethics and Grievances, to advise its
members as to the Code's interpretation. The American Arbitration
Association and the Federal Mediation and Conciliation Service will
apply the Code to the arbitrators on their rosters in cases handled
under their respective appointment or referral procedures. Other arbitrators and administrative agencies may, of course, voluntarily
adopt the Code and be governed by it.

10   In interpreting the Code and applying it to charges of professional misconduct, under existing or revised procedures of the National Academy of Arbitrators and of the administrative agencies, it
should be recognized that while some of its standards express ethical
principles basic to the arbitration profession, others rest less on ethics

than on considerations of good practice. Experience has shown the difficulty of drawing rigid lines of distinction between ethics and good practice and this Code does not attempt to do so. Rather, it leaves the gravity of alleged misconduct and the extent to which ethical standards have been violated to be assessed in the light of the facts and circumstances of each particular case.

1. Arbitrator's Qualifications and Responsibilities to the Profession

A. General Qualifications

1. **Essential personal qualifications of an arbitrator include honesty, integrity, impartiality and general competence in labor relations matters.**   11

An arbitrator must demonstrate ability to exercise these personal qualities faithfully and with good judgment, both in procedural matters and in substantive decisions.   12

   a. Selection by mutual agreement of the parties or direct designation by an administrative agency are the effective methods of appraisal of this combination of an individual's potential and performance, rather than the fact of placement on a roster of an administrative agency or membership in a professional association of arbitrators.   13

2. **An arbitrator must be as ready to rule for one party as for the other on each issue, either in a single case or in a group of cases. Compromise by an arbitrator for the sake of attempting to achieve personal acceptability is unprofessional.**   14

B. Qualifications for Special Cases

1. **An arbitrator must decline appointment, withdraw, or request technical assistance when he or she decides that a case is beyond his or her competence.**   15

   a. An arbitrator may be qualified generally but not for specialized assignments. Some types of incentive, work standard, job evaluation, welfare program, pension, or insurance cases may require specialized knowledge, experience or competence. Arbitration of contract terms also may require distinctive background and experience.   16

   b. Effective appraisal by an administrative agency or by an arbitrator of the need for special qualifications requires that both   17 parties make known the special nature of the case prior to appointment of the arbitrator.

C. Responsibilities to the Profession

18   **1. An arbitrator must uphold the dignity and integrity of the office and endeavor to provide effective service to the parties.**

19   a. To this end, an arbitrator should keep current with principles, practices and developments that are relevant to his or her own field of arbitration practice.

20   **2. An experienced arbitrator should cooperate in the training of new arbitrators.**

21   **3. An arbitrator must not advertise or solicit arbitration assignments.**

22   a. It is a matter of personal preference whether an arbitrator includes "Labor Arbitrator" or similar notation on letterheads, cards, or announcements. *It is inappropriate, however, to include memberships or offices held in professional societies or listings on rosters of administrative agencies.*

23   b. *Information provided for published biographical sketches, as well as that supplied to administrative agencies, must be accurate.* Such information may include membership in professional organizations (including reference to significant offices held), and listings on rosters of administrative agencies.

2. Responsibilities to the Parties

A. Recognition of Diversity in Arbitration Arrangements

24   **1. An arbitrator should conscientiously endeavor to understand and observe, to the extent consistent with professional responsibility, the significant principles governing each arbitration system in which he or she serves.**

25   a. Recognition of special features of a particular arbitration arrangement can be essential with respect to procedural matters and may influence other aspects of the arbitration process.

26   **2. Such understanding does not relieve an arbitrator from a corollary responsibility to seek to discern and refuse to lend approval or consent to any collusive attempt by the parties to use arbitration for an improper purpose.**

B. Required Disclosures

1. **Before accepting an appointment, an arbitrator must disclose** 27
directly or through the administrative agency involved, any current
or past managerial, representational, or consultative relationship
with any company or union involved in a proceeding in which he
or she is being considered for appointment or has been tentatively
designated to serve. Disclosure must also be made of any pertinent
pecuniary interest.

> a. The duty to disclose includes membership on a Board of 28
> Directors, full-time or part-time service as a representative or
> advocate, consultation work for a fee, current stock or bond
> ownership (other than mutual fund shares or appropriate trust
> arrangements) or any other pertinent form of managerial, finan-
> cial or immediate family interest in the company or union
> involved.

2. **When an arbitrator is serving concurrently as an advocate** 29
for or representative of other companies or unions in labor rela-
tions matters, or had done so in recent years, he or she must dis-
close such activities before accepting appointment as an arbitrator.

An arbitrator must disclose such activities to an administrative 30
agency if he or she is on that agency's active roster or seeks place-
ment on a roster. Such disclosure then satisifies this requirement
for cases handled under that agency's referral.

> a. It is not necessary to disclose names of clients or other spe- 31
> cific details. It is necessary to indicate the general nature of the
> labor relations advocacy or representational work involved,
> whether for companies or unions or both, and a reasonable ap-
> proximation of the extent of such activity.

> b. *An arbitrator on an administrative agency's roster has a continuing* 32
> *obligation to notify the agency of any significant changes pertinent to this*
> *requirement.*

> c. When an administrative agency is not involved, an arbitrator 33
> must make such disclosure directly unless he or she is certain
> that both parties to the case are fully aware of such activities.

3. **An arbitrator must not permit personal relationships to af-** 34
fect decision-making.

Prior to acceptance of an appointment, an arbitrator must dis- 35
close to the parties or to the administrative agency involved any
close personal relationship or other circumstance, in addition to
those specifically mentioned earlier in this section, which might rea-
sonably raise a question as to the arbitrator's impartiality.

36   a. Arbitrators establish personal relationships with many company and union representatives, with fellow arbitrators, and with fellow members of various professional associations. There should be no attempt to be secretive about such friendships or acquaintances but disclosure is not necessary unless some feature of a particular relationship might reasonably appear to impair impartiality.

37   **4. If the circumstances requiring disclosure are not known to the arbitrator prior to acceptance of appointment, disclosure must be made when such circumstances become known to the arbitrator.**

38   **5. The burden of disclosure rests on the arbitrator. After appropriate disclosure, the arbitrator may serve if both parties so desire. If the arbitrator believes or perceives that there is a clear conflict of interest, he or she should withdraw, irrespective of the expressed desires of the parties.**

C. Privacy of Arbitration

39   **1. All significant aspects of an arbitration proceeding must be treated by the arbitrator as confidential unless this requirement is waived by both parties or disclosure is required or permitted by law.**

40   a. Attendance at hearings by persons not representing the parties or invited by either or both of them should be permitted only when the parties agree or when an applicable law requires or permits. Occasionally, special circumstances may require that an arbitrator rule on such matters as attendance and degree of participation of counsel selected by a grievant.

41   b. *Discussion of a case at any time by an arbitrator with persons not involved directly should be limited to situations where advance approval or consent of both parties is obtained or where the identity of the parties and details of the case are sufficiently obscured to eliminate any realistic probability of identification.*

42   A commonly recognized exception is discussion of a problem in a case with a fellow arbitrator. *Any such discussion does not relieve the arbitrator who is acting in the case from sole responsibility for the decision and the discussion must be considered as confidential.*

43   Discussion of aspects of a case in a classroom without prior specific approval of the parties is not a violation provided the arbitrator is satisfied that there is no breach of essential confidentiality.

44   c. *It is a violation of professional responsibility for an arbitrator to make public an award without the consent of the parties.*

An arbitrator may request but not press the parties for consent to pub-   45
lish an opinion. Such a request should normally not be made until
after the award has been issued to the parties.

d. It is not improper for an arbitrator to donate arbitration   46
files to a library of a college, university or similar institution
without prior consent of all the parties involved. When the circumstances permit, there should be deleted from such donations
any cases concerning which one or both of the parties have expressed a desire for privacy. As an additional safeguard, an arbitrator may also decide to withhold recent cases or indicate to the
donee a time interval before such cases can be made generally
available.

e. *Applicable laws, regulations, or practices of the parties may permit*   47
or even require exceptions to the above noted principles of privacy.

D. Personal Relationships with the Parties

1. An arbitrator must make very reasonable effort to conform   48
to arrangements required by an administrative agency or mutually
desired by the parties regarding communications and personal rela-
tionships with the parties.

a. *Only an "arm's-length" relationship may be acceptable to the parties*   49
in some arbitration arrangements or may be required by the rules of an
administrative agency. The arbitrator should then have no contact of
consequence with representatives of either party while handling a case
without the other party's presence or consent.

b. *In other situations, both parties may want communications and per-*   50
sonal relationships to be less formal. It is then appropriate for the arbi-
trator to respond accordingly.

E. Jurisdiction

1. An arbitrator must observe faithfully both the limitations   51
and inclusions of the jurisdiction conferred by an agreement or
other submission under which he or she serves.

2. A direct settlement by the parties of some or all issues in a   52
case, at any stage of the proceedings, must be accepted by the arbi-
trator as relieving him or her of further jurisdiction over such
issues.

F. Mediation by an Arbitrator

1. When the parties wish at the outset to give an arbitrator au-   53
thority both to mediate and to decide or submit recommendations

regarding residual issues, if any, they should advise the arbitrator prior to appointment. If the appointment is accepted, the arbitrator must perform a mediation role consistent with the circumstances of the case.

54   a. Direct appointments, also, may require a dual role as mediator and arbitrator of residual issues. This is most likely to occur in some public sector cases.

55   **2. When a request to mediate is first made after appointment, the arbitrator may either accept or decline a mediation role.**

56   a. *Once arbitration has been invoked, either party normally has a right to insist that the process be continued to decision.*

57   b. *If one party requests that the arbitrator mediate and the other party objects, the arbitrator should decline the request.*

58   c. *An arbitrator is not precluded from making a suggestion that he or she mediate. To avoid the possibility of improper pressure, the arbitrator should not so suggest unless it can be discerned that both parties are likely to be receptive. In any event, the arbitrator's suggestion should not be pursued unless both parties readily agree.*

G. Reliance by an Arbitrator on Other Arbitration Awards or on Independent Research

59   **1. An arbitrator must assume full personal responsibility for the decision in each case decided.**

60   a. *The extent, if any, to which an arbitrator properly may rely on precedent, on guidance of other awards, or on independent research is dependent primarily on the policies of the parties on these matters, as expressed in the contract, or other agreement, or at the hearing.*

61   b. When the mutual desires of the parties are not known or when the parties express differing opinions or policies, the arbitrator may exercise discretion as to these matters, consistent with acceptance of full personal responsibility for the award.

H. Use of Assistants

62   **1. An arbitrator must not delegate any decision-making function to another person without consent of the parties.**

63   a. *Without prior consent of the parties, an arbitrator may use the services of an assistant for research, clerical duties, or preliminary drafting under the direction of the arbitrator, which does not involve the delegation of any decision-making function.*

64   b. *If an arbitrator is unable, because of time limitations or other reasons, to handle all decision-making aspects of a case, it is not a violation of*

professional responsibility to suggest to the parties an allocation of responsibility between the arbitrator and an assistant or associate. The arbitrator must not exert pressure on the parties to accept such a suggestion.

I. Consent Awards

1. Prior to issuance of an award, the parties may jointly request the arbitrator to include in the award certain agreements between them, concerning some or all of the issues. If the arbitrator believes that a suggested award is proper, fair, sound, and lawful, it is consistent with professional responsibility to adopt it. 65

    a. *Before complying with such a request, an arbitrator must be certain that he or she understands the suggested settlement adequately in order to be able to appraise its terms. If it appears that pertinent facts or circumstances may not have been disclosed, the arbitrator should take the initiative to assure that all significant aspects of the case are fully understood. To this end, the arbitrator may request additional specific information and may question witnesses at a hearing.* 66

J. Avoidance of Delay

1. It is a basic professional responsibility of an arbitrator to plan his or her work schedule so that present and future commitments will be fulfilled in a timely manner. 67

    a. *When planning is upset for reasons beyond the control of the arbitrator, he or she, nevertheless, should exert every reasonable effort to fulfill all commitments. If this is not possible, prompt notice at the arbitrator's initiative should be given to all parties affected. Such notices should include reasonably accurate estimates of any additional time required. To the extent possible, priority should be given to cases in process so that other parties may make alternative arbitration arrangements.* 68

2. An arbitrator must cooperate with the parties and with any administrative agency involved in avoiding delays. 69

    a. *An arbitrator on the active roster of an administrative agency must take the initiative in advising the agency of any scheduling difficulties that he or she can forsee.* 70

    b. *Requests for services, whether received directly or through an administrative agency, should be declined if the arbitrator is unable to schedule a hearing as soon as the parties wish. If the parties, nevertheless, jointly desire to obtain the services of the arbitrator and the arbitrator agrees, arrangements should be made by agreement that the arbitrator confidently expects to fulfill.* 71

    c. *An arbitrator may properly seek to persuade the parties to alter or eliminate arbitration procedures or tactics that cause unnecessary delay.* 72

73   **3. Once the case record has been closed, an arbitrator must adhere to the time limits for an award, as stipulated in the labor agreement or as provided by regulation of an administrative agency or as otherwise agreed.**

74   a. *If an appropriate award cannot be rendered within the required time, it is incumbent on the arbitrator to seek an extension of time from the parties.*

75   b. If the parties have agreed upon abnormally short time limits for an award after a case is closed, the arbitrator should be so advised by the parties or by the administrative agency involved, prior to acceptance of appointment.

K. Fees and Expenses

76   **1. An arbitrator occupies a position of trust in respect to the parties and the administrative agencies. In charging for services and expenses, the arbitrator must be governed by the same high standards of honor and integrity that apply to all other phases of his or her work.**

77   **An arbitrator must endeavor to keep total charges for services and expenses reasonable and consistent with the nature of the case or cases decided.**

78   **Prior to appointment, the parties should be aware of or be able readily to determine all significant aspects of an arbitrator's bases for charges for fees and expenses.**

79   a. *Services Not Primarily Chargeable on a Per Diem Basis*

By agreement with the parties, the financial aspects of many "permanent" arbitration assignments, of some interest disputes, and of some "ad hoc" grievance assignments do not include a per diem fee for services as a primary part of the total understanding. *In such situations, the arbitrator must adhere faithfully to all agreed-upon arrangements governing fees and expenses.*

80   b. *Per Diem Basis for Charges for Services*

(1) *When an arbitrator's charges for services are determined primarily by a stipulated per diem fee, the arbitrator should establish in advance his or her bases for application of such per diem fee and for determination of reimbursable expenses.*

81   *Practices established by an arbitrator should include the basis for charges, if any, for:*
(a) hearing time, including the application of the stipulated basic per diem hearing fee to hearing days of varying lengths;
(b) study time;

(c) necessary travel time when not included in charges for hearing time;

(d) postponement or cancellation of hearings by the parties and the circumstances in which such charges will normally be assessed or waived;

(e) office overhead expenses (secretarial, telephone, postage, etc.);

(f) the work of paid assistants or associates.

(2) *Each arbitrator should be guided by the following general principles:*   82

(a) *Per diem charges for a hearing should not be in excess of actual time spent or allocated for the hearing.*   83

(b) *Per diem charges for study time should not be in excess of actual time spent.*   84

(c) *Any fixed ratio of study days to hearing days, not agreed to specifically by the parties, is inconsistent with the per diem method of charges for services.*   85

(d) *Charges for expenses must not be in excess of actual expenses normally reimbursable and incurred in connection with the case or cases involved.*   86

(e) *When time or expense are involved for two or more sets of parties on the same day or trip, such time or expense charges should be appropriately prorated.*   87

(f) *An arbitrator may stipulate in advance a minimum charge for a hearing without violation of (a) or (e) above.*   88

(3) *An arbitrator on the active roster of an administrative agency must file with the agency his or her individual bases for determination of fees and expenses of the agency so requires. Thereafter, it is the responsibility of each such arbitrator to advise the agency promptly of any change in any basis for charges.*   89

Such filing may be in the form of answers to a questionnaire devised by an agency or by any other method adopted by or approved by an agency.   90

Having supplied an administrative agency with the information noted above, an arbitrator's professional responsibility of disclosure under this Code with respect to fees and expenses has been satisfied for cases referred by that agency.   91

(4) *If an administrative agency promulgates specific standards with respect to any of these matters which are in addition to or more restrictive than an individual arbitrator's standards, an arbitrator on its active roster must observe the agency standards for cases handled under the auspices of that agency, or decline to serve.*   92

93   (5) *When an arbitrator is contacted directly by the parties for a case or cases, the arbitrator has a professional responsibility to respond to questions by submitting his or her bases for charges for fees and expenses.*

94   (6) *When it is known to the arbitrator that one or both of the parties cannot afford normal charges, it is consistent with professional responsibility to charge lesser amounts to both parties or to one of the parties if the other party is made aware of the difference and agrees.*

95   (7) *If an arbitrator concludes that the total of charges derived from his or her normal basis of calculation is not compatible with the case decided, it is consistent with professional responsibility to charge lesser amounts to both parties.*

96   **2. An arbitrator must maintain adequate records to support charges for services and expenses and must make an accounting to the parties or to an involved administrative agency on request.**

3. Responsibilities to Administrative Agencies

A. General Responsibilities

97   **1. An arbitrator must be candid, accurate, and fully responsive to an administrative agency concerning his or her qualifications, availability, and all other pertinent matters.**

98   **2. An arbitrator must observe policies and rules of an administrative agency in cases referred by that agency.**

99   **3. An arbitrator must not seek to influence an administrative agency by any improper means, including gifts, or other inducements to agency personnel.**

100   a. It is not improper for a person seeking placement on a roster to request references from individuals having knowledge of the applicant's experience and qualifications.

101   b. Arbitrators should recognize that the primary responsibility of an administrative agency is to serve the parties.

4. Prehearing Conduct

102   **1. All prehearing matters must be handled in a manner that fosters complete impartiality by the arbitrator.**

103   a. The primary purpose of prehearing discussions involving the arbitrator is to obtain agreement on procedural matters so

that the hearing can proceed without unnecessary obstacles. If differences of opinion should arise during such discussions and, particularly, if such differences appear to impinge on substantive matters, the circumstances will suggest whether the matter can be resolved informally or may require a prehearing conference or, more rarely, a formal preliminary hearing. When an administrative agency handles some or all aspects of the arrangements prior to a hearing, the arbitrator will become involved only if differences of some substance arise.

b. *Copies of any prehearing correspondence between the arbitrator and either party must be made available to both parties.*   104

5. Hearing Conduct

A. General Principles

1. An arbitrator must provide a fair and adequate hearing which assures that both parties have sufficient opportunity to present their respective evidence and argument.   105

a. *Within the limits of this responsibility, an arbitrator should conform to the various types of hearing procedures desired by the parties.*   106

b. An arbitrator may: encourage stipulations of fact; restate the substance of issues or arguments to promote or verify understanding; question the parties' representatives or witnesses, when necessary or advisable, to obtain additional pertinent information; and request that the parties submit additional evidence, either at the hearing or by subsequent filing.   107

c. *An arbitrator should not intrude into a party's presentation so as to prevent that party from putting forward its case fairly and adequately.*   108

B. Transcripts or Recordings

1. Mutual agreement of the parties to use or non-use of a transcript must be respected by the arbitrator.   109

a. *A transcript is the official record of a hearing only when both parties agree to a transcript or an applicable law or regulation so provides.*   110

b. An arbitrator may seek to persuade the parties to avoid use of a transcript, or to use a transcript if the nature of the case appears to require one. *However, if an arbitrator intends to make his or her appointment to a case contingent on mutual agreement to a transcript, that requirement must be made known to both parties prior to appointment.*   111

112   c. If the parties do not agree to a transcript, an arbitrator may permit one party to take a transcript at its own cost. The arbitrator may also make appropriate arrangements under which the other party may have access to a copy, if a copy is provided to the arbitrator.

113   d. Without prior approval, an arbitrator may seek to use his or her own tape recorder to supplement note taking. The arbitrator should not insist on such a tape recording if either or both parties object.

C. Ex Parte Hearings

114   **1. In determining whether to conduct an ex parte hearing, an arbitrator must consider relevant legal, contractual, and other pertinent circumstances.**

115   **2. An arbitrator must be certain, before proceeding ex parte, that the party refusing or failing to attend the hearing has been given adequate notice of the time, place, and purposes of the hearing.**

D. Plant Visits

116   **1. An arbitrator should comply with a request of any party that he or she visit a work area pertinent to the dispute prior to, during, or after a hearing. An arbitrator may also initiate such a request.**

117   a. *Procedures for such visits should be agreed to by the parties in consultation with the arbitrator.*

E. Bench Decisions or Expedited Awards

118   **1. When an arbitrator understands, prior to acceptance of appointment, that a bench decision is expected at the conclusion of the hearing, the arbitrator must comply with the understanding unless both parties agree otherwise.**

119   a. *If notice of the parties' desire for a bench decision is not given prior to the arbitrator's acceptance of the case, issuance of such a bench decision is discretionary.*

120   b. *When only one party makes the request and the other objects, the arbitrator should not render a bench decision except under most unusual circumstances.*

121   **2. When an arbitrator understands, prior to acceptance of appointment, that a concise written award is expected within a stated time period after the hearing, the arbitrator must comply with the understanding unless both parties agree otherwise.**

6. Post Hearing Conduct

A. Post Hearing Briefs and Submissions

1. An arbitrator must comply with mutual agreements in respect to the filing or nonfiling of post hearing briefs or submissions.   122

a. An arbitrator, in his or her discretion, may either suggest the filing of post hearing briefs or other submissions or suggest that none be filed.   123

b. When the parties disagree as to the need for briefs, an arbitrator may permit filing but may determine a reasonable time limitation.   124

2. An arbitrator must not consider a post hearing brief or submission that has not been provided to the other party.   125

B. Disclosure of Terms of Award

1. An arbitrator must not disclose a prospective award to either party prior to its simultaneous issuance to both parties or explore possible alternative awards unilaterally with one party, unless both parties so agree.   126

a. Partisan members of tripartite boards may know prospective terms of an award in advance of its issuance. Similar situations may exist in other less formal arrangements mutually agreed to by the parties. In any such situation, the arbitrator should determine and observe the mutually desired degree of confidentiality.   127

C. Awards and Opinions

1. The award should be definite, certain, and as concise as possible.   128

a. When an opinion is required, factors to be considered by an arbitrator include: desirability of brevity, consistent with the nature of the case and any expressed desires of the parties; need to use a style and form that is understandable to responsible representatives of the parties, to the grievant and supervisors, and to others in the collective bargaining relationship; necessity of meeting the significant issues; forthrightness to an extent not harmful to the relationship of the parties; and avoidance of gratuitous advice or discourse not essential to disposition of the issues.   129

D. Clarification or Interpretation of Awards

1. No clarification or interpretation of an award is permissible without the consent of both parties.   130

131   2. Under agreements which permit or require clarification or interpretation of an award, an arbitrator must afford both parties an opportunity to be heard.

E. Enforcement of Award

132   1. The arbitrator's responsibility does not extend to the enforcement of an award.

133   2. In view of the professional and confidential nature of the arbitration relationship, an arbitrator should not voluntarily participate in legal enforcement proceedings.

References

Aaron, Benjamin
    1955   "The Uses of the Past in Arbitration." *Arbitration To-day*. Washington, D.C.: Bureau of National Affairs.
    1978   *Final Offer Arbitration Awards in Michigan 1973–1977*. Ann Arbor, Mich.: Institute of Labor and Industrial Relations, University of Michigan–Wayne State University.

Barnum, Darold T.
    1971   "From Private to Public Labor Relations in Urban Transit." *Industrial and Labor Relations Review* 25, 95.

Bloch, Richard I.
    1978   "Some Far-Sighted Views of Myopia." *Arbitration—1977*. Proceedings of the Thirtieth Annual Meeting, National Academy of Arbitrators. Washington, D.C.: Bureau of National Affairs.

Bowers, Mollie Heath
    1973   "A Study of Arbitration and Collective Bargaining in the Public Services in Michigan and Pennsylvania." Ph.D. diss., Cornell University.

Brown, Douglass V.
    1949   "Management Rights and the Collective Bargaining Agreement." Proceedings of the First Annual Meeting of the Industrial Relations Research Association. Champaign, Ill.: IRRA.

Cardozo, Benjamin N.
    1921   *Nature of the Judicial Process*. Lecture 4. New Haven: Yale University Press.

Cox, Archibald
    1958   "The Legal Nature of Collective Bargaining Agreements." 57 *Michigan Law Review* 1.
    1959   "Reflections upon Labor Arbitration in the Light of the Lincoln Mills Case." In *Arbitration and the Law.* Washington, D.C.: Bureau of National Affairs.

Cox, Archibald, and Dunlop, John
    1950   "The Duty to Bargain Collectively during the Term of an Existing Agreement." 63 *Harvard Law Review* 1097.

Derber, Milton; Chalmers, W. E.; and Stagner, R.
    1958   "The Labor Contract: Provision and Practice." *Personnel Magazine* (Jan.–Feb.).

Edwards, Harry T.
    1976a   "Arbitration of Employment Discrimination Cases: An Empirical Study." Proceedings of the Twenty-eighth Annual Meeting, National Academy of Arbitrators, Washington, D.C.: Bureau of National Affairs.
    1976b   "Arbitration of Employment Discrimination Cases: A Proposal for Employee and Union Representatives." 27 *Labor Law Journal* 265–77 (May 1976).
    1977a   "The Coming of Age of the Burger Court: Labor Law Decisions of the Supreme Court during the 1976 Term." 19 *Boston College Law Review* 1.
    1977b   "Labor Arbitration at the Crossroads: The 'Common Law of the Shop' versus External Law." 32 *Arbitration Journal* 65 (June 1977).
    1980   "Affirmative Action or Reverse Discrimination: The Head and Tail of *Weber.*" 13 *Creighton Law Review* 713 (1980).

Edwards, Harry T., and Zaretsky, Barry L.
    1975   "Preferential Remedies for Employment Discrimination." 74 *Michigan Law Review* 1 (1975).

Elkouri, Frank, and Elkouri, Edna Asper
    1960   *How Arbitration Works.* Washington, D.C.: Bureau of National Affairs.
    1973   *How Arbitration Works.* 3d ed. Washington, D.C.: Bureau of National Affairs.

Feller, David
    1976   "The Coming End of Arbitration's Golden Age." In *Arbitration-1976.* Proceedings of the Twenty-ninth Annual Meeting, National Academy of Arbitrators. Washington, D.C.: Bureau of National Affairs.

Fletcher, Betty
    1982   "Arbitration of Title VII Claims: Some Judicial Perceptions." In *Arbitration Issues for the Eighties*. Proceedings of the Thirty-fourth Annual Meeting, National Academy of Arbitrators. Washington, D.C.: Bureau of National Affairs.

Frank, Jerome
    1934   "Experimental Jurisprudence and the New Deal." 78 *Congressional Record* 12412.
    1949   *Law and the Modern Mind*. New York: Coward-McCann.

Goldberg, Arthur J.
    1956   "Management's Reserved Rights: A Labor View." In *Management Rights and the Arbitration Process*. Proceedings of the Ninth Annual Meeting, National Academy of Arbitrators, edited by Jean T. McKelvey. Washington, D.C.: Bureau of National Affairs.

Gorman, Robert A.
    1976   *Basic Text on Labor Law*. St. Paul: West Publishing Co.

Harvard Law Review
    1982   "The Supreme Court 1981 Term." 96 *Harvard Law Review* 287–88.

Hill, James C.
    1956   "Summary." In *Management Rights and the Arbitration Process*. Proceedings of the Ninth Annual Meeting, National Academy of Arbitrators, edited by Jean T. McKelvey. Washington D.C.: Bureau of National Affairs.

Hill, Lee H., and Hook, Charles L., Jr.
    1945   *Management at the Bargaining Table*. New York: McGraw-Hill.

Holly, J. Fred
    1957   *The Arbitration of Discharge Cases: A Case Study in Critical Issues in Labor Arbitration*. Washington, D.C.: Bureau of National Affairs.

Jones, Edgar A., Jr.
    1966.   "Evidentiary Concepts in Labor Arbitration: Some Modern Variations on Ancient Legal Themes." 13 *U.C.L.A. Law Review* 1241.
    1968.   Series on discovery procedures in collective bargaining disputes. 116 *University of Pennsylvania Law Review* 571, 830, 1185 (1968).

1978 " 'Truth' When the Polygraph Operator Sits as Arbitrator (or Judge): The Deception of 'Detection' in the 'Diagnosis of Truth and Deception.' " In *Truth, Lie Detectors, and Other Problems in Labor Arbitration*, Proceedings of the Thirty-first Annual Meeting, National Academy of Arbitrators, edited by Stern and Dennis. Washington, D.C.: Bureau of National Affairs.

Kennedy, Thomas
1963 "Merging Seniority Lists." In *Labor Arbitration and Industrial Changes*. Proceedings of the Sixteenth Annual Meeting, National Academy of Arbitrators. Washington, D.C.: Bureau of National Affairs.

Kerr, Clark
1954 *Labor Mobility and Economic Opportunity: Essays*, by E. Wight Bakke and others. New York: MIT Press and John Wiley.

Kramer, Jay
1956 "Seniority and Ability." In *Management Rights and the Arbitration Process*. Proceedings of the Ninth Annual Meeting, National Academy of Arbitrators, edited by Jean T. McKelvey. Washington, D.C.: Bureau of National Affairs.

Kuhn, Alfred
1952 *Arbitration in Transit*. Philadelphia: University of Pennsylvania Press.

Loewenberg, J. Joseph
1975 "The Pennsylvania Experience." In *Final Offer Arbitration*. Lexington, Mass.: Lexington Books.

Long, Gary, and Feuille, Peter
1974 "Final Offer Arbitration: Sudden Death in Eugene." *Industrial and Labor Relations Review* 27, 2 (January 1974): 186.

Lykken, David T.
1980 *A Tremor in the Blood: Uses and Abuses of the Lie Detector*. New York: McGraw-Hill.

Murphy, W.; Getman, G.; and Jones, J.
1979 *Discrimination in Employment*. Washington, D.C.: Bureau of National Affairs.

Phelps, James C.
1956 "Management's Reserved Rights: An Industry Perspective." *Management Rights and the Arbitration Process*. Proceedings of the Ninth Annual Meeting, National Academy of Arbitrators, edited by Jean T. McKelvey. Washington, D.C.: Bureau of National Affairs.

Platt, Harry H., et al.
 1973   "Arbitration of Interest Disputes in the Local Transit
         and Newspaper Publishing Industries." *Arbitration of
         Interest Disputes.* Proceedings of the Twenty-sixth An-
         nual Meeting, National Academy of Arbitrators.
         Washington, D.C.: Bureau of National Affairs.
Rehmus, Charles M.
 1975   "The Michigan Experience." *Final Offer Arbitration.*
         Lexington, Mass.: Lexington Books.
Reilly, Gerard D.
 1957   "Labor Law for Practitioners." 8 *Labor Law Journal* 19
         (CCH, Jan.)
Reynolds, Lloyd G.
 1974   *Labor Economics and Labor Relations.* 6th ed. New York:
         Prentice-Hall.
Ross, Arthur
 1964   "The Criminal Law and Industrial Systems." In *Labor
         Arbitration Perspectives and Problems.* Proceedings of the
         Seventeenth Annual Meeting, National Academy of
         Arbitrators. Washington, D.C.: Bureau of National
         Affairs.
Rothschild, Donald P.; Merrifield, Leroy S.; and Edwards, Harry T.
 1979   *Collective Bargaining and Labor Arbitration.* 2d ed. Indian-
         apolis: Bobbs-Merrill.
Rubin, Alvin
 1979   "Arbitration: Toward a Rebirth." In *Truth, Lie Detec-
         tors, and Other Problems in Labor Arbitration.* Proceedings
         of the Thirty-first Annual Meeting, National Academy
         of Arbitrators, edited by Stern and Dennis. Washing-
         ton, D.C.: Bureau of National Affairs.
St. Antoine, Theodore
 1978   "Judicial Review of Labor Arbitration Awards: A Sec-
         ond Look at *Enterprise Wheel* and Its Progeny." In *Arbi-
         tration–1977.* Proceedings of the Thirtieth Annual
         Meeting, National Academy of Arbitrators. Washing-
         ton, D.C.: Bureau of National Affairs.
Seward, Ralph
 1957   "Arbitration in the World Today." *The Profession of La-
         bor Arbitration.* Washington, D.C.: Bureau of National
         Affairs.
 1964   *Labor Arbitration: Perspectives and Problems.* Proceedings
         of the Seventeenth Annual Meeting, National Acad-
         emy of Arbitrators. Washington, D.C.: Bureau of Na-
         tional Affairs, p. 242.

Shulman, Harry
    1956   "Reason, Contract, and Law in Labor Relations." Reprinted in *Management Rights and the Arbitration Process.* Proceedings of the Ninth Annual Meeting, National Academy of Arbitrators, edited by Jean T. McKelvey. Washington, D.C.: Bureau of National Affairs.
Slichter, Sumner H.; Healy, James J.; and Livernash, E. Robert
    1960   *The Impact of Collective Bargaining on Management.* Washington, D.C.: Brookings Institution.
Stessin, Lawrence
    1973   *Employee Discipline.* Washington, D.C.: Bureau of National Affairs.
Taylor, George
    1957   "Effectuating the Labor Contract through Arbitration." In *The Profession of Labor Arbitration.* Washington, D.C.: Bureau of National Affairs.
Whitney, F.
    1973   "Final Offer Arbitration: The Indianapolis Experience." *Monthly Labor Review* 96, 20.
Williston, Samuel
    1936   *Contracts,* rev. ed., vol. 3. New York: Baker, Voorhis & Co.
Young, Dallas M.
    1966   "Arbitration of Terms for New Labor Contracts." 13 *Western Reserve University Law Review* 1302 (June 1966).

Index to Cases Cited

General Index

Contributors

Harry T. Edwards is Circuit Judge, United States Court of Appeals for the District of Columbia. He has taught in the law schools at the University of Michigan and at Harvard University, where he also taught at the Institute for Educational Management. He has been a member of the board of directors of the National Academy of Arbitrators and a presidential appointee to the International Women's Year Commission. Among his previous works are *The Lawyer as a Negotiator, Collective Bargaining and Labor Arbitration, Labor Relations Law in the Public Sector,* and *Higher Education and the Law.*

Robben W. Fleming, president emeritus and professor of law, University of Michigan, is senior consultant to the Annenberg/CPB Project. A past president of the Corporation for Public Broadcasting, he is a fellow of the American Academy of Arts and Sciences and has been chairman of the board of the Carnegie Fund for the Advancement of Teaching and of the American Council on Education. He was a charter member of the council's Business-Higher Education Forum. Fleming has directed the Institute of Labor and Industrial Relations, University of Illinois, and served as president of the National Academy of Arbitrators. He is the author of a number of articles on trends in labor law and collective bargaining.

Ronald W. Haughton is a member and former chairman of the Federal Labor Relations Authority. He has been a permanent umpire in a number of industries and has drafted public employment legislation for the states of Michigan and California, jurisdictions in which he worked as a factfinder. He is a former vice president of Wayne State University, where he was also codirector of the Institute of Industrial Relations. Having served as president of the Board of Mediation for Community Disputes in New York City, and chaired several presidential emergency boards, Haughton is a member of the board of directors of the American Arbitration Association.

Robert G. Howlett is an arbitrator and attorney in the firm of Varnum, Riddering, Schmidt, and Howlett. He is chairman of the Federal Service

Impasses Panel and a former chairman of the Michigan Employment Relations Commission. He has been a visiting professor at Michigan State University and is the author of many articles on public employment and on dispute resolution.

Edgar A. Jones, Jr., is professor of law at the University of California, Los Angeles. A past president of the National Academy of Arbitrators, he is the author of numerous law review articles, the most recent of which focus on decisional thinking by triers of fact.

Charles C. Killingsworth is University Professor, Michigan State University, where he was founder and first director of the School of Industrial and Labor Relations. He is a permanent umpire in the steel, rubber, and automobile industries. A former chairman of the National Wage Stabilization Board, Killingsworth is a charter member and past president of the National Academy of Arbitrators. He is the author of a monograph on jobs and incomes for blacks, as well as a number of articles on technological change and the work force.

Jean T. McKelvey is professor at the New York State School of Industrial and Labor Relations, Cornell University, where she teaches collective bargaining, labor law, and arbitration. She is a mediator and arbitrator who has been appointed to the Federal Service Impasses Panel and the Public Review Board of the United Auto Workers. She is the author of many works on industrial relations and the editor of *The Duty of Fair Representation*.

Richard Mittenthal is an arbitrator in private practice. He is a permanent umpire for various private sector industries as well as for the U.S. Postal Service. Mittenthal is a member of the Foreign Service Grievance Board and a past president of the National Academy of Arbitrators. He has taught at the University of Michigan Law School and written on various aspects of arbitration.

Charles M. Rehmus is dean of the New York State School of Industrial and Labor Relations, Cornell University. He has served as chairman of the Michigan Employment Relations Commission, commissioner of the Federal Mediation and Conciliation Service, labor adviser to the secretary of commerce, and chairman of four presidential emergency boards. Among his previously published works are *Labor and American Politics, Final Offer Arbitration,* and *The Railway Labor Act at Fifty.*

Theodore J. St. Antoine is the James E. and Sarah A. Degan Professor of Law at the University of Michigan and a former dean of the law school there. He serves on the Public Review Board of the United Auto Workers and on numerous bar association committees. He is a coauthor of *Labor Relations Law: Cases and Materials.*

Jack Stieber is professor of economics and director of the School of Labor and Industrial Relations, Michigan State University. He is, in addition, an arbitrator and author. His recent books concern wage structure and union governance.

Clyde W. Summers is Fordham Professor of Law at the University of Pennsylvania School of Law. He taught previously at the Yale University School of Law. He was secretary, section on labor relations law, of the American Bar Association, an alternate member of the Connecticut State Labor Relations Board and of the Connecticut State Mediation Board and a hearing officer for the Connecticut Human Rights Commission. He is the author of *Rights of Union Members*, as well as a number of case books on labor law.

Rolf Valtin is an arbitrator in private practice. He has been a permanent umpire in the steel, auto, and coal industries and has worked as a mediator in the federal sector. Having served as president of the National Academy of Arbitrators and as a member of several presidential emergency boards, Valtin is at present chairman of the Energy Labor-Management Relations Panel. He is the author of a number of previous articles on arbitration.

Arnold M. Zack is an arbitrator in private practice. A past vice president of the National Academy of Arbitrators, he is the recipient of the American Arbitration Association's Whitney North Seymour Award. He is also a member of the Foreign Service Labor Relations Board. Zack has many previous publications; his most recent writing focuses on the grievance process.